Creating
GI Jane

Sexuality and Power

in the

Women's Army Corps

During

World War II

D0888958

Creating
GI Jane

Sexuality and Power

in the

Women's Army Corps

During

World War II

Leisa D. Meyer

Columbia University Press

New York

Columbia University Press
Publishers since 1893
New York   Chichester, West Sussex
Copyright © 1996 Columbia University Press
All rights reserved

Library of Congress Cataloging-in-Publication Data
Meyer, Leisa D.
  Creating GI Jane : sexuality and power in the Women's Army Corps
during World War II / Leisa D. Meyer.
    p. cm.
  Includes bibliographical references and index.
  ISBN 0–231–10144–9 (cl) — ISBN 0–231–10145–7 (pbk.)
  1. United States. Army Women's Army Corps. 2. Sociology.
Military—United States. 3. World War, 1939–1945—Women.
I. Title.
UA565.W6M48   1996
940.54'0973'082—dc20   96–13858
                                              CIP

Casebound editions of Columbia University Press books are printed on permanent
and durable acid-free paper.
Printed in the United States of America
c 10 9 8 7 6 5 4 3 2 1
p 10 9 8 7 6 5 4 3 2 1

Cartoons on pages 27 to 29 appeared in Vic Herman's *Winnie the Wac* (New York:
Random House); cartoons on pages 30–31: "Tin Hats" (Bell Syndicate); "You're in the
Army Now" (Register and Tribune Syndicate); "Something New Has Been Added"
(New York Tribune Inc.); "Crosstown" (Register and Tribune Syndicate); cartoon on
page 154 from Milton Caniff's *Male Call*, reprinted with special permission of Milton
Caniff Estate by Toni Mendez, Inc.

For Maureen

Contents

Acknowledgments

I am indebted to a number of people and institutions for providing me with the financial and emotional support necessary to complete this book. The University of California, Santa Barbara, furnished me with important financial support through their Women's Studies predoctoral dissertation fellowship. In addition, I thank the History Department of the University of Wisconsin-Madison for a one semester fellowship and the College of William and Mary for a summer research grant that enabled me to finish the book.

This project would have been impossible without the expertise and guidance offered me by the many archivists I encountered during my research. especially Charlotte Seely and Edward Reese of the Military Reference Branch, National Archives and Records Administration. I owe a special debt of gratitude to Chief Master Sergeant Mary Sheehan (U.S. Army, ret.) of the WAC Museum, Fort McClellan, Anniston, Alabama. She offered me support and friendship during my stay there and highlighted for me the importance of my study to former members of the WAC. I am extremely grateful to all of these archivists for their willingness to search for information I required, and for sharing with me their passion for and understandings of the importance of the Women's Army Corps.

I have benefited enormously from the support of WAC veterans throughout this project. Helen Allen, president of the WAC Veteran's Association (1989), and Helen Bill, a WAC veteran of World War II, made it possible for me to develop a list of contacts for my questionnaire project. I would be remiss if I also did not thank the members of the Florida Sunshine Chapter of the WAC Veteran's Association. In September 1989, they welcomed me as their guest to the annual WAC Veteran's convention held at the old WAC Training Center, Fort Des Moines, Iowa. They shared with me their stories and songs from World War II and I am extremely grateful for their candor and overwhelming support.

This book has profited from the intellectually stimulating environment and exchange among students and faculty of the Graduate Program in Women's History at the University of Wisconsin-Madison and subsequent dicussions with new colleagues. I would especially like to thank Andrea Friedman, Laura McEnaney, and Mary Peckham, for their friendship and emotional support throughout this process. My conversations with Beth Hillman, who still struggles within the instititution, have been critical to shaping this book. This project has also benefited from the close scrutiny of Linda Gordon, whom I owe a special debt for many years of support and advice, and Gerda Lerner, whose vigorous vision of women's history inspired those of us who shared time with her at Wisconsin. I must also give heartfelt thanks to Allan Berube for his advice and support of this project, as well as his willingness to share materials and evidence with me. This book would not have been possible without my editor at Columbia University Press, Kate Wittenberg, whose insight and patience I have greatly appreciated.

Finally, I want to thank my family—my parents, my sister, Dayna, and my brother, Andrew, whose acceptance of my choices has been a constant affirmative presence in my life, and most importantly my partner, Maureen Fitzgerald. Her encouragement and friendship kept and still keep me going and her spirited support of me when I had the greatest doubts was crucial to me finishing this project. Thank you, Maureen.

Creating
GI Jane

Sexuality and Power

in the

Women's Army Corps

During

World War II

Prologue

Today, the national public is grappling with a host of questions concerning women in the military and the sexual orientation of servicemen and servicewomen. Should servicewomen be trained for combat positions? What should be done about sexual harassment within the military, a problem brought to national attention by the 1991 "Tailhook scandal?" Should the historic ban on gays and lesbians in the military be lifted, and if so does the current "Don't Ask, Don't Tell, Don't Pursue" policy serve this function?

Although these questions are not new, the debates about them are situated in a different ideological and material context, than that of the 1940s. The strong and visible civil rights, feminist, and lesbian and gay liberation movements of the previous decades have changed practices and altered the terms of the discussion in the civilian sector to a much greater degree than is apparent in the military itself. Yet, like the 1940s, the 1990s are a time of transition, and there is public and military resistance to allowing women access to the highest echelons of male state and economic power, and to affording gay men and lesbians protection from systematic harassment and discrimination.

These current questions, ostensibly about military men and women, are not being debated popularly because the public is inherently concerned about the military itself. Rather, because the military is a critical bastion of state power and service within it a determinant of the rights of citizens, allowing heterosexual women, lesbians, and gay men to participate within it fully and without harassment or discrimination increases expectations that those same groups will be treated with fairness and respect in the public sector. For some, raising the status and increasing the opportunities of heterosexual women, gay men, and lesbians in the military is viewed as a way to bring the military in line with public thought and practice. For others, these same actions seem a profoundly disturbing and irrevocable sanction of feminism and lesbian and gay rights, a substantial threat to what they believe to be a "natural" or divinely ordained gender and sexual order.

To fully understand contemporary debates over these issues, one must first appreciate the historical foundation for these discussions located in World War II and bound up with the permanent establishment of a women's military presence. In this book I investigate this foundation by analyzing the creation and history of the Women's Army Corps (WAC) during World War II. Understanding the process by which women were accepted into this "masculine" institution, and a new category of "female soldier" was constructed, helps us to evaluate better the challenges to gender and sexual hierarchies mounted during the war and the consequence of these challenges for twentieth-century American culture.

This book is not intended to serve as a broad-based social history of the women's army corps. Instead, using archival records, popular media coverage of the WAC, and oral histories I examine the "women's army" as a means through which to evaluate the discussions and debates over men's and women's "proper" roles during wartime. The formation of the Women's Army Auxiliary Corps (WAAC)* in May 1942, crystallized public fears that the mobilization of women for war would undermine the established sex/gender system, and both men and women's places within it. Thus, analyzing military and civilian attempts to create a place for women without disrupting contemporary definitions of "masculinity" and "femininity" is crucial to understanding the impact of World War II on gender and sexual ideology and the struggles around gender and sexual identity taking place in American society.

Over fifty years ago, women's entrance into the Army was accepted by male Army leaders under the banner of expedience. Supporting the formation of a "women's corps" seemed a reasonable solution to the expected

---

*The Women's Army Auxiliary Corps (WAAC) existed from May 1942 to September 1943, when it was replaced by the Women's Army Corps (WAC). Throughout this book I use the acronym WAC to refer to the organization and Wac ("ac" lowercase) to refer to an individual or individuals within the corps. In addition, to avoid repetition I use the terms "corps" and "women's corps" interchangeably with WAC. To avoid confusing terminology, in the text I use the acronym WAC in most discussions of the women's corps throughout World War II. When I discuss material that is specific to the early auxiliary years of the corps, I will specifically note this by referring to the corps as "the auxiliary" or the WAAC. In direct quotations, I use WAAC as called for by the source material.

increase in the numbers of "women's jobs" involving tasks such as clerking, typing, and communications, and enabled the Army to maintain control over this labor and its employment. Moreover, sponsoring the creation of such a corps allowed the Army, not civilian legislators, to dictate the terms of female military participation.

In the civilian sector, women's entrance into the Army was advocated by some who believed that women's rights and duties as citizens should not be limited. Yet it was also restricted by opponents who argued that women's participation must be tolerated and encouraged only to the degree that it did not disrupt systems of male dominance and power. Supporters of the WAC constructed the female soldier as a symbol of American women's patriotism, self-sacrifice, and courage. Some, like Representative Edith Nourse Rogers, saw the corps as a long-awaited symbol of recognition for all the women who had worked with the military in previous American war efforts; an important step toward women's status as full citizens, deserving of the rights and benefits long enjoyed by men. Others constructed the female soldier as a modern Molly Pitcher who, in response to a national emergency, left her home and family temporarily to lend a hand. In contrast, opponents characterized the female soldier as a dire threat to this home and family, and to the privatized gender relationships within them, especially to the husband's status as breadwinner and head of household. To these commentators, the female soldier epitomized the wartime antiheroine, a figure whose potential sexual and economic independence from men subverted the "natural order" and whose position as a female protector usurped men's status and power, both within and outside of the home.

Public fears of the consequences of establishing a women's army were rooted in a cultural inability to reconcile the categories of "woman" and "soldier." This oppositional division is based on both constructions of military service as a critical measure of cultural "masculinity,"[1] and the asymmetrically gendered relationship between the male "protector" and the female "protected." In the 1990s, the possibility that male soldiers might seek to defend and protect military women instead of carrying out their assigned missions continues to be cited by military experts as a primary example of the potential "dangers" in incorporating women fully into the military structure. Brian Mitchell, author of *Weak Link: The Feminization of the American Military*, argues "Men simply cannot treat women like other men. And it's silly to think that a few months' training can make them into some kind of sexless soldiers."[2] Mitchell's statement clearly reflects the assumption that soldiers are male, that women's full participation in the military could be accomplished only by making them sexless, and that a female soldier remains an impossibility. By arguing that male bonding is crucial to the definition of the military, opponents of women's military service reinforce constructions of "soldier" as male, and woman as "other," and destructive to masculine culture. Women's entrance into the military disrupts the dichotomies between woman and soldier by raising questions about exactly what a "woman" is, what a "soldier" is, and what a "female soldier" could possibly be.

The difficulty of reconciling the categories of woman and soldier has meant that women in the military have received little attention either from military or women's historians. Military historians who concentrate on social history sometimes address issues of race and class, but rarely conceptualize the military as gendered, and consequently view women's entrance into the military as, at most, a marginal development. At the same time, feminist historians have discussed women's opposition to the military as a masculine institution that wields coercive power for the state, but have rarely tackled the question of how to analyze and interpret women's military service. Feminist scholars' unwillingness to address women's position *within* the military, especially given the growing literature on women's relationship to and work within the "state," indicates their own discomfort with the combination of the "feminine" and the "martial," a discomfort that reinforces ideological constructions of gender that define "soldiers" as male, and "women" as essentially nonmilitary. While military and feminist historians would likely be at odds on most issues, the frameworks they utilize conspire collectively to render military women invisible or "othered." To the degree that servicewomen are discussed by feminists, they are characterized primarily as victims. As feminist scholar Cynthia Enloe reflected:

> Those women exerting so much energy inside the military establishment to overcome barriers to training and promotion may find it insulting when a civilian feminist like me argues that a military is so fundamentally masculinized that no woman has a chance of transforming that military . . . when a 'feminist-in-khaki' hears another woman arguing that the military is basically misogynist, she hears someone telling her that she can't accomplish what she's set out to do, that she's letting herself be duped if she persists in trying. The message reeks of condescension.[3]

I am not the first to notice the absence of military women from the fields of women's and military history. In fact, the lack of scholarly attention paid to female military service has catalyzed the development of the burgeoning field of women's military history. The work of these scholars has both increased the visibility of women's past military participation, and has raised new questions concerning the meanings of that participation. In turn, the growth of the field of women's military history itself has benefited from the heightened public attention to the social and cultural questions arising from a female presence in what remains a masculine institution.[4]

I do not contest that the military is among the most powerful masculine institutions, or that women's entrance into and interactions with it present dangers and sometimes insurmountable difficulties. Yet, military women, during World War II and today, did not and do not perceive themselves as exclusively victims. Women's reasons for entering the military were and remain complex, and their struggles are both similar to and distinct from those faced by civilian women who struggle to obtain legitimacy in bastions of male power. The increasing number of young women, especially African-American women, who are entering the military for jobs, education, or as a career, underlines the need to historicize both American women's role in the U.S. military and the process by which G.I. Jane or the female soldier was created and continues to be constructed.

While black men's service as soldiers, for instance, has often been characterized as crucial to shifting conceptions of citizenship rights for African-American people, black women's military participation must be situated within a similar framework. African-American servicewomen had to contend not only with the Army's system of segregation, but also with racial constructions of gender and gendered constructions of race that influenced the jobs they were allowed to perform, their living conditions, and the ways in which female sexuality was regulated and controlled. I will demonstrate that black women saw their involvement in the military as critical to the larger struggle for racial justice, and that much of their resistance to racist WAC policies foreshadowed the actions of civil rights activists in the 1950s and 1960s.

The historical criteria usually accompanying an increase in female sexual autonomy were exaggerated during World War II. Increasing mobility, as women joined the military or left hometowns for war jobs, sparked a decrease in parental control. In turn, the need to mobilize the entire populace to support the war effort offered many women increasing access to wages, and a semblance of economic autonomy.[5] Consequently, it is not surprising that during World War II, the female soldier, who epitomized a more generalized female deviance, was frequently the subject of public concerns specifically with female sexual deviance.

The loss of femininity many civilians feared might result from women's entrance into the Army linked women's assumption of the masculine duties of soldiering with their potential assumption of a more aggressive and assertive masculine sexuality. While female sexual agency was a symbol of service-women's gender deviance, Army women's violation of contemporary gender norms by joining the WAC and donning "male uniforms" also indicated their potential sexual deviance. As a result, while women's presence within a male institution raised concerns about their sexual interactions with male soldiers, the sex segregated nature of WAC units also raised concerns about their sexual interactions with one another.

In fact, the most resilient and entrenched historical images of female soldiers are those of the camp follower and cross-dresser. During World War II, images of female soldiers as camp followers were articulated in accusations of sexual promiscuity among Wacs and allegations that the WAC was simply an organized cadre of prostitutes enlisted to fulfill the sexual needs of male soldiers. These allegations were supported by military sexual paradigms that condoned and at times encouraged the heterosexual activity of male soldiers while condemning any such activities among women. The WAC leadership responded to the assumptions of servicewomen's heterosexual promiscuity by creating a framework within which Wacs and female officers were depicted as sexually respectable. This strategy was directed at gaining protection for women from negative publicity, sexual harassment and sexual violence. The Army's paradigm of protection, however, focused on shielding men from any responsibility for their heterosexual encounters, including venereal disease and fatherhood, and instead putting the blame on the women with whom they were involved. Taken together, these two different sexual systems reinforced the sexual double standard, marginalized service-women and female officers, and minimized the limited protections available to them.

The historic image of female soldiers as cross-dressers was also articulated during World War II in public allegations that the WAC both attracted or produced "mannish" women. The mannish woman was a cultural symbol of lesbians prior to the war. During World War II, however, the association of mannish women with the WAC was not focused on a tiny minority of individuals who would assume this identity, but on how the state's encouragement of women to move into a preeminently masculine institution could, in fact, encourage large numbers of women to assume a masculine identity. Indeed, public assumptions that military women would be mannish, when joined with the cultural equation of mannishness with lesbianism, meant that women joining the Army during World War II were popularly perceived as having the potential to be lesbians.

Given the widespread public anxiety over the creation of the WAC both female and male military leaders, as well as civilian proponents of the women's corps, agreed that "female soldiers" must not seem to threaten either male power in the military or the notion that masculinity was integrally tied to the definition of "soldier." Army and WAC leaders' desires to present the women's corps to the public, and servicewomen to their male counterparts and commanders, in the most nonthreatening way possible formed the basis for Army and corps' policies addressing work conditions, race relations, and sexual regulation within the WAC. The Army's employment of servicewomen in so-called feminine job categories, for instance, was designed to differentiate women from male soldiers in terms of both duties and status. In addition, the women's corps' adherence to Army segregation rulings, and its employment of African-American women in racially stereotyped jobs, made distinctions in terms of status between Black women and their white counterparts. Further, the Army's system of rank and authority guaranteed that women occupying the lower ranks of the military structure would be more likely to be employed in menial duties. Thus, the Army and WAC's framework resulted in a work system closer to the prewar sex, race, and class segregated labor market, than that occurring in the wartime civilian labor force.

The control and regulation of the lives of military personnel was not unique to female soldiers. During World War II the Army, as a total institution, tried to control the entirety of servicewomen's and servicemen's lives. In describing the Army as a "total institution" I am referring to the formal regulations, policies, and procedures as well as the informal practices and long-standing military customs that circumscribed virtually every aspect of servicemen's and women's lives. It could be argued that such control over military men and women was necessary given the huge task of mobilization facing the Army. Indeed, enlisting, training, and employing millions of young men and thousands of young women required a fairly rigid structure and disciplinary system.

First, Army and WAC regulations dictated when and where all military personnel would eat and sleep, provided uniforms for them, told them how to dress, defined the training for which male soldiers and Wacs were eligible, and the jobs they could and must perform. Second, Army and WAC policies defined "misconduct" and the punishments that could be invoked if servicemen and women "misbehaved"; the military regulated their social and sexual lives to an extent even greater than families. Virtually nothing a soldier did while in the military was considered private. Last, the Army's hierarchical system of command meant that officers had the authority to determine how these regulations would be interpreted for both male and female enlisted personnel.

The questions of how servicewomen's lives would be regulated, and whether Army policies would be applied in the same manner to both female and male soldiers, were the subjects of debate and conflict between male and female military leaders throughout the war. Male military commanders often wanted to treat servicewomen just as they did male soldiers, which would have encompassed a great deal of freedom from gender and sexual restraints specific to women. In contrast, the female WAC leadership, guided by Colonel Oveta Culp Hobby, insisted on differential treatment for women, especially in the arenas of public relations and sexual regulation. In these areas, the corps' female leadership within the Army was often more powerful than their male counterparts in determining how servicewomen's sexuality would be regulated and how the female soldier would be presented to the public. Hobby and other WAC leaders believed that not controlling the construction of the female soldier would prove either harmful to WAC legitimacy or harmful to particular women who were not protected within an overwhelmingly male institution.

The entire construction of the WAC by corps' leaders was organized to limit public fears that the state was advocating changes in sexual, gender, race, or class hierarchies. The WAC leadership attempted to assuage public concerns about the potential sexual independence and victimization of servicewomen, for example, by depicting female soldiers as feminine and chaste. This insistence, by WAC leaders, on the need for different rules of conduct and behavior for servicewomen vis-à-vis male soldiers was shaped in part by public beliefs that loss of sexual respectability was inherent in female military service. In the 1940s, sexual respectability was a fluctuating category for women. Sexual respectability, however, continued to be contingent on women acting or appearing to act within certain prescribed limits of sexual behavior. While women could engage in some extramartial heterosexual petting and necking without becoming "bad" women, and even intercourse with fiancees or in the context of love and commitment, promiscuity, including casual sexual encounters or multiple sexual partners, was not popularly accepted as appropriate for women. Women's entrance into the military raised the question of whether military women would engage in the same types of promiscuous heterosexual activity presumed to occur among male soldiers; men did not lose "respect" by engaging in these activities, but women did. In formulating distinct WAC regulations and arguing for differential applications of general Army policies intended to control men's sexual and social lives, the corps' female leadership reinforced existing sexual, gender, race, and class norms and explicitly articulated what they believed these norms to be.

The WAC female leadership believed that claiming sexual respectability for female soldiers was necessary to gain legitimacy for the corps and to protect individual women within it. Key to the philosophy of the WAC administration was their equation of sexual respectability with feminine appearance and sexual restraint. WAC leaders believed, moreover, that sexual respectability was more likely to be found in white middle-class women than in nonwhite or lower-class women. Consequently, they focused corps' recruiting efforts and publicity on portrayals of the WAC as an organization of white middle-class women. Further, "misconduct" discharges were approved for servicewomen for behaviors that were not only condoned but encouraged in male soldiers. As I will show, within the tight cloak of respectability draped around the WAC, even the appearance of sexual or social misconduct could be grounds for dismissal from the corps.

In itself, not having sex with men was insufficient to counteract public concerns with female sexual agency. During World War II, the most potent symbol of servicewomen's gender and sexual deviance was the mannish woman and her sexual flipside, the butch lesbian. Although regulations intended to control servicewomen's sexual behavior addressed both heterosexual and homosexual activities, the latter were prioritized as a threat to the legitimacy of the corps. In particular, butch lesbians' masculine appearance and demeanor in an environment which privileged and emphasized feminine appearance, and the association of butch women and butch/femme dyadic relationships with a working-class culture that was explicitly sexual, made mannish women highly visible and extremely suspect. While butch women were likely to be targeted as lesbians, however, their visibility also served as both an anchor and rallying point for the formation of lesbian communities within the corps.

While World War II marked a turning point in both the development and consolidation of lesbian subcultures, in contrast to some historians, I do not see military "tolerance" of lesbians as either an adequate characterization of lesbians' military experience during World War II or the sole reason for the consolidation of these subcultures. Historians Lillian Faderman and Allan Berube have cited the "tolerant" wartime attitudes toward lesbians and the "lenience" of official military policies as crucial to this development. As Faderman has argued, "War and especially military life fostered some tolerance regarding lesbianism among young women who, perhaps for the first time in their lives, came in contact with sexuality between women in the close confines of the barracks."[6] At the same time, the WAC, a sex-segregated institution, attracted women who enjoyed the company of other women and oth-

ers who were drawn to the masculine status of soldiers. Although WAC policies toward lesbians appeared to espouse toleration, there were a number of
informal methods utilized by WAC officials to address and eliminate the "lesbian problem" within the women's corps without drawing public attention.
Because the label of "lesbian" was such a visible sign of gender and sexual
deviance and public associations of lesbian with female soldier threatened the
legitimacy of the WAC directly, lesbians were harassed and discharged for a
broad range of misconduct. Official policies on lesbians and records referring
explicitly to "lesbian" problems, therefore, do not tell the whole story.

The WAC leadership's attempts to control how often lesbians were associated with women's military service, moreover, underlines their efforts to control the public discussion about lesbians in the military. Indeed, while invisibility of lesbians seemed the goal of WAC leaders, what was particularly note-
worthy was the proliferation of discourses concerning lesbians generated
within the military. Servicewomen positioned themselves within these discussions by defining themselves or "others" as lesbians. While these actions
were occasionally repressive, they also allowed for the beginnings of common
identification among lesbians.[7]

Like the above example, Wacs and WAC officers throughout the war made
their own contributions to the constructions of "female soldiers." By protest-
ing gender and racially stereotyped work assignments and refusing to accept
exclusion from certain jobs and training, some Wacs served notice that they
would not passively accept the limitations placed on their service by the Army
and the corps' female leadership. By contesting and maneuvering around regulations designed either to control their sexual behavior or punish them for it,
service women's opposition threatened prevailing definitions of female sexual
respectability and was crucial to the development of lesbian communities
within the corps. In the long run, Wacs' attempts to shape their own military
experience sometimes challenged and other times reinforced the very racial,
sexual, and gender norms used to proscribe, as well as support, their participation in the armed forces.

1

"What Has Become of the Manhood of America?" Creating a Woman's Army

Republican Congresswoman Edith Nourse Rogers (Mass.) introduced the bill to create a Women's Army Auxiliary Corps (WAAC) on May 28, 1941.[1] Rogers considered her legislation a long overdue acknowledgment of those women who worked for the military in the previous world war.[2] Because most women who served with the military during World War I were civilians, they were not eligible for the same benefits as the men in uniform with whom they worked. Invoking her own World War I military experience Rogers described this arrangement as "most unsatisfactory" because these women "received no compensation of any kind in the event they were sick or injured—and many were."[3] Rogers desired to prevent a similar "tragedy" during World War II, wherein women worked with the military in jobs similar to those performed by male soldiers but from which women derived no comparable compensation or power. She was determined that during this war women's service with the military *would* be recognized and that as "patriots" they would be entitled to the same rewards from the state as men for the "faithful" discharge of their duties.[4] Throughout World War II Rogers and other WAAC proponents argued that women were not demanding the right to do work in the military other than the clerical and communications tasks in which they were already engaged as civilians. What they contended and what proved threatening to many, however, was that such work constituted military service and should be officially recognized as such.

In proposing a women's corps Rogers acknowledged the degree to which definitions of American citizenship were contingent on a prescribed exchange of duties and rights and that all women's treatment as full and equal citizens would be tied to their eligibility for military service.[5] Such an exchange was historically prescribed for men only, despite women's record of military service; so long as women remained apart from the military itself, even if their service was obvious, the corollary rights guaranteed to men would not be forthcoming. As members of the Women's Overseas Service League (WOSL), Rogers and others had worked for two decades to achieve recognition of women's service with the U.S. armed forces overseas during World War I. Crucial to this recognition were members' attempts to secure veterans benefits, disability pensions, and hospitalization privileges for themselves and other women. In defending her WAAC Bill, Rogers used arguments similar to those used by League leaders, depicting women's service as selflessly motivated and thus deserving of some reward. She also departed from this conventional framework by arguing that women who served with the military not only *deserved* rewards similar to those of men but that by performing the same *duties* as male soldiers, female citizens were *entitled* to the same *rights* as their male counterparts, in the form of veteran's benefits, pensions, and equal pay.[6]

The progress of the legislation creating the Women's Army Auxiliary Corps (WAAC) highlights the potential challenge female soldiers offered to the gendered and raced constructions of citizenship at work during World War II. The right to bear arms and the corresponding benefits and rewards that the state grants those who fulfill this duty, have been delimited by race as well as sex. The historical exclusion of all women and African-American men from arms-bearing in effect prohibited them from making claims on the state as full citizens. In fact, during the war black leaders argued that the future status of African-Americans as *citizens* in the United States depended upon their service as *equals* in the armed forces.[7] Thus, historical constructions of the military as a bastion of white male power and the male "warrior" as white meant that the construction of the female soldier in general and the category "Waac" in particular was an essentially raced as well as gendered process.

While the creation of the WAAC marked a first move toward official acknowledgment of women's military service, it also highlighted the centrality of military service as a criterion that structured the rights of citizens into a hierarchichal system that privileged white men. Thus, although women's entrance into the Army in some ways paralleled women's movement into nontraditional jobs in the civilian labor force, it was also more threatening because of the military's cultural function as one of the rites of passage to manhood. Like women, most men who served in the military during World War II functioned solely in noncombat support roles. Yet the ideological construction of "soldier" as a man with a weapon who fights, and the military as a preeminently masculine institution, continued to include all white men, whether or not they saw combat, and black men who were active combatants, while excluding all women entirely.[8] The tensions between these concepts — "woman" and "soldier" — and the attempts to untangle and reconstitute this dichotomy underlay much of the public and congressional debate about women's military service.

The congressional debate was ostensibly about the most appropriate wartime duties for male and female citizens. Beneath this rhetorical surface, however, the debate centered more precisely on the profound concerns generated by the militarization of women, especially the potential defeminization of women and the emasculation of men, with all that might mean. As Congressman Somers (D, N.Y.), one stalwart opponent of the WAAC bill, argued: "A women's Army to defend the United States of America! Think of the humiliation. What has become of the manhood of America, that we have to call on our women to do what has ever been the duty of men?"[9] To Somers, female soldiers conjured up visions of female protectors and undercut the more comfortable, familiar scenario of weeping women sending their men in uniform off to war and watching over the homefront while they awaited the soldiers return. The "humiliation" that Somers believed inhered in a woman's army was rooted in his fear that women would derive from military service some power over men, not just in the military but elsewhere.

Military leaders first contemplated making women formal participants within the armed services during World War I, primarily because the American Expeditionary Forces (AEF) needed women's labor in overseas theaters. General Pershing's inability to borrow the necessary numbers of British servicewomen to fill his army's need for clerical, communications, and laundry workers prompted him to demand that the War Department recruit American civilian women who could be assigned to the AEF. Pershing's and other such requests were approved piecemeal by the War Department; by war's end several hundred civilian women served overseas working as telephone operators attached to the Army Signal Corps and as clerical workers and laundresses with other Army departments.[10]

The War Department explored but did not develop the possibility of increasing the numbers of American women at the Army's disposal by organizing an auxiliary corps similar to that used by the British. Secretary of War Newton Baker was vehemently opposed to any such action and blocked tentative congressional efforts in this direction.[11] It is probable that had World War I lasted even a few months longer the Army's shortage of clerical and administrative personnel would have demanded Army leaders take action to fully incorporate women's labor. As it was, Army and War Department officials' breathed a collective sigh of relief at narrowly averting this prospect.

Thus, while women served with the Army during World War I, their service was largely unrecognized because they were civilians. Army and War department reluctance to give official sanction to women's military participation not only reinforced female invisibilty but also made women ineligible for the benefits and services provided to male soldiers by the Veterans Administration for identical work.

While War Department leaders sought to maintain distinctions between male and female citizens working with the Army, Secretary of the Navy Josephus Daniels' action to meet the staffing needs of the Navy was a first step toward breaking down this differentiation. Daniels simply interpreted enlistment law covering "any citizen of the United States" to include women. His assumption that "citizen" could include women might have reflected contemporary political discourse over the nature of the "woman citizen" in which some suffragists were arguing for their rights as full and equal citizens.[12] Under his guidance, the Navy recruited and officially enlisted 13,305 white women during World War I. Daniels' act exposed the presumption that the "citizen" identified in enlistment law was male and his suggestion that women might be included in both this definition of "citizen" and the military threatened white male citizens' status as "protectors." Congress replied to this threat by amending the legislation guiding military enlistment procedures to read "any male citizen of the United States" thereby closing Daniels' loophole. Congressional clarification of the sex of citizens eligible for military service explicitly defined soldiers as male and forced the military to get congressional approval for any future use of women within the armed forces.[13]

While not challenging constructions of military service as the duty of male citizens, after World War I Army and War department officials believed it necessary, in light of women's newly won right to vote, to gain their support for the military as an institution. Secretary of War Newton Baker was especially concerned with what he called the "dangerous combination" of female pacifism and female suffrage and believed it was important to convince women that the Army was "a progressive and socially minded human institution" not a "ruthless military machine" that must be disbanded.[14] Baker subsequently created a position within the Army's administrative division for a female liaison to the "women of America," an intermediary who Baker believed would insure that at least some women would see their political interests as connected with, and not in opposition to, those of the Army and the War department.[15]

Baker envisioned this liaison as a public relations spokeswoman influencing women and women's groups to support the Army and their own exclusion from this institution. In contrast, Anita Phipps, who held the position for ten years, set out to empower women within the Army by developing a workable plan for the military's future employment of women. Despite her efforts, the actions of War Department and Army administrators not only made it clear that she was not taken seriously, but also on many occasions alienated the women's groups she had so carefully cultivated. In 1930, an increasingly frustrated Phipps asked the Secretary of War to clarify her duties and authority. She was forced to resign due to illness before she received this clarification, but the new Chief of Staff, General Douglas MacArthur, recommended abolishing her position as it had "no military value."[16] Phipps managed to develop a blueprint for a corps of women soldiers before her resignation, but military officials shelved her designs and did not use them once serious discussion of the issue again surfaced after World War II began.[17]

The creation of the WAAC in 1942 was in large part the legacy of the work of women during World War I and the interwar years. Anita Phipps' service as the War Department's Director of Women's Relations was one aspect of this work, as was the pressure brought to bear by women's groups as U.S. involvement in World War II seemed imminent. By 1939 some women's organizations were demanding that the War Department allow women to serve their country as citizens and patriots by granting them the right to participate in the military establishment. Other women's insistence that they be included in the state's plans for national defense were manifest in the hundreds of female defense leagues that appeared before the war. Thousands of women joined organizations like the Chicago Women's League of Defense and the Washington, D.C. Green Guards, designed to serve as conduits for women eager to play not only crucial roles in the U.S. preparation for war but specifically in the military defense of the nation.[18]

The most significant pressure was brought to bear by white women with access to state power, particularly First Lady Eleanor Roosevelt and Representative Edith Nourse Rogers. In early 1941, with her husband's informal support for her efforts, Roosevelt sent several proposals to the War Department suggesting that American women be employed by the armed forces as auxiliaries in a system similar to that used by the British. A short time later Representative Rogers informed Army leaders that she intended to introduce a bill in Congress to establish a women's corps.[19]

The prospect of Congress passing a bill to create a women's corps without the input and control of Army officials generated a great deal of alarm in the

War Department. Army leaders were unwilling to allow civilians to make decisions as to the most appropriate and effective way to incorporate women into the military. General Marshall (COS) asked Rogers to delay initiating this legislation while Army officials examined her proposal to determine if he could support such a measure. Instead of perusing Rogers' recommendations, Marshall ordered Army planners to design a counterproposal that the Army could "safely sponsor" and "run . . . our way."[20]

The resulting Army plan indicated that "running it our way," meant not only controlling a women's corps, but also limiting to auxiliary, not full military, status women serving with the Army. By initially granting women status as "militarized civilians," but not as "soldiers," Army planners deferred the issue of formally incorporating women into the military, "avert[ing] the pressure to admit women to actual membership in the Army."[21] The Army's bill, as in the past, denied women equal rank, benefits, and pay as male soldiers and officers. Although Rogers' initial proposal would have placed women formally in the Army, she compromised and introduced the Army's bill for a corps of female auxiliaries.[22]

The WAAC bill was supported by the Roosevelt administration, the War Department, and the Chief of Staff, and presented to Congress as a necessary piece of the entire war mobilization package.[23] Despite the initial reluctance of War Department and Army officials to actively support the legislation, by late 1941, Marshall had come to believe that access to women's occupational skills would be crucial for the Army to effectively prosecute the imminent U.S. military effort. As a result, Marshall used his considerable power and influence to assure the passage of the pending legislation to create a women's corps. Part of his efforts involved pressuring agencies that were holding up the bill's passage to issue favorable reports. To help him in these endeavors, he recruited Oveta Culp Hobby.[24]

Oveta Culp Hobby was one of the few women who held positions of power within the state during World War II. While New Deal programs and the corresponding expansion of government services had opened opportunities for women in government during the 1930s, similar opportunities were not forthcoming during World War II. Most women who worked with and in the federal government during the war served in an advisory capacity and had minimal direct input in formulating and developing wartime policies and programs. As director of the WAAC Hobby was an exception to this general trend.[25] Oveta Hobby was not part of the earlier network of elite, predominantly white women who assumed power within the state during the 1930s. Born in 1905, she did not share their history and lacked their experience in social reform and suffrage during the Progressive Era that had shaped both their politics and their feminism. She did, however, share some of her predecessors' assumptions and, like this prior generation of feminists, she did not challenge contemporary gender ideologies that characterized women as "family oriented." While she would work for equal treatment of servicewomen and was determined to integrate the WAAC as fully as possible within the Army, she viewed the women's corps as a temporary entity which should be disbanded when the war was over and whose members should be returned to their families and their primary duties as wives and mothers.[26]

Oveta Culp Hobby assumed the position of WAAC director at the age of thirty-seven. Born in Killeen, Texas, Hobby was the daughter of a Texas lawyer and legislator. Privately educated at Mary Hardin-Baylor College, she followed her father's lead, attending law school and becoming extensively involved in Texas state politics throughout the 1920s. After her marriage in 1931 to the former governor of Texas, William Pettus Hobby, she began a new career with the *Houston Post*, which her husband edited and they eventually co-owned. During the 1930s Hobby joined her husband on the editorial staff of the *Post* and worked with him in orchestrating and influencing state and national politics from gubernatorial to presidential elections.[27] Like her husband, Oveta Hobby was a Southern Democrat but, as the 1930s progressed, an increasingly disaffected one. Both she and William Hobby believed that Roosevelt's social programs were far too sweeping. Although they supported Roosevelt during the war years, after the war Oveta Hobby set up several statewide organizations aimed at garnering the votes of Democrats for Republican presidential contenders.[28]

Oveta Hobby's career in newspaper editing and publishing had a tremendous effect on her work for the federal government during World War II. Her first position with the War Department was largely due to her experience with the *Houston Post* and her reputation as a "savvy politician." She was recruited in 1941 by Secretary of War Henry Stimson to organize and head the new Women's Interest Section of the War Department's Bureau of Public Relations and with her husband's support left Texas and her two small children and headed for Washington, D.C.[29]

Hobby's post as the first chief of the War Department Women's Interest Section, like Anita Phipps as director of Women's Relations in the 1920s, was purportedly to help "tell the story of the Army" to American women in ways that would gain their support for military efforts. In her role as "translator" for the War Department Hobby was expected to understand and sympathize with the military's positions while also as a woman gain the support and trust of prominent women's organizations for military efforts. One of her first actions in this position was to establish the Advisory Council of the Women's Interests Section, composed of thirty-three nationally organized women's groups, to cooperate with the War Department in national defense.[30]

While Hobby cultivated and maintained a cooperative relationship with prominent women's groups throughout the war she was not explicitly affiliated with any one women's organization. The criteria for the WAAC directorship demanded that all candidates for the position not only have executive experience involving the "successful management of both men and women assistants" but also, and most importantly, have no previous affiliation with any pressure group. Women's organizations, especially those perceived as feminist, whether local or national, were prominently featured in the War Department's definition of "pressure group."[31]

Marshall's recruitment of Oveta Culp Hobby marked the beginning of a professional relationship that would serve Hobby well during her tenure as WAAC director. Impressed with Hobby's savvy as head of the Women's Interest Section, Marshall asked her to represent the War Department in government hearings on the WAAC legislation. During these hearings Marshall became convinced that Oveta Hobby was the woman who could most effectively direct and manage the new women's corps, and in March 1942 he recommended her for the position of WAAC director.[32] Marshall's early work with Hobby and his confidence in her judgment and abilities made it possible for Hobby to call on him for help when she encountered hostility and opposition from members of his staff during the war. The fact that Hobby had the ear and support of the most powerful man in the Army insured that the opinions of female administrators would be taken seriously and allowed her to successfully meet the various challenges to her authority that would occur in the war years.

Expediency, not public or congressional acknowledgment of women's rights to military service, proved the impetus behind the passage of the WAAC bill. The sluggish progress of the legislation was drastically altered after the Japanese attack on Pearl Harbor in December 1941, and the WAAC bill was before the full House and Senate by March 1942. The battle to pass the WAAC measure, however, was postponed as opposition to the legislation developed and members decided to put off serious discussion of the act, citing their need to pass "more important war measures" first.[33]

Initial congressional reluctance on the bill foreshadowed the complex and often hostile reactions of civilians to the inclusion of women in the military. Despite Marshall's utilitarian analysis of Army labor power or Rogers' plea that women simply be rewarded for work they had done or were doing, many congressional representatives and their constituents judged the measure as one that might disrupt gender and racial order in the larger society.[34] In fact, the WAAC, as the first of the women's services, became the focus of broader public concerns with the potentially disruptive effect of the war on "normal" relations between the sexes and races.

The opposition of "soldier" and "woman," homefront and battlefront, posited by the opponents of the legislation framed most of the discussion surrounding women's presence in the U.S. military throughout World War II. For the most part, the congressional debate focused on gender issues and did not delineate between different racial/ethnic groups of women. Yet the persistent oppositional positioning of "male soldier" versus "woman" more clearly reflected the gendered tensions of the white community. These oppositions rested upon the distinct wartime duties most clearly ascribed to the white female and male citizen. Men were expected to bear arms in order to protect and defend their country and their women. Women were expected to support and sustain this effort by keeping the homefires burning, bearing children, and filling the role of the "girl back home," the symbol for which the "boys in uniform" were fighting.[35] These reciprocal obligations of citizenship rested upon the privatized gender relationships between women and men in the "home" and the particular asymmetrical relationship between the male protector and the female protectee.[36]

The debate on the floor of the House and Senate over the WAAC bill indicated the degree to which many members of Congress viewed women's military service, and the rights and privileges such service was assumed to accord women, as profoundly threatening. Some congressional opponents of the legislation questioned whether military service was the most effective mode of mobilizing women in support of the war effort. Others focused their concerns on the possible problems arising from the "masculine" environment that would be the Waacs' new home. At issue were the implications of women's military service for American "manhood" and "womanhood."[37]

The most striking characteristic of the factions supporting and opposing the WAAC legislation was their bipartisan composition. Congressman Somers' (D, N.Y.) characterization of "defense of country" as the "duty" of men, was seconded by his Republican colleague, Congressman Hoffman of Michigan. Expressing his disapproval of the WAAC bill, Congressman Hoffman (R, Mich.) articulated what he considered to be the "duties" of female citizens during war by criticizing women's potential abdication of the duties of the domestic sphere for military service.

Take the women into the armed service . . . who then will maintain the home fires; who will do the cooking, the washing, the mending, the humble, homey tasks to which every woman has devoted herself; who will rear and nurture the children; who will teach them patriotism and loyalty; who will make men of them, so that, when their day comes, they, too, may march away to war?[38]

The WAAC bill threatened to upset these gender relationships and the construction of citizenship they represented. Thus, congressional opponents viewed the potential upheaval in gender relationships and gendered wartime duties resulting from an influx of women into the Army as having serious consequences for wide-ranging issues far removed from the military itself.[39]

In response, most advocates of the WAAC bill articulated their support within conventional constructs, often framing their arguments in defensive ways and trying to assure the public, and perhaps themselves, that the creation of a women's corps would not threaten gender order or male citizens' duties as soldiers. Proponents of the bill did not argue explicitly for the legislation as progress in women's rights as citizens. Most supporters distinguished between female auxiliaries and soldiers with rhetoric that maintained a bifurcated construction of citizenship which reified wives and mothers and defined the primary female duty during wartime as that of supporting men, particularly soldiers, while locating the most important duties of male citizens in military service.

Proponents initially depicted women's service in the WAAC as an extension of women's duty to be active in home defense. The home defense argument was undergirded by the American public's fascination with and support of the employment of women with the British armed forces. Many Americans viewed women serving with the British military as heroines, forced from their homes to defend themselves, their families, and their country from the aerial attacks launched against their "island nation."[40] Within this framework congressional and military advocates argued that women's military service was simply an extension of their duties within the home. "Total war," Representative Rogers contended recognized "no limitations of battlefields, no gender of its participants. . . . To win . . . every resource, every service must be utilized."[41]

Congressional supporters were especially careful to head off any accusations that women's duties in the WAAC would encourage young women to renounce responsibilities as wives and mothers. Several members of Congress even erroneously declared that mothers would not be allowed entrance into the WAAC. This line of reasoning played well with Southern Democrats like Representative Thomason of Texas, who argued that while in peacetime women's place was in the home, the women volunteering for the WAAC "don't have husbands or children" and should be allowed to do their part.[42] Despite Thomason's statement, the WAAC legislation carried no restrictions on married women's entrance.[43]

Many WAAC supporters also argued that women's entrance was not a threat to male privileges and honor associated with soldiering, but rather a means by which some male soldiers could be utilized as fighting men. Republican Congresswomen Rogers (Mass.) and Bolton (Ohio) assured their male colleagues that military women would not be usurping the positions of male soldiers. They and other supporters depicted women's role in the military as one of "assisting," not "displacing," those in combat, particularly by filling jobs considered "women's work" in civilian life. Women's military service would therefore not threaten gender order in the military but rather rectify the practice of having men do work in the Army that was considered "feminine."[44] "We do not want your jobs," Bolton claimed, "We want to make your jobs easier, and we want to make them fit in better to the present day, which is a fighting world for you and an assisting one for us."[45] By legitimating and espousing a system within the military in which a sex-segregated labor force would relieve men of "women's work," proponents of the WAAC bill reinforced distinctions between "women" and "soldiers." Men were better able to do the clearly masculine work of the military, soldiering, if women assumed the work associated with assisting soldiers in a modern war, especially clerical and communications jobs.

The most effective rhetoric supporting and defending the WAAC was that associated with patriotism, women's capacities for patriotic duty, and the corollary accusation that those who did not support the WAAC were questioning women's historical and contemporary service to their country. Opponents of the WAAC bill had no choice but to respond with similar rhetoric, and most of the arguments against the measure contained assurances that this opposition did not derive from any doubts as to American women's patriotic motives.[46] Those opposing the bill were uncomfortable being cast in the role of villains who did not respect the patriotic desires of the women of America.

By invoking this type of patriotic discourse, proponents of the bill created a situation in which the debate centered on the most appropriate ways for American women, as citizens, to serve the U.S. war effort. With the backing of the War Department and the Chief of Staff, as well as thousands of women writing in support of the measure, it was a difficult task for male members of the House and the Senate to argue that they "knew better."[47] On several occasions opponents of the WAAC bill were chastised by the women in Congress for their intransigence. Bolton, recalling women's service during World War I, remarked that the time for women serving without recognition or status "has long since passed."[48] Rogers joined in and berated several congressmen who wished to prohibit women's service overseas asking, "Do you think for one moment . . . that the sisters of the men who have given their lives overseas for us would hesitate for one moment to go overseas if they could be of service?"[49]

Framing the debate in this way not only made it easier for supporters of the legislation to argue in favor of the bill, but also called into question the "patriotism" and "loyalty" of those who opposed it. Several congressional opponents suggested that they were defeated from the outset, arguing that if a secret ballot was taken on the measure it would fail, but that most were afraid of being accused of "aiding Hitler and our enemies across the sea."[50] Representative Hoffman lambasted the Democratic administration for forcing legislation on Congress in the name of the war effort and contended that Congress had reached the stage in which anything the armed forces or administration demanded must be conceded. He ended his harangue by declaring that members had no choice but to agree to the bill or be "classified as one who opposes the war effort" and concluded his opposition by voting against the bill in the final roll call.[51]

The frameworks congressional supporters employed to argue for the WAAC bill deflected opposition to the legislation but also insured that the Army would not be required to treat female soldiers the same as their male counterparts. Equal treatment of all women hinged in part on their eligibility for the same benefits granted all male soldiers including equal pay, and equal access to hospitalization, medical care, and other services offered by the Veteran's Administration. In keeping with WAAC supporters' assertions that Waacs would do work associated with civilian life, not soldiering, the WAAC bill provided for women to receive compensation for injury and medical benefits under the Federal Employees Compensation Act, a law addressing civil, not military, service. Women as civilian employees of the federal government were already eligible for such benefits outside their service with the Army. The question before Congress was whether in discharging the duties previously ascribed to male citizens women would then be granted the same veteran's *entitlements* as their male counterparts.[52]

Congressional debate on this issue focused on the status of women entering the WAAC; were they soldiers or civilians? Clearly the WAAC bill in its original form classified them as militarized civilians serving with, not in, the Army. Nevertheless, several congressmen argued that the legislation should be amended to make Waacs eligible for veteran's benefits like male soldiers.

Some claimed women had rights to veteran's benefits based on the work they would perform. The fact that many of these jobs would be exactly the same as those already held by male soldiers prompted Congressman Clason (R, Mass.) to call on his colleagues to grant Waacs "exactly the same consideration" as male soldiers, offering no benefits to men "that are not given to women."[53] Others chose to frame their positions with traditional rhetoric highlighting the importance of "protecting" women. Congressman Nichols (D, Okla.) couldn't understand why his colleagues would be "blind" to their "responsibility to give these women the same protection that we give the men."[54]

The most effective opposition to the amendment was presented by Congressman Kilday (D, Texas), who bypassed a direct discussion of the rights of "militarized women" by focusing on the drastic impact any such amendment would have on the status of all civilians working with the Army. He argued that it would be "complicated and expensive" to open the Veteran's Administration insurance system to civilians, and claimed that amending the WAAC legislation in this manner would set an "unwise" precedent in this direction.[55]

The amendment was precisely centered on the issue of granting female soldiers the same citizenship rights as defined by benefits as their male counterparts. To begin to characterize female participation in and with the military as having the same meanings as men's service was too bold a move for Congress to contemplate. Even most supporters of the WAAC bill opposed the amendment, fearing that its consideration would indefinitely delay the passage of the WAAC bill itself.[56] Although Congress dispatched the question of veteran's benefits relatively neatly at this time, the issue would be raised again one year later when members discussed passage of a subsequent bill to grant women full military status.

For African-American women, "equal treatment" was a question not only of their status and opportunities relative to male soldiers, but also relative to their white female counterparts within the WAAC. The Army's Jim Crow policies that segregated all African-American military personnel from their Euro-American counterparts and included the provision of separate and often unequal housing, dining, and recreational facilities, were clear indicators of the lesser status and authority afforded black men and women in the Army during World War II.[57]

Senate debate about equal treatment of servicewomen focused not only on the gendered nature of the benefits they might receive but also on preserving racial distinctions among female auxiliaries. Several senators argued that amendments prohibiting racial discrimination were necessary to guarantee "colored" women equal treatment within the Army, and Senator Johnson (D,

Colo.) offered an amendment to this effect.[58] Senator Austin (R, Vt.), chair of the Senate Committee on Military Affairs, persuaded his colleagues to oppose Johnson's amendment, not "on the merits of the policy it represented" but rather because the War Department did not want any "question of discrimination" raised.[59] Army and War department officials feared any direct mention of racial discrimination would serve only to heighten suspicions concerning the Army's treatment of "colored" male personnel as well.

Senators' concerns about racial discrimination were focused on the question of whether "colored" women would be allowed to enter the WAAC. No Senator argued that segregation per se was a form of racial discrimination; in the minds of military officials and most senators "fair and equal" did not preclude segregation. During committee hearings and discussions before the full Senate most members made clear that they believed the Army was best equipped to decide "where they are going to put the colored and where they are going to put the white people."[60]

Proponents of the WAAC feared that any implied challenge to the Army's segregation policies would be enough for Congress to reject the bill altogether. Senator Johnson subsequently retracted his objections after Senator Austin agreed to state for the record that entrance to the corps would not be prohibited because of race. Thus, the issue of "equal treatment" in terms of both benefits for all female citizens serving with the Army, and bans on racial discrimination to insure equal opportunities for African-American women, were bypassed in favor of a policy of expedience to guarantee passage of the unamended WAAC bill.[61]

The WAAC bill was eventually passed on May 14, 1942. Its difficult journey through Congress reflected not so much by its fate in the House, which passed the bill on March 27, 1942, by a substantial margin, but by its arduous passage through the Senate, whose members delayed passage of the bill until May 14, 1942, and then sent it on with an 11-vote margin of victory.[62] On May 15, 1942, President Roosevelt signed the bill into law, establishing a women's auxiliary for service with the Army.

This first battle, fought on the floors of Congress, was won; however, the corps would soon find itself tested again, this time in the arena of public opinion. Despite the assurances of the War Department that women would be utilized in limited ways and that their service as auxiliaries would be predominantly in jobs that women had previously performed in the civilian labor force, the Edith Nourse Rogers Bill creating the female auxiliary was the center of heated public debate. Echoing the congressional debates over the WAAC bill, public discussion centered on fears that the establishment of the auxiliary and the creation of a corps of "female soldiers" would lead women to abdicate their responsibilities within the home in order to usurp the male duty of protecting and defending home and country.

The potential upheaval in public understandings of exactly what constituted proper "manhood" and "womanhood" was viewed by some as having serious consequences for the American family, either because military service encouraged women to leave the home or because it challenged gender order within the home. Some of these concerns were articulated by conservative religious and secular organizations opposed to military service for women. An article in *Time* magazine reported that the National Catholic Women's Union described the WAAC as a "serious menace to the home and foundation of a true Christian and democratic country." The Brooklyn *Tablet,* a Catholic weekly, characterized women's military service as an "opening wedge" in breaking down "traditional American opposition to removing women from the home."[63] Still other organizations, such as the isolationist America First movement, focused on women's responsibilities as caretakers of American values and morality and as mothers of the next generation. Leaders of America First portrayed the auxiliary corps as an "unnatural" organization, demanding as it did that women "give up" motherhood for the duration of the war.[64]

The fear that women's military service would lead to a falling birthrate was manifest in various editorials published shortly after the creation of the auxiliary corps. "Is it advisable," one editorialist queried, "long before the supply of manpower shows any sign of running short, to take a lot of young, vigorous women into a vaguely defined noncombatant branch of the Army; and is it advisable then to tell them they must not have children? Wouldn't it be wiser just to leave them out of the armed forces, and encourage them to marry, produce children, and thus contribute in the old, natural way to the war effort?"[65]

Those opponents of the WAAC who focused on the military itself drew on public beliefs that the "feminine" and the "martial" were wholly incompatible. Some reasoned that because the military was such a completely masculine institution, if women remained unchanged, they could not possibly function as soldiers within its structures. Others emphasized the potential masculinization of those women who took soldiering seriously. In their view the only way that women could perform efficiently within the Army was if they laid aside their femininity and acted like men. A good soldier epitomized conventional masculine qualities; he was "authoritative," "strong," "logical," and "well-disciplined." All white men had the potential to be good soldiers; the War Department and much of the American public, however, did not believe that such attributes were possible for women and many African-American men.

The conviction that women, because of their femininity, would not perform well in a military environment was evident in media coverage of the auxiliary in its first year of existence which focused on the humorous consequences of a feminine auxiliary. The exaggerated definitions of femininity framing these editorials included a lack of intelligence, an inability to perform simple tasks or to endure any kind of hardship, a preoccupation with trivial issues, and a general tendency to be illogical or scatterbrained.[66] One piece in *Newsweek* poked fun at servicewomen learning to salute, characterizing it as the "chief amusement" for the men stationed with them and noting that even the corps' director, Colonel Hobby, had difficulty with the maneuver. The author went on to describe Hobby's dismay at the early rising hour prescribed by the Army and the post commandant's assurances that she would be exempt from this requirement.[67] This "news" article was joined by a number of nationally syndicated cartoons which gave amusing renditions of women's attempt to fit into the Army. These depictions included a woman who resorted to dumping her purse all over a general's desk to find a message requested by him, and another falling out for reveille with her hair in curlers and clothed only in a bathrobe.[68] These portrayals of auxiliaries demonstrated an unwillingness to take seriously a corps of female soldiers and supported the contentions of those who saw the corps as nothing but a ridiculous Army experiment, with no purpose or function.

The featherbrained Waac found her counterpart in the mannish woman who flourished in a martial environment. The belief that women could not be good soldiers without losing or rejecting their femininity was integral to the construction of the mannish Waac. This image was rooted predominantly in public speculation as to the type of woman who would choose military service, as well as fears of the impact the masculine environment of the Army would have on women. Many mainstream journalists evinced conern over the potential development of masculine appearance and characteristics in Army women. Some of these editorials were supportive of the WAAC and countered the stereotypes of mannish Waacs with reports that servicewomen were maintaining their feminine appearance and attractiveness. "They might be called amazons," one reporter remarked, "Yet those trim martial young women at Des Moines, Iowa, to train as officers in the WAAC look feminine enough in their 'civvies.' And even in their uniforms too."[69] Other journalists urged women not to join the corps warning,"Stay as feminine as possible. Who wants to go out with an ersatz man?"[70]

"My boy friend knitted it for me."

"Give me 4 soldiers, please!"

While appearance was a key aspect of the mannish Waac stereotype, equally important was the fact that most of the women who were portrayed as lacking femininity were in positions of authority, the WAAC sergeant drilling her female troops or the WAAC commanding officer in control of a company. A woman with status and power was by definition "unfeminine" and represented a threat to male authority. Military women's perceived usurpation of men's duties as "protectors" was also symbolic of a potential shift in women's relationships to and power over men in the Army. The consequences of such a shift were starkly addressed in a series of nationally syndicated cartoons caricaturing the new "female protector." In visual illustrations of the potential results of women's presence within the Army, large manly Waacs towered over diminutive service men. These men were not only smaller and shorter than their female counterparts but they were always of lower rank than the Waacs with whom they interacted. The text of these cartoons revealed the emasculation of men at the hands of empowered women, made smaller not only in physical stature but also by servicewomen's assumption of the duties crucial to constructions of American manhood. In one popular series, *Private Breger Abroad*, a tiny GI with glasses sat at a desk typing a report as a mannish WAAC sergeant strode out of the office. Another male soldier in the office turns to him and says: "Stop Griping! SOMEBODY had to be chosen to release her for combat!"[71]

That female power within the military might influence women's interactions with men in their homes was clear in popular media depictions portending the subversion of men's position as head of the household and women's role as "supporter" and "helpmeet" to men. Nationally syndicated cartoons provided graphic illustrations of this possibility with drawings that included a man sitting at home knitting a sweater for his Waac wife, as well as a frail-looking bespectacled husband wearing an apron and wielding a broom while asking his Army wife at the door if she had his monthly dependency allowance.[72] In these examples women assumed the male role of breadwinner and the male obligation of military service and men were relegated to the domain of the home. These paired constructions, breadwinner/helpmeet, protector/protected, did not represent "different but equal" functions but gave men considerable power over women. To give women traditionally male responsibilities then threatened women's power over men both within and outside the home.

While the initial response of the white public and mainstream press to the formation of the WAAC ranged from guarded approval to dismay and focused on the gendered implications of women's military service, the opening reaction of the African-American press and black leaders centered on the selection of Oveta Culp Hobby, a white Southern woman, to head the corps. Hobby's appointment was especially opposed by the National Association for the

"One confirmed—two probables!"

"Can't you forget I'm a first-class private?"

"Column right!—MARCH!"

"It was awfully nice of you boys to give us your seats."

Advancement of Colored People (NAACP) and the National Council of Negro Women (NCNW), led by Mary McLeod Bethune. Bethune and other national black leaders pointed to William Hobby's actions when he was governor of Texas as evidence that African-American women would not be well-served with Oveta Hobby as WAAC director. According to NAACP Director Walter White, on one occasion during Governor Hobby's tenure a black man was beaten in broad daylight by a gang of white men. In response, several African-American groups, including the NAACP, called on the governor to take action. Governor Hobby subsequently told White that black organizations could "contribute more to the advancement of both races by keeping your representatives and their propaganda out of this state." According to White and Bethune, Oveta Hobby's husband's position on race relations made many people "apprehensive lest Mrs. Hobby share the views which her husband expressed at that time." Colonel Hobby's subsequent announcement that 10 percent of the first WAAC group would be black women was met with skepticism by Walter White of the NAACP, who remarked, "the general feeling in Washington is that this was in large measure due to the opposition to her appointment."[73]

The 10 percent quota for black women as well as the WAAC's policies of segregating its white and African-American members did little to quiet these concerns and were the subject of protests throughout the war.[74] The black press became one of the main forums for criticism of Army treatment of African-American male and female personnel. Many elements of the black press engaged in a "Double V" campaign, advocating victory abroad in the war against fascism, as well as victory at home against racial injustice. Editorials in Black newspapers, such as the *Pittsburgh Courier* and the *Philadelphia Afro-American*, echoed the arguments of the NAACP and African-American leaders who asserted that the future status of Black people in the United States depended upon their service as equals in the armed forces.[75] African-American women's service was situated within this larger framework that characterized the military during World War II as one of the major arenas in which the fight for racial equality must take place.

The more positive reaction of the black press, relative to the white press, to women's entrance into the WAAC can be partially explained by this framework. Another part of the explanation lies in the greater acceptance by the African-American community of black women's participation in the paid work force. African-American women's role in the labor force had historically been much greater than white women's, and definitions of "respectability" for black women did not preclude workforce participation.[76]

The black press' supportive reception of African-American women's enrollment in the WAAC can been seen in the coverage of black women's service

"I'm certain I have a message for you in here somewhere, general!"

by national and local black newspapers. The *Philadelphia Afro-American*, for example, carried updates on the numbers, assignments, and performances of African-American Waacs in regular columns such as Charles Howard's "At Home and Abroad with the WAAC."[77] Articles on black women in the military lauded their efforts as akin to that of black men in improving the position of the race.

National African-American women's organizations, especially the National Council of Negro Women (NCNW) and black sororities like Alpha Kappa Alpha (AKA), among others, also provided support and sympathy for African-American servicewomen. Many African-American Waacs wrote of their struggles to the NCNW and its president, Mary McLeod Bethune, asking Bethune to take action on their behalf. While the NCNW supported the corps as an "opportunity for . . . women of the race," Bethune simultaneously cautioned that their endorsement of the organization should not be interpreted as an endorsement of segregation: "This . . . is the other half of our battle. [But] it must not, in any way, lessen our support or participation in our country's victory effort." Bethune, like the African-American press, framed the battle against segregation and prejudice within a larger support of the war effort.[78]

The congressional debates and public discussion about the WAAC highlighted the gendered and raced constructions of male and female citizenship underpinning the positions of both supporters and opponents of a women's corps. The issues raised in these exchanges, and their heatedness, portended the storm of controversy that would surround the women's corps throughout World War II, as well as the cultural anxieties raised with the inclusion of Euro-American women and women of color within the white male military. In response, Waacs felt it necessary to prove that they were needed for vital military purposes and that they were not mannish women attempting to usurp male soldiers' authority.

Public concerns with a corps of female soldiers were eased somewhat by the many ways the WAAC legislation differentiated servicewomen from the male soldiers with whom they would serve. Because of the corps' "semimilitary" status, the Army did not retain full control of its operation. This authority was located instead with the female director, Oveta Culp Hobby, and in the female command structure she supervised. In addition to women's ineligibility for veteran's benefits, the grade and rank structure of the WAAC differed from that of the male Army.[79] These distinctions allayed public fears of both women's authority over men and the more disturbing implications of Army control of young women; clearly women in the WAAC were not really soldiers and Hobby and her staff, as women, would see to the special needs and protection of Waacs.

The Army's return to Congress in 1943 with a plan to place women formally within its ranks renewed public debate and attention to the WAAC. Seeking to gain fuller control of the women's corps and eliminate the confusion created by the differential regulations mandated by the WAAC bill, the Army proposed that servicewomen's status be changed from "auxiliary" to "full military." "In other words," the head of the Army's administrative branch remarked, "in the Army we want one category of people."[80]

To Congress and the American public "one category of people" implied treating Waacs exactly like male soldiers. Public and congressional responses focused on the threat to sexual norms and women themselves that such "equal treatment" implied. Would the Army's bill mean that servicewomen would be free to engage in the same kinds of behavior as their male counterparts? Would Waacs lose the female advocacy and protection of Colonel Hobby? Would the Army now move to more fully exploit women within its ranks? These questions and others framed public and congressional discussion over the creation of a new entity—the Women's Army Corps.

2

"Ain't Misbehavin' "?
The Slander Campaign Against the WAC

John O'Donnell's syndicated column, "Capitol Stuff," hit the streets June 8, 1943. In his article, this staff writer for the *New York Daily News* "revealed" that corps' leaders, in cooperation with the War Department, would be furnishing Army women with "contraceptive and prophylactic equipment."[1] Portions of the public understood this as a sign that the Army was luring women into the corps under false pretenses and in reality intended to use them as prostitutes. Other citizens saw the issuance of prophylactics to Waacs as a continuation of the Army practice of dispensing condoms and setting up prophylaxis stations for male GIs. Since prevailing norms dictated that respectable, unmarried women were not supposed to be sexually active, the suggestion that birth control information and devices would be furnished to women within the Army was interpreted as proof that the military was either encouraging heterosexual promiscuity in women or using Waacs to provide sexual services to male GIs and officers.

World War II was a moment of transition, a snapshot of changing values, behaviors, and discourses concerning female sexuality. In fact, American mobilization for the war, with its attendant disruption of traditional systems of social order, catalyzed popular fears about women's sexual and economic independence. U.S. participation in the war accelerated the shift to city living and provided millions of young people with opportunities for economic autonomy and freedom from constraining social environments, creating new possibilities for extramarital sexual experience.[2] Popular focus on the sexual threat such changes might pose was never divorced from broad concerns about the simultaneous dangers to gender order mobilization entailed. In fact, the potential increase in female power publicly perceived as flowing from women's full integration within the Army prompted accusations of sexual immorality within the WAC.

Public concerns with women's sexual agency and fears of women's sexual victimization emerged in part as a reaction to this new mobility and were fueled by the removal of women from more traditional protective networks, namely the control and guidance exercised by their parents and their husbands. In fact, many contemporary social commentators attributed the perceived rise in heterosexual promiscuity among young women to women's greater freedom outside the home in the twentieth century. One public health officer even claimed that problems with female heterosexual promiscuity began with the passage of the 19th Amendment, "when women gained the same political privileges and freedom held by men," contending that women's presence in previously masculine realms had resulted in their acceptance of "the same masculine freedom in relation to sex."[3]

During the war the breakdown of previous systems of protection for women, as well as established modes of controlling and regulating sexuality, coincided with an increasing public focus on and visibility of alleged female sexual agents. Public concerns over the potential escalation in female heterosexual promiscuity were engendered in part by the belief that joining the workforce or the military might prompt women to claim rights to sexual freedoms associated with male economic independence and power; women who "behaved" like men would also earn the right to "misbehave" like men, especially sexually.[4] "Female soldiers," working in the most masculine wartime arena, found themselves the most frequent targets of these anxieties.

Public and state attention to the potentially negative consequences of an increase in women's sexual agency had a profound impact on societal attitudes toward and response to the WAC. During World War II public discussions of sexual norms and behavior were integral to popular cultural constructions of "masculinity" and "femininity." As such, concerns with the impact of women's military service on gender norms and relationships were paralleled by fears of the similarly disruptive influence the WAC might have on sexual norms.[5] The potentially masculinizing effect of the military on women was not only in women's taking on male characteristics, appearance, and power, but also in women adopting an aggressive, independent and masculine sexuality. Worries that servicewomen might become sexual victims were joined by depictions of Wacs as sexual actors and agents engaging in the same types of promiscuity, drunkenness, and sexual adventure tacitly encouraged in male GIs. Rumors as to the nature of this sexual adventure did not focus solely on heterosexual escapades but also alleged that the women's corps was full of homosexuals. In all cases the fear was that the WAC would either attract women who were sexually deviant, or that service in the Army would make them that way. Sexual agency in itself was seen as masculine; thus, the Army's masculinizing influence on women would cause them to engage in extramarital heterosexual activity, as was encouraged in their male counterparts, or turn them into "men" who took women lovers.

The slander campaign targeting the women's corps, and most powerful from early 1943 through early 1944, was the most visible articulation of these anxieties. Columnist John O'Donnell gave public voice to some of the rumors and sexual innuendo that had been swirling around the women's corps since the early spring. Spread largely by word of mouth in neighborhoods and on Army posts nationwide, occasionally picked up by the white mainstream press, and repeated and reinforced by members of Congress and the Army, this whispering campaign had far-reaching consequences for military women as it sculpted a series of sexual images of female soldiers that shaped popular perceptions of the Corps during and after the war.

During the war popular fears of the consequences of perceived changes in female sexual behavior were also driven by the continuing deterioration of conventional ideological systems of protection. The long-standing equation of female passionlessness and sexual passivity with respectability had been breaking down since the early twentieth century.[6] By the early twentieth century the increasing availability of birth control meant that sexuality was becoming more and more separated from reproduction. Young women's increasing opportunities for economic independence also meant that some women no longer depended on men for their financial security.[7] Additionally, nineteenth-century sexual commentators' emphasis on sexual restraint was being replaced by a modern focus on the importance of sexual fulfillment within marriage, for both men and women. As a result, contemporary sexual ideology, although continuing to posit the greater sexual aggressiveness and stronger sexual desire of men than women, began to acknowledge female desire and women's capacity for sexual interest.[8]

The erosion of nineteenth-century emphases on sexual restraint was not necessarily liberating for women. As historian Christina Simmons argues, the new sexual discourses of the 1920s and 1930s, while allowing for and acknowledging female desire, also contained new forms of sexual regulation focused on women. Twentieth-century sexual commentators' affirmation of female desire, for instance, was combined with their criticism of women who sought to withdraw from men sexually, thereby enhancing the specifically sexual power of men both before and within marriage.[9] Severing sexuality from reproduction, moreover, while enabling some women to engage in extramarital heterosexual relationships without the risk of pregnancy, deprived other women of the ability to reject sex because of fear of pregnancy, and allowed for increased criticism of women who withheld sex from their husbands.

Women's ability to make choices in sexual relationships was shaped by their continuing ability or lack thereof to claim "protection" from sexual exploitation and/or victimization once they consented to some forms of extramarital sex. The past use of "passionlessness" as a mode of protection for women against the dangers of heterosexual expressions of desire had been based on a constructed dichotomy between "good" and "bad" women, the former usually white and middle to upper class, while the latter included poor and working-class women and women of color, all of whom were excluded from its limited security.[10]

Within this protective paradigm then female sexual respectability was always determined by race and class as well as behavior. As such, working-class women were assumed to be more sexually active than middle-class and upper-class women and African-American women were stereotyped as sexually promiscuous by nature.[11] Given these racialized sexual stereotypes it is not surprising that the black press, unlike its white counterparts, did not attack the sexual respectability of female soldiers and officers. Still, both black and white women felt the impact of the rumors and many have since commented on the frustration and anger they felt living through the period "with its cartoons, and dirty jokes and vile insinuations."[12]

Despite the new acknowledgment of women's desire, engaging in extramarital heterosexual relationships put middle- and upper-class young Euro-American women beyond the pale of protection previously offered by strict Victorian standards. The penalties that all women faced for having extramarital sex—including pregnancy, stigma, and even rape—remained in force. The "double standard" was as visible as ever; men took no more responsibility for extramarital sex than they ever had, while sexual availability for women continued to carry with it the label of "bad girl."[13]

Women's historical relationship to the military was fraught with cultural representations of "bad girls" and is crucial to understanding the sexualized constructions of "female soldier" that emerged during World War II. In general, women's nonmedical military service prior to World War II has been framed by the cultural meanings attached to past female military participation as "camp followers," and "cross-dressers."[14] The term "camp follower" was used by American military commanders in the eighteenth and nineteenth centuries to describe civilian women who traveled with armies, providing needed goods and services. Some of these women were the wives, widows, or companions of individual male soldiers; others eked out a living performing duties that would later be subsumed under the Army's quartermaster corps, including cooking, sewing, and laundering.[15] Despite the military's dependence on women's assistance for nonsexual services, the duties of camp followers were often assumed by military and civilian leaders to include prostitution. Equally important, this term, when used to identify women traveling with the army, perpetuated the belief that only immoral women would associate with the military, and that the only valuable service a woman could provide the military was sexual in nature.[16] In popular usage of the mid-twentieth century, the term "camp follower" was frequently synonymous with that of "prostitute" and usually implied a woman of "loose sexual morals." Consequently, women's past nonsexual work in the military was rarely visible or acknowledged when this term was publicly invoked to discredit Waacs during World War II.

The camp follower was joined by the uncounted and sparsely documented cross-dressers who had historically "passed" as men in order to take part in combat.[17] While their exploits were celebrated, once detected many found it necessary to portray their experiences in ways that did not violate contemporary gender and sexual norms. Some, like the early cross-dressing soldier Deborah Samson, assured the public that she "preserved her chastity inviolate" and in a later speaking tour apologized for the "uncouth" actions of her masquerade.[18] By the turn of the twentieth century cross-dressing was increasingly viewed with hostility and clinical suspicion as a manifestation of "sexual deviance."[19] Like cross-dressing women in civilian life, the sexual deviance of women who passed as men in the military was associated with "gender inversion," a medical term linking female masculine behavior and appearance with female homosexuality. The perceptions of the dangers involved in this undertaking would surface again during World War II as women were formally incorporated into the Army as soldiers.

These past constructions of military women guaranteed that they would remain largely invisible and the crucial work they did in and with the military would remain undervalued and unacknowledged. Thus, although their work was integral to the existence and survival of military units, women themselves were ideologically and formally marginal to the military's identity as a fighting force.[20]

While the WAAC bill's differentiation between soldiers and female auxiliaries had been effective in quieting public concern about sanctioning the use of female soldiers, the Army's subsequent move to incorporate women completely within its ranks sparked renewed scrutiny of the women's corps. The second Army bill, offered in January 1943, was prompted in part by the dissatisfaction of Waacs, who found themselves neither "soldiers or members of the military team."

The deficiencies of auxiliary status were made especially visible and objectionable by Navy officials' successful efforts, after passage of the WAAC bill, to grant women full military membership rights in the Navy. As in World War I, during World War II Navy officials arranged for the acceptance of women as official members of the Navy and Marines, with the corresponding rights, benefits, and compensation granted male sailors and officers. Navy officials had waited to see how the Army's WAAC bill would fare before offering their own proposal. After supporters of the WAAC bill had fielded most of the attacks in Congress, the Navy, facing little resistance, pushed through their own legislation giving women full military status. Consequently, the pay scale of Navy women kept pace with that of their male counterparts. When the new Army pay scale went into effect soon after the WAAC was established, Army women found themselves locked into a pay scale by the initial WAAC legislation, resulting in their doing the same work but making far less pay than either male Army soldiers or their counterparts in the naval women's organization, the WAVES.[21] The real impetus for this change, however, was male Army leaders' frustration with the confusion and duplication of effort required to administer two different sets of regulations for Waacs and male soldiers.[22]

It was no coincidence that the whispering campaign against the women's corps gained momentum at the precise moment that the WAAC was trading its marginal status for full membership in the Army. The conversion to full military status for servicewomen represented the formal inclusion of women within the male bastion of the Army. This change in status meant that military women moved from having a partial role as auxiliaries *with* the Army to an official and recognized role *in* the Army as soldiers. The official inclusion of women in the Army was seen by many to mean that women would be completely under the control of male military officers and no longer protected by Colonel Hobby and her WAAC female command apparatus. The conversion of the Women's Army Auxiliary Corps into the Women's Army Corps (WAC) then resurrected earlier questions as to the impact of a state-sanctioned and state-controlled organization taking women away from their families and placing them within a wholly male institution. Once subsumed into the Army proper could the WAC continue to act en loco parentis to protect women and regulate their sexual behavior? Or would women be endangered by their male counterparts and the Army's more lax attitudes toward the heterosexual behavior of soldiers generally?

Military men had historically acted in ways that proved dangerous to women, with implicit if not explicit encouragement by Army officials and the larger masculine culture of the military. For parents and concerned citizens therefore, the Army's support of the women's corps suggested a potentially hazardous sexual exploitation of women within its ranks. Based partially in the invisibility of women's past work with the military, these uncertainties were voiced in public allegations that the Army had no real military need for women and was simply trying to develop an organized cadre of prostitutes that would function to boost male morale and help combat male GIs' soaring venereal disease rates.

In addressing the new military status of the WAC, many citizens focused on women's lack of sexual protection within the Army. The hundreds of letters that flooded the War Department and WAAC headquarters expressed concern with the vulnerability of servicewomen within the Army generally and the "sexual advances" of male officers particularly. "If the pending bill to make the WAAC *of the* Army (not auxiliaries) goes through," one male doctor argued, "then some evil-minded officer may (under the guise of military discipline), order a WAAC to his private tent plus her contraceptive."[23] Some male enlisted personnel were also wary of the new control the Army would have over its female soldiers. Within the Army's strict division between officers and enlisted personnel, some enlisted men considered themselves at the mercy of officers' whims; this was bad enough for men but could have even more serious consequences for women. "The main need for WAACs overseas is to provide them (officers) with women," a male corporal warned a WAAC friend, "There is no absolute means of forcing them to become playthings for the officers, but the power is there to make things unpleasant if they don't."[24] Implicit in these statements was a concern with the possibly tragic results of servicewomen's lack of traditional familial and kin protection and the potential for sexual harassment, leaving them susceptible to the advances of ill-intentioned men.

While some servicemen were concerned with the threats to women's person and reputation in the new WAC system, the antagonism of other male GIs and officers toward female soldiers became clear when Army investigations into the whispering campaign found that most of the rumors and negative accounts about the women's corps originated with and were spread by male military personnel. The creation and dissemination of slanderous stories about the WAC was one expression of men's resentment of women's entrance into a previously male-only preserve. A number of servicemen argued that the WAC was surplus, simply a "women's organization for show," and as service-women began to take over jobs, male soldiers disapproval of the corps actively increased. Some in noncombat positions feared that servicewomen might supplant them and many preferred their present assignments to combat duty overseas. Some enlisted men and officers who did not wish to be relieved of their stateside jobs refused to show Wacs how the work should be done and generally discouraged women they knew from joining the organization.[25] It might have been easier to slander female soldiers sexually than to admit that all men were not excited at the opportunity of serving their country on one of the fighting fronts. Articulating yet another reason for male resentment, one African-American WAC officer recalled:

> The presence of women in the Army was resented by many because, tradi-
> tionally, the military was male . . . Negro males had been systematically
> degraded and mistreated in the civilian world, and the presence of success-
> fully performing Negro women on the scene increased their resentment.
> The efforts of the women to be supportive of the men was mistaken for com-
> petition and patronage.[26]

Surveys by the Army's research branch indicated that servicemen believed that the WAC was not really needed, that women could be employed in civil-ian defense work or as nurses, and that military service was not appropriate for women because it took them away from their homes. Some of the men who responded felt generally that the Army was "full of wolves" and close associa-tion with male soldiers would lead women to have declining moral standards and to lose their femininity, while others felt the problem lay in the WAC itself and the "kind of women" who joined. In general the majority of male respon-dents described the WAC as "bad for a girl's reputation." One male GI remarked that he would rather stay in the Army longer and then when the war was over "be able to return to normal civilian life and *feminine* women . . . I feel that this would not be possible if many girls joined the Wacs." Army opin-ion surveys also found that the majority of enlisted men would advise their sis-ters or girlfriends *not* to join the WAC, while only 12 to 17 percent would advise them to join.[27]

These attitudes had a great impact on women who considered enlisting in the women's corps. A Gallup Poll of civilian women in early 1944 showed that the majority of the respondents felt that men did not approve of women in military service. Of these, 16 percent felt men didn't respect the WAC and thought it was "immoral," "coarse," and had a "poor reputation"; 15 percent thought men resented women in service because they didn't want to feel equal to women; 9 percent believed men did not like women in uniform because it wasn't feminine, and another 9 percent thought men believed that women's place was in the home and that they should stay there. The overwhelming majority (72 percent) stated that Army men's attitudes had given them an unfavorable impression of the women's corps and had been a major factor in their decisions not to enlist.[28]

The most frequently recurring accusation leveled at the Army was that the role male leaders envisioned for women was not one of soldier, but of "morale booster" to male GIs. These questions concerning the function of the WAC were in part shaped by earlier cultural images of camp followers. Although morale boosting did not necessarily imply prostitution or sexual service, the two were often linked in the public consciousness, and explicit in this type of allegation was the belief that boosting male morale involved providing sexual services to GIs and officers. As one army investigator reported, residents of Kansas City, Kansas, generally believed that "Waacs were issued condoms, and enrolled solely for the soldiers' entertainment, serving as 'morale builders' for the men and nothing more."[29] The fear was that in establishing the WAC the Army was simply creating an organized cadre of prostitutes to satisfy male soldiers' needs for heterosexual companionship and keep their morale high. In other words, the Army itself might pose the most serious threat to women, exploiting rather than protecting female soldiers.

Letters to WAC headquarters and the War Department made it clear that portions of the public, particularly those with female relatives or friends in service, were especially concerned with this possibility. "If my daughter is a member of an organized uniformed group of whores," wrote one father of an auxiliary, "I want to know it and get her out of the WAAC."[30] Army investigations of these rumors and accusations, carried out through the summer and fall of 1943, found that at many posts where Wacs were stationed, the pervasive assumption of military and civilian personnel was that the Corps existed to provide companionship for soldiers.[31] Wacs, although largely rejecting these rumors, were nevertheless affected by them and sometimes articulated their own uncertainty with Army purposes. "A satisfied soldier can learn and fight better than a restless, nerve wracked man," wrote one auxiliary, "You can't change human nature so why not supply a healthy source of entertainment for our gallant men, and win the war?"[32]

Civilians frequently assumed that the alleged issuance of contraceptives to Wacs was proof that sexual services were an integral component of their mission.[33] In addition, the media, especially cartoonists, had a field day with the theme of Wac morale boosting. Perhaps one of the most explicit renditions of the subject was drawn by Corporal Vic Herman in his Army camp newspaper cartoon series, "Winnie the Wac." In one episode, "Winnie," a character drawn as white and extremely sexualized, is shown sitting on a soldier's lap in a dentist's office with the caption "I just came in to cheer your patients."[34] Some GIs were also uncertain as to the purpose of the women's corps; one report noted that a white soldier "expressed great surprise when refused a date by a Waac who he attempted to 'pick-up' as he thought that was the duty of the Corps."[35]

At the heart of the negative publicity was the belief that Army recruitment of women and women's enrollment in the WAC were evidence of dangerously misplaced priorities and values that left women unprotected and their reputations ruined. In turn, the persistence and pervasiveness of reports of Wac "immorality" seemed to confirm the worst fears of the effect military service would have on women as individuals and, through them, on the family. One recruiting officer summed up the negative images prevalent at her post: "The WAC is made up of women who are tired of living with their husbands, give their children away for someone else to care for and seek adventure and chase around with GIs."[36] The depiction of women leaving their husbands and children and abandoning all responsibilities within the home to pursue military service epitomized the contradiction between the traditional duties of women as wives and mothers and the new opportunities made available to them through American mobilization for war.

Women's intemperance and sexual immorality were closely linked in the disparaging descriptions of Wac behavior and character throughout World War II.[37] At a number of posts local civilians characterized Wacs as "two-fisted" drinkers who frequented taverns and drank until they fell off the bar stools.[38] Even one supporter of the Corps wrote to Colonel Hobby that she had heard that often Wacs on overnight passes went to hotel rooms, bought liquor to drink in their rooms, and invited men up for the night.[39] Gossip and speculation as to the number of illegitimate pregnancies and cases of venereal disease in the WAC which might result from this behavior captured the popular imagination. False information of hundreds of Wacs being discharged for illegitimate pregnancy was the subject of editorials in the mainstream press and speculation in the civilian population.[40] Thus, one of the potentially disastrous outcomes of women's military service was inscribed in the image of the drunken Wac engaging in indiscriminate heterosexual activity with any available man, spreading VD or bringing forth a generation of illegitimate children who, like their mothers, were destined to be social outcasts.

Fears of women's sexual independence were also manifested in accusations of homosexuality within the WAC. The lesbian was the epitome of the sexually autonomous woman, not even requiring a male presence to satisfy her sexual desire. Assumptions of predilection, however, rather than individual sexual acts were most critical overall in the public discourse addressing the lesbian "threat" in the World War II Women's Army Corps. A woman's expressed desire to join the military could in itself be cause for suspicion, because "real women" would not want to be "soldiers" at all. Articulated fears of the kind of woman who might flourish in a martial environment, regardless of suspicion of particular sexual behaviors, were rife with allusions to lesbianism and followed the corps from its inception. Jack Kofoed, a reporter for the *Miami* (Fla.) *News*, could imagine no "female soldiers" other than "the naked Amazons . . . and the queer damozels of the isle of Lesbos."[41] Another female reporter, pleasantly surprised at the appointment of the "feminine" Oveta Culp Hobby to head the women's corps, wrote, "Left to guess, most of us would have said that if ever a woman's army got under way in this country a man or an unmarried woman with worlds of experience and a *Gertrude Stein haircut* [my emphasis] would direct it."[42]

Although during the whispering campaign explicit references to female homosexuality in the WAC were seldom made in the mainstream press, the reports of rumors submitted to WAC headquarters by recruiting officers in the field demonstrated that public concern with lesbianism was pervasive.[43] Within the WAC the issue of female masculinity or mannishness became one of the major frameworks under which issues of lesbianism were addressed. Women's entrance into the military and the assumed usurpation of men's duties also became a symbol of women claiming traditionally male power. Fears that the WAC would either attract or produce lesbians were in part generated by what historian Esther Newton has called the "fusion of masculinity, feminist aspirations, and lesbianism."[44] The connection between mannishness, female power, and lesbianism was also made by Colonel Oveta Hobby in a postwar interview in which she drew an analogy between women's claim to suffrage and women's entrance into the military: "Just as a startled public was once sure that woman's suffrage would make women unwomanly, so the thought of 'woman soldiers' caused some people to assume that WAC units would be hotbeds of perversion."[45] As WAC historian Mattie Treadwell recalled, during the war there was a "public impression that a women's corps would be the ideal breeding ground for [homosexuality]" because of the "mistaken" popular belief that "any woman who was masculine in appearance or dress" was a homosexual."[46]

The slander campaign was exacerbated by the words and actions of state officials, both civilian and military, who often lent credibility to the rumors concerning the women's corps. The greatest opposition to the Women's Army
Corps (WAC) bill took place in the House of Representatives, as the Senate
passed the measure quickly and with little comment barely a month after it
was first introduced. This opposition was led by, but not exclusively composed
of, Southern Democrats, who delayed the bill with extended filibusters and by
offering substantive amendments to the legislation that resulted in lengthy
congressional discussions.

The first successful amendment to the WAC bill was drafted by the House
Committee on Military Affairs, and was intended to clarify women's authority vis-à-vis their male counterparts within the Army. While the original WAC
bill simply included the women's corps in the Army and provided no limitations on women's military authority, several congressmen expressed horror at
the idea of "women generals" running around commanding male troops. This
potential threat to male control was averted by an amendment prohibiting servicewomen or female officers from commanding male soldiers. The chair of
the House committee, Congressman Andrew May (D, Ky.), reported that
women's authority was thereby "limited to the command, control, and direction of those in the WAC and does not apply to the male members of the U.S.
Army."[47] The limitations this amendment placed on women's status and
power within the Army was clearly intended to bolster the increasingly murky
divisions between female and male "soldiers," and to insure that conversion to
full military status for female auxiliaries did not mean granting them power
over or the *same* status as male "soldiers."

The most vocal opponent of the WAC bill, Congressman Vincent (D, Ky.),
characterized his disapproval of the measure as a defense of American
women. In offering an amendment to prohibit overseas service for Wacs,
Vincent enumerated the many "dangers" women might face overseas. Citing
a recent *Times-Herald* article Vincent raised the specter of both Wacs pregnancy and the sexual victimization of Wacs by servicemen when he remarked,
"I'm sure all of you saw the statement in the paper about the trouble that had
developed in north Africa, where the girls had to be given protection."[48] By
injecting this unsubstantiated insinuation into the congressional discussion
Vincent lent credibility to the rumors that were currently plaguing the
women's corps.

Although Vincent's remarks represented the most extreme form of opposition to the WAC bill, his position was vigorously supported by several congressional colleagues. "The man does not live who holds in higher respect the

womanhood of the world than I do," remarked Congressman Folger (D, N.C.), "On account of that pedestal upon which I have always placed her and which position she has occupied in my life always, I am opposed to this bill."[49]

The rhetoric fashioned by Vincent and his allies demonstrated the ways in which female military service threatened both women's status as "protectees," men's as "protectors," and the gender, racial, and sexual systems based on this duality. By invoking women's "cherished" place on a "pedestal" to frame their opposition, Vincent and others defended male power under the guise of female protection. Moreover, by contending that one of the most "drastic consequences" of the "militarization" of women was that it placed them in situations in which "all male commands must be recognized," Vincent's concern, was focused on the "protection" of white, not black, women. His definition of "protection" included not only the need to safeguard women's sexual reputation, but also revealed his desire to defend the racial and class status of white Southern "ladies" as "good" women. Racial and class status were crucial to contemporary definitions of female sexual respectability and embedded in Vincent's criticism of the Army. He objected to making "servants" out of women by requiring them to say "Ma'am" after every statement, language that "down South we expect our servants to use . . . not the young ladies of the land." Clearly Vincent intended to extend the traditional protections of race and class status only to white upper and middle-class women.[50]

Supporters of the WAC bill were quite willing to vie with Vincent for the right to speak for American women. Congressman Thomason (D, Texas), took the "moral high ground" and accused Vincent of treating the legislation as a "matter of levity." He went on to "defend American womanhood" from what he termed as Vincent's attacks and blasted him for subjecting "50,000 fine young women in this country, who have volunteered, if you please, to a certain form of criticism and sarcasm, to which I do not think they are entitled, and which I know they do not deserve."[51] Others supported the bill by arguing that opponents' claims to want to "protect" women were a thinly veiled effort to deny female soldiers rights and benefits. Thomason was joined in his defense of the WAC bill by Congressman Sparkman (D, Ala.), who responded directly to Vincent's claim that overseas service was "dangerous" for women by asserting that civilian women employed in the U.S. were "working in places just as dangerous as the places they [Wacs] will be sent over there. . . . You do not object to their working in those places of danger. Is it anymore dangerous to drive a jeep or an ambulance or a truck or to do some clerical work miles and miles back of the front lines?"[52]

Representative Vincent's agenda became more clear as he began to concentrate on the issues of benefits and status derived from military service, insisting that women should under no circumstances have access to them. One amendment he offered denied servicewomen access to the veteran's benefits and privileges that their new status in the Army would grant them. Vincent based his proposal on the fact that women were ineligible for combat, noting, "The whole theory of pension and compensation is to take care of our veterans who fight our wars, who put themselves in danger, and become thereby disabled." He presented his motion as important in assuring that Wacs who served within the United States would not be compensated in the same manner as male soldiers, "especially when they stay here in good jobs, in the country at home, not in any more danger than I am right now."[53] In offering this amendment Vincent appeared to want to play both sides of the fence, earlier arguing that women should be "protected" from overseas service, and here contending that those who remained within the United States should be denied the "protection" found in veteran's benefits.

WAC supporters used the contradictions in Vincent's protection rhetoric to highlight the injustice of not insuring that women in the military be entitled to benefits comparable to those of men. Vincent's newest attack against the WAC bill was countered by several congressmen who contended that Vincent's stated rationale of opposing the WAC bill in "defense of American womanhood" was not borne out in his actions on the floor of the House. Pointing out that Vincent's desire to "protect" women was hardly served by an amendment that would deny them compensation and medical benefits, Congressman Miller (R, Conn.) underlined the problems with Vincent's proposal by reminding him that his logic for denying women disability benefits might also apply to male soldiers who either served within the U.S. or did not participate in combat.[54]

In recognizing the importance of not undermining male power by denigrating male noncombatants, members demonstrated their understanding that if they did so they would be impugning a huge portion of the male military. Vincent's amendment was defeated as it was clear that no one would take away benefits from male soldiers even though they were not combatants. Members of Congress were not about to eliminate the construction of veterans' benefits as an "entitlement" to all men who served in the military, whether or not they actually offered their lives in "defense of country."

The controversy above points to the conflicting logic of arguments against affording benefits and status to women in the military. While much of the discussion centered on the inability and impropriety of women acting as soldiers, there was also a second and more important protective discourse at work. All men, regardless of combat experience, were entitled to entrance to the military and the state-funded veteran's benefits accruing from military service. To allow women into the Army, even as noncombatants, was to threaten the gender hierarchy that guaranteed only men the status and power associated with military service.

Although defeating Vincent's amendment, House members made clear their own concerns with the effect female integration might have on male power outside the Army; they let stand an amendment that would deny Wacs the dependency allotments available to male soldiers.[55] Dependency allotments allowed soldiers to provide for their spouses, children, and family who might otherwise face economic hardship as a result of their military service. These allowances were crucial to the construction of male soldiers as both protectors and breadwinners. By barring female soldiers from access to these allotments House members revealed their uneasiness with the idea of either female protectors or female breadwinners. Although a few members objected to the "discrimination" they argued was inherent in this provision, most sided with Congressman Elston (R, Ohio), who invoked the specter of dependent husbands to support the committee's recommendation.[56] The vision of "dependent husbands" suggested the emasculation of men, just as the image of "female soldiers" pointed to the defeminization of women. Therefore, women's eligibility for dependency allotments was a direct threat not only to male authority within the Army but also to privatized gender and sexual relationships within families and male power outside the military.[57]

Perhaps the greatest impact of this second round of congressional debates was to fan the flames of the ongoing slander campaign against the women's corps. On the one hand, journalist John O'Donnell's claim in his June 9 editorial that a female legislator was the source for his explosive allegations provoked the House to go on record refuting his statements. On the other hand, O'Donnell's description of the Army's allocation of prophylactics to women as a protective policy was extremely close to Representative Vincent's remarks before the House only days earlier. Vincent's name stayed in the public eye when *Newsweek* followed up on O'Donnell's allegations by reporting that Vincent opposed assignment of Wacs abroad because, "He said there had been 'trouble' about the women soldiers in North Africa, and he had read somewhere that they 'had to be given protection.' "[58] The nature of this rumor campaign, like any other, was circular. Vincent read an article about Wacs in North Africa and reported it to his colleagues as fact. Although refuted, his statements were picked up by a reporter for a mainstream news periodical who then printed his assertions for thousands to read. What should the public assume? Why not believe O'Donnell when a U.S. congressman seemed to agree with him?

Civilian officials were not alone in fueling public speculation about the women's corps. In a similar fashion the actions of Army leaders sometimes reinforced public fears that the only "real uses" the Army had for women were sexual. Concerns with the potential sexual victimization of servicewomen were intensified, for instance, by male officers who claimed that the most important function of the WAC was not the soldierly duties it performed, but the positive impact the women had on the morale of male soldiers.[59] Given the public presumption that morale boosting by female soldiers might include sexual service, statements of this type did little to alleviate and much to aggravate popular concerns with women's role in the military.

More devastating than individual officers' statements was the Army's occasional use of WAC units to control male sexuality, moves which seemed to confirm suspicions that the role the Army envisioned for women *was* sexual. African-American WAC units were in general stationed only at posts where black male soldiers were present. In part this practice was a product of the Army's policy of segregating its troops by race. White officers, particularly at Southern posts, however, also referred explicitly to the assignment of African-American WAC units with black male troops as a means of discouraging African-American servicemen from forming liaisons with white women in the surrounding communities.[60] The inspector general at Sioux Falls Army Air Base suggested that "large groups of Negro Wacs be brought by truck from Des Moines" to make up for the "recreational deficiencies of Negro men at the air base."[61] In these instances, African-American WAC units were used by the Army as a means of upholding and supporting prohibitions on interracial relationships.

White Wacs were also deployed in areas in which male soldiers' sexual contact with civilian women was deemed a threat to national security. In December 1944, Field Marshall Sir Bernard L. Montgomery proposed using white U.S. WAC and British Auxiliary Territorial Service units in the Allied occupation of Germany to curb the fraternization of male GIs in the American and British armies with enemy (German) women, especially prostitutes. Field Marshall Montgomery's proposal was made public in a number of articles and editorials and harshly criticized by WAC headquarters, as well as by Wacs stationed overseas in the European Theater of Operations.[62]

The public reaction to Montgomery's proposal demonstrated the clear links made by many between such actions and the sexualized use of female soldiers as morale boosters. In one national radio program the broadcaster claimed that a recent Army order was taking Wacs from "clerical and steno-graphic jobs and moving them to the same camps as the men in order that companionship would curb the too frequent visits to German brothels of our soldiers."[63] That such actions were seen as pervasive and understood to repre-sent the sexual availability of Wacs to male soldiers is illustrated in a letter from an Army officer to an enlisted male friend. Commenting on a recent order from Army headquarters prohibiting the association of officers with prostitutes, the officer observed: "First they issue a directive saying no officers will be allowed to be seen with girls of that character or in the houses of pros-titution—the next day the same colonel issues a directive saying that the offi-cers can now date Wacs. Nuf sed."[64]

The difficulty of clearly distinguishing "female soldiers" from civilian women who were involved sexually with Army men was exacerbated when white general officers directly commissioned their white civilian secretaries into the women's corps. One incident incited both white male soldiers' resentment and public comment. In early 1944, Lt. General Kenny, sta-tioned in Australia, arranged for the direct commissioning of three Australian women who had worked for him as civilians, ostensibly to allow him to move them to his headquarters in New Guinea.[65] WAC headquarters was notified of the incident when they received complaints not only from Wacs but from the parents of enlisted men who took exception to the appointment of civil-ian women as captains, while their sons remained privates. One father wanted to know what the newly commissioned WAC captain "did up in New Guinea to earn her wage."[66] There was a great deal of suspicion on the part of both WAC administrators and public commentators that the actions of General Kenny signaled a mistress relationship between him and one of the newly commissioned Australian women, Mrs. (now Captain) Clark. This suspicion seemed to be confirmed by Army investigations into the allega-tions.[67] Whether true or not, the actions of General Kenny directly violated WAC regulations and brought a new round of negative publicity to corps.[68] The practice of general officers commissioning their enlisted and civilian secretaries gave rise to renewed public suspicion that servicewomen's func-tion was primarily sexual and generated a new series of GI rumors that Wacs were used only as "morale boosters."[69]

At the heart of the slander campaign lay the issue of who or what would be responsible for protecting military women from military men, the Army, and themselves. Images of female soldiers as either sexual victims, exploited by the

Army and their male counterparts, or sexual agents, victims of lax regulations and their own bad judgment, propelled public concerns and determined the parameters of the WAC response. In this response, corps' administrators were convinced of the need to reestablish the WAC, even after conversion, as a protector of young women and an organization that would act both as a guardian of their morals and welfare and to regulate and control their sexual behavior.

This characterization of the WAC as acting en loco parentis led one disgruntled general to remark that Hobby ran the WAC as if it were an all-girls' boarding school and not a military entity. Despite his annoyance, it was exactly this boarding school image that Colonel Hobby had in mind—an elite, cloistered, enclave of young women eligible to enter male public space because of their inherent respectability and difference from other "questionable" women.[70] And it was this image that drove WAC recruiting and public relations campaigns throughout the war.

3

The WAC Strikes Back:
Constructing the "Respectable" Female Soldier

Even without the impetus of the rumors targeting the WAC, Colonel Hobby's decade of experience with the mainstream media had already heightened her consciousness of how critical the "presentation" of the women's corps was to its public reception and legitimacy. In fact, she expected that initial press coverage and controversy about the women's corps would be influenced by contemporary stereotypes of women entering nontraditional fields. She believed that "female soldiers" would probably be portrayed in one of several ways: "giddy, featherbrain(s) engaged in powder-puff wars with no interest beyond clothes, cosmetics, and dates"; "hen-pecking old battle ax(es) who loved to boss the male species"; "sainted wives and mothers until they left the kitchen, then scarlet women;" or "amazons rushing to battle."[1] While Hobby was not surprised by this type of negative publicity or press descriptions trivializing the women's corps she was taken aback by the vitriol of the slander campaign.

Under the director's supervision, WAC and Army administrators responded to public concerns that women's military service threatened gender, racial, and sexual hierarchies by constructing images of "female soldiers" that upheld these systems of power relations. In doing so Army and WAC administrators found themselves engaged in a precarious balancing act. To convince Americans of the "real military need" for women, and deflect fears that women would be exploited sexually, the Army was forced to make a persuasive case that it required female labor and women's military service as "soldiers" to effectively prosecute the war. Simultaneously, any suggestion that female soldiers would have the same status or be treated identically to male soldiers exacerbated concerns with female heterosexual agency, lesbianism, and women's power within and outside the military.

Colonel Hobby and her staff, working through the Army and WAC Bureaus of Public Relations (BPR), sought a solution to this paradox by portraying the corps as guarding young women's welfare and morals, and presenting female soldiers as feminine in appearance, sexually respectable, and less powerful than their male counterparts. The WAC female leadership sought to insert into the public consciousness a feminine, controlled, young woman—comparable to a college girl—as an antidote to the "female protector" or sexual agent. The women's corps was also recast, not as a threat to the home, but rather as an organization that nurtured and supported women's love of home and desire to return to it at the close of hostilities. Most importantly, WAC leaders constructed the "female soldier" as white, middle-class, and educated, invoking cultural connections between race and class status and sexual respectability to counter public antagonism.

The military's efforts to mobilize women for the WAC were similar in several ways to the War Manpower Commission's attempts to encourage civilian women, especially married women, to enter the paid labor force. The propaganda used by the Army and civilian agencies to support some women's movement into war industry in nontraditional jobs and others' entrance into the military framed women's participation in both arenas as temporary responses to the crisis. Mobilization propaganda for both groups also depicted women's desires to accept these new opportunities as patriotically motivated and rooted in a traditional feminine theme of self-sacrifice. Military women, like their civilian counterparts, were characterized as making the ultimate sacrifice, giving up the possibility of home and family for a short time to aid the war effort.[2] Thus, the recruitment of women for war industry and the military were both constructed as short-term solutions to "total war" mobilization and explicitly denied that women had a right in peacetime to either access to those positions or the benefits and status they accrued from them.

While the "gains" women made by being accepted into the military were in some ways offset by the conventional feminine images and limiting ideological frameworks used to win public acceptance of women's military service those attempting to sell the concept of a women's army to the U.S. public were also forced to do a large-scale reeducation of the populace, stressing the necessity of women's service in the army and familiarizing civilians and male soldiers with the corps itself. This broad education campaign worked to counter some public antagonism and to create a space, albeit a tiny one, for women within the military that had not existed prior to the war.

It is too simple then to characterize World War II as a period whose gains for women were abruptly ended because repressive ideologies on women's place within the home were never displaced.[3] The war was a period when several discourses concerning women's status in the United States met and clashed.[4] For servicewomen this meant that themes of self-sacrifice and patriotism were joined by self-interest as important recruiting and publicity tools. The Army Recruiting Service and the Bureau of Public Relations (BPR) defined this "self-interest" not only in terms of women's desire to bring the war to a quick end and "bring their men home," but also in the opportunities for training, new skills, education, travel, and adventure women would find in the service. It was also clear from the outset that African-American women's service within the WAC was lodged within a framework of group-interest, as part of a movement for racial justice and race and gender equality. In one public statement the National Council of Negro Women placed African-American women's military service within the context of advances occurring for all women and black people during the war:

> The role of the Negro woman . . . is immediately connected to the strategic gains made by all women in the present world situation. These general gains must be expanded and consolidated. There must be no recession from the encouraging advances already made by women. . . . Sex must never again be a determinant affecting broad opportunities for women. Prejudice based on sex has no place in the present scheme of social activity—where it is accentuated by the factor of color, affirmative steps must be taken to eliminate both.[5]

The greatest problem faced by WAC recruiters and public relations personnel was the need to change public consciousness and convince the majority of Americans, especially young women, that women's military service was not radical or threatening but instead necessary and expedient to eventual victory in the war. To do so, the WAC director was convinced of the need to "package" and recruit "female soldiers" differently than their male counterparts. Hobby's perspective was shaped in part by her discussions with officials of the Canadian and British women's military organizations prior to the passage of the initial auxiliary legislation. These officials' descriptions of the negative publicity their corps had encountered convinced the director that public relations and recruiting policies were key to gaining public acceptance of women's military service. As a member of Hobby's staff recalled, "One major effect of the Canadian visit upon the headquarters was that it became what its members called 'public-relations conscious.' "[6]

The War Department BPR initially followed WAC female leaders' outlines and assured civilians that women serving in the Army were not abdicating their position and responsibilities within the home. WAC officials and civilian supporters of the corps argued that complete mobilization of all portions of the population were necessary to insure victory and that military women were not so much stepping out of the home as they were simply meeting the conflict encroaching on their private sphere. "The American family is the kernel of democracy," a writer for the *Ladies Home Journal* observed, "and that's why U.S. women are entering the armed forces, sacrifice to save the family and democracy."[7] These arguments paralleled those of early women's rights activists who framed calls for women's increased power in the state with rhetoric asserting that women's active participation in the state was simply an extension of their duties within the home.[8] As former suffragist Alma Lutz contended, service in the auxiliary corps "will not wipe out women's inherent love of home and the making of a home. If anything it will make them value home more."[9] This line of reasoning redrew the lines separating men's and women's domains, expanding women's sphere to include the entire home front in an effort to legitimize women's entrance into the war effort and the military. Thus, the view of the WAC as a threat to the family and U.S. society was countered by arguments that affirmed the value of the home and women's place within it and characterized women's role in the military as a way of protecting the family, not destroying it.

One of the key foundations of this paradigm as developed by WAC public relations officials was a portrayal of women's military service as organized around familial relationships as daughters, mothers, sisters, wives, and sweethearts. The Army eagerly seized on and fed to the press various stories of servicewomen who joined because of their connections to men who had been killed, were prisoners of war, or who were fighting overseas. "The reason behind most enlistments is a man in the armed forces," reported one male writer after a visit to a WAC post. He went on to observe that, like male GIs, women kept pictures of the opposite sex in their lockers, but in contrast to the men, "There are no movie stars. Every picture is there by right of kinship— either blood or heart."[10] Servicewomen were depicted as enlisting not for personal gain but in order to hasten the war's end, and public acceptance of Wacs was made conditional on them giving first priority to the men in their lives.[11]

Female Army leaders viewed women's position within the home as crucial to contemporary definitions of femininity. In arguing that military service did not rob women of their feminine appearance or attributes, WAC leaders emphasized servicewomen's actions to create homelike environments at their posts.[12] Several correspondents used this information to highlight the feminine actions of female soldiers who planted flowers, painted their barracks a soft green, and added attractive matching curtains. They also found them "sprucing up" the "unglamorous" Army foot lockers and field tables by decorating them with chintz skirts, thereby turning them into "smart dressing tables." Corps' newsletters reported that the materials that servicewomen used to feminize their barracks were supplied by male GIs in exchange for women's sewing and ironing, thus, replicating familiar, gendered patterns of labor and exchange.[13]

Although WAC publicity stressed that Army life did not inhibit women's desire to create a "home," it also made clear that most servicewomen wanted nothing more than to return to the "real thing" once the war ended. On one occasion Colonel Hobby even implied that public concern should actually be focused on civilian women war workers, not on Wacs, since civilian women earned more money and had more independence while "a girl's experience in the Wacs . . . serves to accentuate her desire for home . . . and children. When you put on a uniform you don't change nature."[14] Several supporters of the corps also suggested that military service would actually make women better wives, especially to male GIs returning after the conflict, teaching them valuable lessons in discipline and budgeting resources, and resulting in "these girls making a fine bunch of mothers when they come back." For a short time the War Department even used the slogan "The Wac who shares your Army life will make a better postwar wife!" to promote women's military service.[15] Thus, Hobby and the various WAC publicity agencies created a framework of reassurance that portrayed military service as supporting, not inhibiting, women's "femininity."

The necessity of presenting servicewomen as "feminine" to offset concerns with masculinization and rumors of homosexuality also paradoxically reinforced popular fears that the Army had no "real military need" for women's labor and that the Army's intent was to exploit women sexually. Consequently, the importance of depicting servicewomen as feminine was joined by Army and WAC public relations efforts to persuade American civilians of the military's need for women's labor, as soldiers. Throughout the war WAC and Army public relations and recruiting officials focused on the Army's need for the special skills and knowledge of *women* in its prosecution of the war.[16] Army leaders described women's role within the WAC with the same rhetoric used in the early twentieth century to support the movement of women into clerical work. They maintained that women were more skillful than men in these areas because they did not mind routine jobs, had "keen eyes and quick fingers," and were patient, loyal, and conscientious. This logic defined many of the new tasks resulting from changing technology as "women's jobs" and reinforced the sexual division of labor.[17] After the war Army officials pointed to the successful employment of servicewomen in these new tasks, observing that "women's manual dexterity was valuable not only on a typewriter keyboard, but in maintaining and repairing the multitude of intricate small instruments essential to mechanized warfare."[18]

By representing the women's corps as reinforcing the established civilian sexual division of labor, Army and WAC public relations officials indicated their understanding of the tensions between "femininity" and military service and asserted explicitly that it was possible to be a "woman" and a "soldier." Editorials in support of the WAC drew attention to the seeming contradiction: "they are feminine but darn good soldiers," read one. Another assured readers, "you never forget that they are women. But you never forget, either, that they are soldiers."[19]

Army officials' descriptions of the military's need for women's labor as a supplement to men's service in combat were designed to counter public concerns of women's usurpation of men's duties as soldiers. Army and WAC public relations officials' emphasis on the *noncombatant* nature of women's service was crucial to their attempts to distinguish servicewomen from their male counterparts. The first WAC national recruiting slogan, "Join the WAAC! Release a man for combat!," was intended to exploit this framework in order to gain members and greater public support for the women's corps.

The Army's ability to meet its requirements for skilled women and insure the success of the WAC experiment depended in large measure upon its ability to convince the U.S. public and prospective recruits that military service was appropriate and rewarding for women and that the WAC and its female members were absolutely essential to victory in the war. In a wartime economy when the demand for workers far exceeded the supply, the Army's needs for female personnel clashed with those of civilian agencies and industry trying to fill requests from labor short areas. While most civilians believed that women's work in war industries was critical to the war effort, it was harder to convince the public that women's military service per se was essential or even desirable.[20]

Civilian employers and the War Manpower Commission did nothing to help and a great deal to hinder the Army's efforts to recruit women. Instead of coordination between the civilian and military sectors of the federal government, there was outright competition for women's labor, weighted in favor of the War Manpower Commission. WMC officials contended through much of the war that work in war industry, not military service, was the most effective way for women to contribute to the war effort. With control of the Office of War Information, some WMC officials could and did pull preapproved advertising for WAC recruiting campaigns. In doing so they both undermined Army efforts to enlist women and affirmed public beliefs that women were not essential to the Army. At the very least, the WMC's public stance served to obscure the possible options for women in the WAC and muddle the public understanding of national priorities for womanpower.[21]

In October 1942, William Fitzgerald, the State Manpower Commission director, responded to WAC recruiting in Connecticut by issuing a directive forbidding such activities in his six manpower shortage areas, remarking, "The Army will have to decide whether they want the materials first or the men and women behind them." An editorial in a local paper took issue with Fitzgerald's edict, commenting, "it appears . . . that he intends that production shall proceed regardless of the demands by the military for men and women." The article went on to argue that "such conflicting authority serves only to confuse the public mind." and roundly criticized Fitzgerald's "anti-WAC recruiting order."[22]

The national WMC's public claims of greater need for women's labor were echoed by other civilian employment agencies who also refused to recognize the Army's claim on women's labor or promote women's options for military service. A number of states, as well as employers, refused to grant women interested in military service the same incentives which were guaranteed by law to their male counterparts. Since most men who entered the armed forces were drafted, they were covered under the Selective Service Act and the Soldiers and Sailors Relief Act. These acts protected their civilian jobs and guaranteed them the same or equivalent positions upon their honorable discharge from service. In contrast, the WAC at its inception was a volunteer organization, a civilian auxiliary to the regular Army, and its members were not covered by these provisions.[23]

Most employers actively discouraged women from joining the WAC by withholding provisions that would guarantee them their civilian jobs upon discharge. White female teachers employed in Salem, Oregon, reported that the school board was refusing to hold jobs for, or grant leaves of absence to, teachers desirous of entering the WAC; the board required them instead to formally resign their positions. These women noted that their schools employed the tenure system for rating teachers and many were reluctant to give up their standing in seniority and pay without a guarantee of their jobs when they returned. Several women observed that school board members' simply did not feel that women were "especially essential in the armed services." One woman expressed her "keen wish" to join the WAC and requested that WAC headquarters or the War Department issue a statement which would protect them and "give them the freedom to openly apply for enlistment." When a similar situation arose in Utah, the WAC director requested that the National Education Association (NEA) make a public announcement supporting women's military service. The NEA responded by advising WAC headquarters that no national policy had been contemplated or established "to make mandatory the granting of military leaves to teachers entering the military service," and left the matter up to each state's discretion.[24]

Both the subversion of Army recruiting efforts and the blocking of access to military service for women already employed in the civilian labor force were predicated on the belief that while military service was a "manly obligation" for men and a sacrifice deserving of reward, women's military service was at best inappropriate and at worst marked the abandonment of more fitting responsibilities. As a result, it was an option to be discouraged not encouraged, and censured not sanctioned. Even the Army, despite its attempts to argue for its need for women did not at first support that stance with clear policies which would have allowed women to benefit as men did from enlistment. It was not until after the auxiliary was converted to formal military status that some of these entitlements were finally granted to women.[25]

The public relations efforts of the WAC and the Army were especially tested between the summer of 1943, and the spring of 1944, when public opinion of the women's corps plummeted in response to the slander campaign. While the initial reaction of the War Department was to hold back on any concrete denials to avoid lending credence to public rumors, the outrage and disgrace felt by many Wacs forced the Army to reply directly to the attacks. The War Department's strategy for countering the "malicious gossip" included direct denials of the accusations and demands for a retraction from the journalist who began the "whispers." War Department and military officials' major efforts, however, centered around characterizations of the "attacks" on the women's corps as "Nazi-inspired propaganda" that could seriously damage the war effort and condemned those who believed and repeated the "slanderous stories" as unpatriotic and possibly traitorous.[26]

This patriotic discourse was also invoked by civilian supporters of the women's corps, who described women's military service as epitomizing American women's patriotism and defended servicewomen as symbols of female self-sacrifice. Colonel Hobby's position was consistent with this framework and was influenced by her own philosophy, which defined women's service as motivated by self-sacrifice, not self-interest. The WAC director's approach stressed women's moral obligations to others and throughout the war she argued that military service for women should not be portrayed as "glamorous," but rather as a "selfless" act consistent with women's traditional patriotic duties.[27]

Servicewomen expressed their own outrage at the negative publicity by pointing to their sacrifices and patriotic service to defend themselves and the corps. "I couldn't understand," wrote one Wac, "how my eagerness to serve our country could have brought such shame on us all."[28] In a public plea for sympathy and support, a WAC song developed at the height of the slander campaign characterized "John Q. Public" as falling for a Goebbels-inspired public relations campaign:

Oh, pity the lot of the poor little WAC,
Whom the axis decided to stab in the back.
According to them she's a "Frivolous Sal,"
A rug-cuttin', high-livin' kind of a gal
Whom Uncle Sam's paying to play with the boys.
Come now, Herr Goebbels, let's shut off the noise!
And you, John Q. Public, don't be such a jerk!
Don't you realize the Wacs are in the Army to work?
. . . A Wac does a job and a job that is fine,
The Army has praise for them all down the line.
Well, I guess by this time I've said quite enough.
All we ask is, John Public, don't fall for that stuff.[29]

While appeals to Americans' patriotism and depictions of Wacs as self-sacrificing made good press copy, such strategies were less useful in recruiting large numbers of young women into the military. When Young and Rubicam assumed the role as adviser to WAC recruiters in March 1943, they did a series of Gallup public opinion polls whose results suggested that "self-interest," not "patriotism," was the key to increasing numbers in the WAC. Although Colonel Hobby supported Young and Rubicam as the new advertising agency for the corps, she struggled with their representatives throughout the war over this issue and clashed with their staffers on several occasions. The central question was whether recruiting campaigns should focus solely on "patriotism" and "duty," or "glamorize" servicewomen and appeal to young women's self-interest in trying to fill quotas. Beginning in late 1943, representatives from the ad agency recommended that the WAC move away from the "old unsuccessful idea that it's a girl's patriotic duty to join," reporting that, " 'Duty' is not an effective advertising appeal. The most effective is 'self-interest.' " Hobby nonetheless held out for a straight patriotic appeal and a heavy dose of guilt. During the spring and summer of 1943, the director designed recruiting posters showing pictures of dead and wounded male soldiers with captions chastising women for not joining the WAC. Many newspapers refused to run the ads claiming they were "too gruesome" as well as very stressful for families who had already lost men in the war. In the end, Young and Rubicam's approach won out and ads appeared in the fall of 1943 and through 1944 that stressed the attractive jobs and material advantages women gained joining the WAC.[30]

This tension between self-sacrifice and self-interest represented the collision of two discourses on women's position in society. While arguments emphasizing women's self-sacrifice were often used to advance women's quest for rights within the state, by the 1940s this strategy, while still invoked, was being challenged by a discourse that asserted women's prerogatives to make choices which benefited themselves. The resolution of this conflict was not clear or simple. The tension between the two created a compromise position that used images of self-sacrifice and played on women's moral duty, while simultaneously offering attractions aimed at women's self-interest. Thus, while early recruiting campaigns described patriotism as the major motivation of women who joined, under the guidance of the civilian advertising staff of Young and Rubicam these characterizations were joined by publicity that also encouraged prospective WAC candidates to "take advantage" of the "opportunities" available to young women in the Army.[31]

Some recruiting ads began to focus on military service as an opportunity to build a new tradition of women's service and highlighted the potential for new careers and special job training as well as the value of the physical programs included in the WAC course of study. These were supplemented by advertisements featuring attractive, young, white women in WAC uniforms and bearing captions that promised personal gain to the woman who made "sacrifices": "I joined to serve my country . . . and I'm having the time of my life!"[32] Several civilians and journalists, characterized WAC advertising as "inconsistent" because it stressed both "patriotism" and "glamour and excitement." Another suggested that women's self-interest be tied to the political ramifications of defeat, arguing that Germans, upon victory, would "strip women of their rights and return them to separate and inferior roles."[33] WAC recruiting eventually utilized both themes and in the final year of the war advertised, "Every young American woman who has the necessary qualifications should avail herself of this opportunity to serve her country and, in so doing, her own interests as well."[34]

While Colonel Hobby withdrew her insistence that appeals to women's patriotism be the only corps recruiting strategy, she and her female colleagues refused absolutely to support the assumption that women's self-interest in military service could include sexual freedom. Hobby and other WAC leaders worked hard to counter allegations of sexual immorality within the women's corps by constructing the WAC as a "respectable" organization. Crucial to this construction was their effort to gain the support and sponsorship of religious associations and churches during the spring of 1943. WAC headquarters stressed the importance the corps placed on women's attendance at religious services and organized a visit by church leaders to the WAC training centers at Fort Des Moines, Iowa, and Fort Oglethorpe, Georgia. After they inspected the facilities and interviewed a number of Wacs these church representatives issued a statement complimenting the women and condoning the existence of the WAC. Part of this statement reassured parents that the moral and spiritual welfare of their daughters was being provided for via the Army chaplains present at the posts and the opportunities the women had for contact with civilian churches.[35] One possible reason for this blanket support of church leaders could have been the WAC leadership's portrayal of the women's corps as offering a supervised and restricted environment for young women of "good backgrounds." Even the Catholic Church, which had initially condemned the formation of the WAC, changed its tune and claimed that conditions in the WAC were "designed to safeguard family life, and to contribute to the physical and moral welfare of the young women."[36]

WAC administrators also enlisted the aid of nationally prominent women's groups to defend the corps against the allegations raised in the slander campaign. Colonel Hobby believed that getting respected women in various communities to endorse her organization would greatly increase public support of the corps. In response, Emily Newell Blair, chief of the War Department's Women's Interest Section, asked the Women's Advisory Council and all women's clubs to help WAC recruiting by publishing articles supportive of the corps in their club letters and local newspapers, and urged members to serve on the local women's committees for recruiting in their own communities. Many women's clubs went even further and invited WAC officers to speak at their club meetings and community functions in order to acquaint civilians in their areas with the organization.[37] In a June 1943, speech to the

Women's Advisory Council Hobby also urged its members to respond actively to the negative publicity, "Army women are your daughters and the daughters of your friends," she pointed out. "They are the women you meet in business, in offices, in stores, lunching in restaurants. They are—purely and simply— a cross-section of the best of American womanhood."[38]

The Army used Hobby's depiction of Wacs as "girls next door" in its efforts to change military men's negative attitudes toward the women's corps. Once Army investigators discovered that U.S. male GIs and officers were the source of many of the rumors emerging from the slander campaign, Army officials renewed their efforts to convince male personnel of the necessity of the WAC. General Somervell, commander, Army Service Forces, ordered the Army BPR to make a film for the purpose of influencing male soldiers' opinions, create a handbook to provide male soldiers with information about the WAC, and asked the commanding generals of the nine Service Commands to take steps to influence male attitudes.[39]

Stressing that Wacs needed men's "support and respect," commanding officers and chaplains spoke to male soldiers in Basic Training and at reception centers lauding the Wacs and emphasizing the importance of womanpower and the Army's need for women skilled at "women's jobs." Many argued that the reason for low enlistment was "because of men like you" and that negative attitudes toward the WAC would only result in a longer war. These same officials asked male GIs and officers to inform women they knew of the opportunities available to them in the WAC; "prospect cards" were handed out to servicemen, especially those going overseas, and they were asked to get vital information on women they knew who filled the qualifications for the WAC and give this information to the recruiting service so they could contact the women. WAC recruiting and public relations officers also made efforts to use servicemen who had worked with Wacs for radio interviews to describe the importance of WAC jobs and the need for women to join.[40] The education campaign undertaken by the Army to overcome servicemen's objections to the WAC was partly successful, but in general male GIs and officers remained at best ambivalent and at worst openly hostile to women's presence within the Army.

The task of achieving legitimacy for the WAC involved not only creating space within the public arena for "female soldiers" but also creating a place for *women* within the male military. In accomplishing these goals, female military leaders, especially Colonel Hobby, believed it absolutely necessary to construct the "female soldier" as distinct from her male counterpart. WAC leaders argued that these distinctions should be reflected not only in WAC public relations and recruiting campaigns, but also through the implementation of policies and directives that regulated the lives of servicewomen in ways vastly different from service men. Hobby tried to minimize public anxiety about women's sexual agency and victimization by reinvigorating the equation of female sexual restraint with sexual respectability and presenting the corps as an organization composed solely of "good" women.

The director's definition of "good" women was based both on female chastity and cultural connections between sexual morality and race and class status. Throughout the war Hobby and other WAC leaders formulated admission polices and recruiting practices with criteria explicitly linking social background, racial status, and education to their definition of "good" women and good recruits. Hobby, an elite white woman, considered working-class women and women of color as more likely to be sexually active and, within her framework, immoral. Hobby's framework was supported by contemporary sexualized racial stereotypes. Their presence was by extension a threat to WAC legitimacy as their presumed sexual availability made Wacs' potential sexual victimization, and sexual agency, more visible to the American public. White women, especially middle-class, white women, were assumed to have greater sexual restraint as well as greater protection by men of their group, thereby emphasizing their nonavailability and therefore, respectability.[41]

The WAC leadership's emphasis on respectability as a means of gaining public sanction of the women's corps and deflecting criticism and attacks encouraged generation of a classed and raced image of the woman soldier, one who was white and middle-class. To avoid criticism of this direction Hobby insisted publicly that the WAC was open to all women, and that the corps did not discriminate on grounds of "race, creed, or religion." She supported this claim by pointing to the first group of Wacs enrolled, and noting that African-American women were a part of this training class and would always be welcomed into the organization. Further support of the "openness" of the women's corps was provided by WAC public relations efforts that highlighted the enrollment of several Native Americans in the WAC, the first enlistment of Japanese-Americans in the organization, and the recruitment of a squadron composed solely of women of "Spanish-American" heritage. The press release on the creation of the "Benito Juarez Squadron" noted that the WAC received great cooperation from Latin-American groups in their recruiting drive and that a number of Latin-American dignitaries attended the swearing-in ceremony, at which participants were entertained with Latin-American songs and dances.[42] Moreover, the WAC for most of the war required women who wished to be officers in the corps to work their way up through the enlisted ranks and be appointed to Officer Candidate School (OCS), thus allowing no direct commissioning of civilian women as officers. Colonel Hobby contended that this policy was justified because there were very few class differences between women within the corps and to create them artificially was counterproductive.[43]

Despite Hobby's claims, contemporary gender and sexual ideology linking definitions of respectability to class background and education led WAC leaders to define the corps as a space for middle-class, not working-class, women.[44] The initial screening criteria and application procedures for the corps reflected this emphasis. Local interviews of candidates were conducted by a board of two "prominent" local women and one male Army officer. This board was to disqualify those unsuited because of "character" or "bearing" and board members were asked to consider the question "Would I want my daughter to come under the influence of this woman?" A national screening board appointed by WAC headquarters and including women such as the deans of Purdue and Cornell then gave final approval to the first groups of Wacs.[45] The organization Hobby was trying to create was much better served by major WAC recruiting campaigns aimed at white women's colleges and universities, as well as business colleges and technical schools which would enable the corps to obtain the "qualified recruits" they needed with the correct educational background, job skills, class status, and skin color.[46] The white, middle-class definition of respectability WAC leaders sought for their organization was articulated in informational pamphlets which assured parents that the corps took good care of their daughters and compared WAC camps to "women's colleges" with their "libraries, chapels, [and] lovely grounds" while guaranteeing that their daughters would "make the kind of associations you want {them} to have at home."[47]

While, like Hobby, Navy officials operated under the assumption that the recruitment of servicewomen would have to be handled differently from that of servicemen, male Army leaders believed that efforts to recruit and promote Wacs should simply be subsumed under already established agencies within their branch of the armed forces. From the outset the Navy directly commissioned civilian men and women with experience in advertising and publicity to create recruiting campaigns and sales pitches for their corps. In doing so they created a woman's procurement office to handle all WAVES' affairs and separated this section from normal Navy channels for recruiting male personnel.[48] In contrast, the Army felt that its own Bureau of Public Relations and Recruiting Service were sufficient to meet WAC needs.[49]

Colonel Hobby believed that Army methods of and control over WAC recruiting led to the Army Recruiting Service's enrollment of "unsuitable women" and as such was the foundation of the "unseemly" publicity emerging from numerous Army posts. Hobby was convinced that the corps would be better served if her office had authority over these efforts. Her battle to gain control of recruiting intensified in January 1943, when the adjutant general arbitrarily lowered enrollment standards for the corps by eliminating high-school attendance as a requisite for membership, and simplifying many of the screening procedures in an effort to meet the soaring quotas for servicewomen. Horrified, Colonel Hobby and her staff argued that this would greatly harm the public image of the WAC as "some decline of behavior standards was inherent in the acceptance of women of low ability" and that "women were now accepted whose character and past record were questionable." She also felt the corps could not attract "both types of workers," and that "Enlistment of too many low-grade factory, store, and restaurant workers is a problem" because "if low-grade personnel constituted the majority, office workers of good character and acceptable skill would not volunteer."[50]

WAC leaders distinguished between unskilled personnel with little or no secondary education and the skilled and educated women they desired in the WAC. They believed that enrolling the former would make it impossible to meet the needs of the Army for clerical and communications personnel because most of these women would be "untrainable." Hobby also implied that enrolling this "type of woman" would result in a "poor reputation" for all servicewomen because of their inherent inability to meet standards of respectable behavior. Thus, the female WAC leadership conflated respectability and education and indicated that the image of "female soldier" they were trying to create was based on a class ideology that posited sexual immorality and "lower behavior standards" were the province of women with little formal education.[51]

Hobby's attempts to place her headquarters in charge of WAC recruiting and her bid to create a special group under General Surles' (Army BPR) jurisdiction to coordinate WAC publicity eventually succeeded when she called on her powerful ally General Marshall for help. At Hobby's request, the chief of staff stepped into the fray and supported her recommendations by overruling the objections of senior Army officials. As a result, by April 1943, the Army Recruiting Service had been notified that WAC headquarters would henceforth handle the recruitment of women. Marshall also endorsed Hobby's insistence on the restoration of WAC enrollment standards and the requirements for service in the women's corps were raised to a minimum of two years high-school and a higher passing score on the Army standard intelligence test. Hobby was also eventually able to control WAC public relations when Marshall, in March 1944, ordered the formation of a special WAC publicity unit over the objections of the head of the Army Bureau of Public Relations and the commander of the Army Service Forces.[52]

The cultural power of this connection between class status, morality, and respectability was demonstrated in the contrasting public images of the WAC and the WAVES. Several letters from civilians suggested that maintaining extremely "high standards" was the only way to counter the rumors about the WAC.[53] A Gallup survey carried out among civilian women in early 1944 asked the question, "If you were going to enlist which service would you choose?" Seventy percent of the respondents picked the WAVES and gave reasons concerning higher standards, better uniforms, better reputation and treatment, pleasanter duties, more desirable associations, better living quarters, and greater prestige.[54]

The WAVES were from the outset defined as a specialist corps in which women with "sound business and professional experience" were needed. The educational requirements for the WAVES—women must have completed high-school and some college was strongly recommended—were also higher than those of the WAC. Moreover, while Wacs trained at Army forts, the WAVES' training center was located at Smith College. The WAVES' recruiting and public relations officers made much of these differences when presenting their service. One reporter described the WAVE officer barracks as "faintly reminiscent of a swank girls' school dormitory" and depicted the Naval Air Training Center at Pensacola as a "first class summer resort." She went on to note that there were Elizabeth Arden beauty salons available to all WAVES and that while "enlisted personnel are responsible for the care of their own rooms, Negro cleaning women, however, attend to the recreation rooms and for a small fee provide 24 hours laundry service. . . . Also, WAVE officers have their own maid service."[55] Moreover, the WAVES were an entirely white organization until near the war's end while the WAC from the outset included African-American women in their numbers at 10 percent of the total. Although the WAVES had some minor problems with negative publicity, they encountered none of the extreme accusations that plagued the WAC.

Despite WAC assertions that African-American women were welcome in the corps, there is strong evidence to suggest that recruiters made black women's enlistment difficult or impossible. Throughout the war WAC headquarters received numerous complaints from African-American women and

Bethune concerning misinformation given black women at recruiting stations. Many times African-American women were turned away by recruiters who told them that the WAC was not accepting "colored applicants." One black woman alleged that she waited for hours in a recruiting station and was sent on a "wild goose chase" by the white recruiters who claimed that the officer in charge was "unavailable" every time she entered the office. She went on to report that she had heard the same story from several other African-American women. "The thing that these women are practicing are the very things the Allies are fighting against," she remarked, again linking her admission to or exclusion from the WAC to questions of racial and gender justice.[56] The director of housing for recruits to the armed forces in Chicago reported that in Chicago white inductees were put up in loop hotels which were supervised and did not require them to "search around for accommodations in strange neighborhoods," while African-American inductees were given no chaperones or guides and were put up in downtown Chicago, in the worst hotels and with no information or assistance on how to reach their quarters.[57]

WAC officials were also very careful to remove publicity on women of color if such publicity threatened to jeopardize their major recruiting efforts for white women. At the swearing-in ceremony of one of the first groups of Japanese-American Wacs in Denver, Colorado, WAC officers asked an Associated Press reporter not to take pictures or cover the event, claiming it would hurt the overall WAC recruiting effort. The journalist went ahead with his story but was stopped from printing it when the WAC officers eventually got Governor Vivian of Colorado to call the Associated Press and have them "back off."[58]

The most telling illustration of this unstated WAC policy became apparent in April through July 1943, when WAC officials removed most African-American recruiting officers from their positions. In response, the black press and African-American leaders inundated WAC headquarters and the War Department with letters asking why "Negro recruiting officers" were being removed from their communities. "We have noted the closing down of recruiting offices in many or all of our urban communities for the enlistment of Negro Wacs," read a telegram from Walter White of the NAACP. "We would like to know if it is the policy of the War Department to discontinue further recruiting of Negro women?"[59] Colonel Hobby replied to these queries by claiming that a shortage of instructors and administrative personnel for training work had caused a "general reassignment of Negro officers to training centers from other assignments." She went on to say that this was necessary in order to get black WAC units out into the field but that "everything possible" would be done to return the recruiting officers to their posts as soon as the shortage was over.[60]

Internal WAC memos provide a telling contrast to Colonel Hobby's public explanation for the removal of African-American WAC recruiting officers. Summarizing the reasons for this reassignment Major Harold Edlund, chief, WAC Recruiting, stated that "because of adverse public opinion two service commands requested the withdrawal of Negro recruiting officers in early April (1943)." In response, from April 14 to June 14, 1943, corps officials arranged for all black female recruiting officers to be gradually withdrawn from the field. Edlund then went on to describe the "great objections" from African-American leaders in the country to the withdrawal but felt that this "crisis" was now over and he expected "no serious repercussions" as a result of their action. He concluded by reporting that the "use of Negro recruiting officers in some sections of the country is a retardant to recruiting which more than offsets the advantages of their use in the country as a whole." He recommended not returning African-American recruiters to the field, but recognized that the "public policy question involved may dictate that we put them back."[61]

In dealing with racial issues WAC leaders played both sides of the fence, guaranteeing to black leaders that African-American Wacs were treated equally despite segregation, and arguing that although sympathetic to their contentions, segregation was a War Department policy that WAC leaders had no control over and could not change. At the same time Colonel Hobby assured white men and women who wanted segregation maintained that she understood their concerns and that "every effort" was made to insure that black women were housed and messed completely separately from their white counterparts. In response to Texas Representative George Mahon (D), who was upset over reports that segregation was breaking down at Fort Des Moines, Hobby explained that contact between African-American and white service-women was kept at a minimum although some contact was "temporary and practically unavoidable."[62] WAC leaders attempted to straddle a number of different racial discourses, distilling the opposition of African-American male and female leaders and white liberals with sympathetic replies and visits to NCNW meetings, while also reassuring white men and women who supported segregation and rigid racial policies that the WAC was upholding, not challenging, entrenched racial hierarchies.[63]

Most critical to Colonel Hobby's effort to promote the public image of Wacs' sexual respectability was her insistence on strict sexual regulation of women while in the corps. Sexual regulation for women in the military was to be entirely different than that governing male soldiers. The linchpin of her efforts was the "Code of Conduct," which was instituted and formally maintained during the corps' auxiliary status. Central to the Code of Conduct was a provision that any auxiliary who was accused of "conduct of a nature to bring discredit upon the WAAC" could be immediately court-martialed and discharged if found guilty.[64] This broadly worded regulation was used to remove women from the corps whose actions placed them outside the realm of "respectable" behavior and was aimed in particular at servicewomen who engaged in extramarital sexual behavior or public drunkenness.[65]

The Code of Conduct in conjunction with "strict enlistment standards" was central to Hobby's efforts to portray the corps as a haven for "good" women and to characterize women acting outside the bounds of conventional morality as "bad," and therefore not only undeserving of protection, but also dangerous to other servicewomen. Accordingly Wacs whose behavior was deemed to reflect negatively on the corps were depicted as aberrations in the normal composition of the WAC. Their actions, moreover, were largely blamed on their inferior educations and their class and race backgrounds.[66] The Code of Conduct accepted that bad women existed and were the source of constant problems for themselves, the male military, and the larger society. Indeed, bad women were those who acted like male soldiers.

When the corps became a formal part of the Army in 1943 the Code of Conduct was abolished and the women's corps was subsumed under Army regulations. Some high-ranking male officers characterized this as a positive step, arguing that Wacs were soldiers and that it was unfair to punish women more severely than men for similar actions.[67] Hobby squared off with the Army and argued that different standards of conduct were necessary because of public scrutiny and to protect the majority of "good" women within the WAC from the influence of "bad" women acting outside the bounds of propriety. She also pointed out that servicewomen themselves objected to certain kinds of immoral conduct and that their mental and emotional well-being was in danger when differential moral standards were not upheld.[68] This portrayal of Wacs as "exceptional" women who didn't want to associate with anyone not up to their principles was codified in an addition to Army regulations in 1943 which allowed for the discharge of any woman who showed "habits or traits of character which clearly indicate that the individual is not a suitable person to associate with enlisted women." Hobby later noted that though regulations to cover "crude barracks behavior or heavy drinking" could not be put in writing, her office urged Army court-martial boards in judging a case to consider "the morale and efficiency of the total WAC unit involved rather than to consider what comparable behavior in a man would mean on his record."[69]

Inherent in the sexual sterotyping and public expectations that Wacs would be participating in the military only in sexual ways was the invisibility and undervaluing of women's actual labor in the Army. The undervaluing of servicewomen and female officers' military jobs was a product of the general cultural devaluing of work defined as "women's" or "feminine" combined with the actions of male Army officers who believed that Wacs' military labor should be limited to stereotypically "feminine" occupations such as cooking, cleaning, babysitting, and doing laundry for male personnel. Wacs refused to accept this limiting vision of their role, struggling throughout the war to avoid being placed in jobs determined by the gendered and racially segregated job structure of the Army. African-American Wacs were especially vocal and forthright in rejecting the Army's attempts to confine them to menial service jobs. As I will show, the question of how military women would be employed was one of the major issues shaping women's military service and was contested throughout the war.

4

"Women's Work" and Resistance in the WAC: Kitchen Police, Secretaries, and Sit-Down Strikers

The Army's utilization of women during World War II was a logical extension of the changing character of the organization. During the war only 12 percent of all male soldiers participated in combat and fully 25 percent remained stateside throughout the entire conflict. These figures suggest that the function of the Army as well as the actual duties soldiers performed were changing rapidly. Although all men continued to be trained for combat service, World War II was fought as much by the communication and decoding centers of the Signal Corps, on the spotter and interceptor boards of the Aircraft Warning Service, and in the offices of the Quartermaster and Transportation corps as on the battlefields. The increasingly bureaucratic nature of the Army led to the creation of thousands of jobs in clerical and communications fields, jobs largely performed by women in the civilian labor force. As historian Susan Hartmann has concluded, "20th century transformations in warfare produced a military establishment capable of utilizing women and feminization of areas in the civilian economy created an occupational structure which provided women with the skills required by the military."[1]

Most of the histories of women's work during World War II focus on the new opportunities for women in the paid labor force. William Chafe characterizes the war as a watershed in the paid employment of women, especially married women.[2] Other historians have partially revised Chafe's initially optimistic outlook, contending that though women's work during the war was a first step toward making publicly acceptable the idea of women combining home roles and paid employment, the gains made during the war were temporary and did not greatly alter women's secondary status within the paid labor force.[3] Few of these scholars, however, have examined women's military experience, and those that have merely included that experience within an analytic framework created to explain women's work in the civilian sector.[4]

World War II was also a turning point in women's relationship to the military. For the first time women were enrolled under the auspices of the Army, first as auxiliaries and, by 1943, as official members of the Army with full pay and benefits. There are several similarities in civilian and military recruitment and employment. Mobilization propaganda characterized members of each group as "feminine" and defined or redefined their tasks as appropriate for women. In both the civilian and military sectors women's abilities to handle routine, tedious, repetitious work, requiring patience and manual dexterity, were used as justifications for the employment of women in war industry and in military jobs such as clerical and communications work. Additionally, both groups faced hostility from the men with whom they worked and in some instances replaced. Moreover, both arenas had sex and race segregated structures which placed white men at the top and black women at the bottom of the occupational ladder.

There were also some key differences, however. The Army's call for women to enlist and serve with the military came over six months after the United States had declared war and after civilian agencies such as the War Manpower Commission (WMC) had begun their own drive to get every able-bodied man and woman into a war job. Without recourse to a draft for womanpower, the Army was forced to compete with the civilian sector for women's labor and skills. This proved a difficult task and public antagonism to military service for women was a critical factor in the Army's lack of success in meeting its quotas for servicewomen.[5] The great disparity in pay and personal freedom between military and civilian women and the wider range of job opportunities in the civilian labor force also influenced women's decisions.

While both the civilian and Army occupation structures were sex- as well as race-segregated, Wacs had fewer opportunities than their civilian counterparts to engage in nontraditional work. Although the military certainly qualified as a nontraditional occupational field for women, the jobs most servicewomen performed were overwhelmingly "women's jobs," with 70 percent of all Wacs engaged in clerical and communications work. In part this was because Army planners and Colonel Hobby envisioned the WAC as a specialist corps that would provide office skills to the Army. Army leaders believed that their need for clerical and communications workers could be met by enrolling women already competent in these occupations and that it would be inefficient to retrain them in jobs usually done by men as the Army had enough manpower to meet these needs. These factors, when combined with the Army's methods of job classification and assignment, and the prejudices of individual male commanders and personnel officers, resulted in an occupational structure for the WAC that was in many ways even more rigidly sex- and race-segregated than the civilian labor force and certainly more limited in terms of job choices for women.

Individual Wacs and the WAC administration worked throughout the war to contest outright gender and racial discrimination in job assignments. Gendered and racial conflicts were visible in most women's military service, working environments, and daily living conditions. Like their civilian counterparts, Wacs of all races had to cope with male hostility on the job, including sexual harassment and men's unwillingness to train them at particular positions. African-American servicewomen and officers also contended with segregation and racism on a daily basis at both military installations and in the surrounding white civilian communities. Additionally, some Jewish Wacs encountered anti-Semitism within their units, many times expressed by other servicewomen. In grappling with these situations servicewomen's resistance ranged from written complaints to sit-down strikes. The most visible resistance of this kind was articulated by African-American women in response to racial discrimination.

Although Wacs as a group were from varied regional, racial, ethnic, and class backgrounds, they were overwhelmingly single, young, and without dependents. As of May 1943, there were approximately 61,000 women on duty with the corps. Of these, 70 percent were single, 15 percent were married, and 15 percent widowed, separated, or divorced. Most women entering the service were not responsible for any dependents and approximately 70 percent of them were less than 30 years old. These initial trends did not alter very much in later years and the proportion of married women in the Army was always far less than in the civilian labor force.[6] As this group had few if any dependents, and certainly no young children to support, high wages may not have been as important to them as the opportunity to be mobile and active.

Many women who joined the WAC, moreover, may not have had the opportunity to do war industries work if they continued to live at home. Wartime studies indicated that 40 percent of all servicewomen "grew up on farms or in small towns."[7] As most war industries work was centered in urban areas, those women who chose to join the corps may not have chosen military service as an alternative to a high-paying job, but rather as an alternative to living or working in an area in which women had few employment choices.

Because of recruiting policies and WAC leaders' efforts to keep the women's corps "respectable," the educational and class backgrounds of servicewomen and officers as a group tended to be higher than a cross-section of the female civilian population. One third of all servicewomen had fathers who were managers or professionals, thus situating them solidly within the middle-class.[8] Moreover, fewer than 8 percent of all servicewomen had never attended high school, compared to 42 percent of civilian women that age, while 68 percent had graduated from high school and/or had college experience. While white women had a higher rate of high-school graduation than black women surveyed, college graduates made up a slightly higher proportion of African-American Wacs than was the case among their white counterparts.[9]

Although there was no clear overarching economic motivation applicable to all of these women, long-term economic benefits might have outweighed short-term economic motives in choosing the military. Professional women who served as officers may have believed that managerial experience with the military would translate into job options and respect in the postwar period. Other women may have felt that military training in any number of occupations would help them secure better jobs after the war. Moreover, after the corps traded its auxiliary for regular Army status, servicewomen were eligible for the benefits outlined in the GI Bill of Rights. These benefits included reemployment, low-cost housing and business loans, and money for college educations.

While most women cited patriotism, including a desire to contribute to the war effort and "bring the men home," as part of their motivation for joining the military, this general reason could legitimize a great deal of activity associated with self-interest. Desire for change, escape, and adventure were for some women more important than pay. Some Wacs, for instance, fled bad family situations, or simply wanted to get out of a small town and experience something different. "It gave me the opportunity to see and experience things I never could afford coming from a large poor family," explained one Euro-American Wac.[10] " 'It was time to make a change," noted an African-American servicewoman, "and this seemed a good opportunity.' "[11] Others were excited by the possibility of travel and service overseas and saw joining the WAC as an opportunity for gaining valuable education and experience. "Service in the WAAC should broaden my viewpoint," commented another black Wac, "and should be an education in itself."[12] For some childfree, married women, the absence of their husbands due to the draft or overseas service was a circumstance that prompted them to enlist. Several noted their frustration with just "sitting at home and waiting."[13] Finally, many found that offering "ultimate service" to the country, was no less disagreeable, or considerably more reward-ing, than constant "service" to others in their lives.[14] Joining the women's corps, moreover, was not simply a choice of employment, but a choice to live within the institution of the military and not with one's family. For those who could not legitimate a move away from the family sphere, the option of join-ing the military may have represented a means by which they could leave the family and home without incurring disapproval, or at least minimizing it. "Patriotism," duty, and service to country, could in this sense offset the oblig-ations of duty and service to family without challenging the former set of obligations directly.

"Patriotic" motivations were critical to those who identified their military service as part of a broader struggle for gender and racial equality during the war. A number of women reported that their motivations for enlisting were rooted in wanting to be part of a "pioneer venture" for women and believed that their service would aid in opening up opportunities for women in the postwar world.[15] In a public relations radio broadcast, 1st Officer Harriet West, an African-American WAC and a member of Hobby's staff, urged Black women to join the corps. Speaking to those who saw participation in a segre-gated Army as a concession to whites, she argued that "membership in the WAAC and accepting a situation which does not represent an ideal of democ-racy" was not a "retreat from our fight" but rather "our contribution to its real-ization."[16] Similarly, several Nisei women who wanted to enlist in the WAC described their motivations as founded in a view of military service as a mode of attaining full citizenship rights for their race in the United States.[17]

Although military service was certainly a non-traditional occupational field for women, the Army's employment plans for Wacs reflected the race, class, and sex-segregated occupational structure of the prewar civilian labor force. The Army classification system gave women ratings corresponding to specific military jobs based on their scores on Army aptitude tests and their civilian experience and training. Once assigned to a particular post or base the male personnel officer of that station determined how individual women were employed. Although Colonel Hobby and the WAC administration used infor-mal inspections in efforts to insure that women were being placed in jobs for which they were trained, male officers nonetheless had significant power to assign Wacs to "more appropriate" duties. Often these duties were based on stereotyped ideas of gender and race and included assigning black Wacs as domestic servants to clean officers clubs, or white servicewomen to other types of reproductive labor such as cooking or laundry.

Official Army employment policies were founded on Army planners' beliefs that the best use for Wacs was in clerical and administrative positions. Army leaders felt that these jobs were "made to order" for women "because women have been doing similar work in civilian life expertly for many years."[18] They argued that replacing men with women in these occupational categories was the most efficient use of personnel and observed that because of superior skills one Wac could often take the place of two or three enlisted men in these areas. Consequently, Army officials discouraged training female personnel in nontraditional job categories.[19] Colonel Hobby tried to make these routine jobs palatable by characterizing them as "dull" but "nevertheless vital" to the "daily maintenance of countless services necessary to our armed forces" and noted that the ability to perform such service for the military took not heroism but the "courage of commonplace."[20]

Army decisions about what jobs were most appropriate for servicewomen were based on a variety of factors. Practical considerations included the physical strength required to perform certain tasks, the training time necessary for someone to become competent at a specific job, and the Army environment and working conditions for particular job categories. In addition, the Army considered less tangible factors such as whether or not the job in question was "traditionally" acceptable for women. Using these criteria, the Army pared down the 628 noncombat positions available to men to 406 Military Occupational Specialties (MOS) deemed suitable for women. The women's corps actually focused on 142 of these 406 available jobs, 75 percent of which had previously been done by enlisted men and consisted largely of work which required prior civilian training, particularly in communications and administration. These 142 occupations were designated WAC Specialist Jobs and fell into the following civilian occupational groups: office work, service work, communications work, mechanical work, food preparation, technical and professional work, and trade and manual labor.[21]

The sex and race stratified civilian labor force helped determine the skills women brought into the military. Few women came into the corps with professional or managerial experience and their percentage declined from 14 percent to 10 percent between 1943 and 1945, a decline in part due to the slander campaign and other negative publicity that plagued the WAC throughout the war. By far clerical and sales backgrounds predominated throughout the war, with 45 percent of all Wacs having such experience in 1943, increasing to 50 percent by 1945. In keeping with Army policies, over half of all servicewomen performed office and administrative work once enlisted and throughout the war.[22] The percentage of women performing such work was even higher overseas, often approaching 90 percent, reflecting the belief of many male officers that there were enough male soldiers to do the men's jobs.[23]

Rather than increasing chances to be trained and employed in high-skilled work, entrance into the women's corps often resulted in either downward mobility or stagnancy. While only 10 percent of women came into the WAC with a background in service work, close to 18 percent were employed in service-type jobs once enlisted. African-American women were disproportionately represented in these jobs, in part due to their unequal access to economic opportunities in the civilian sector, and in part because of racial stereotyping.[24]

The promotion system within the Army also reflected the race and gender hierarchies in the civilian labor force. Army women in general were considerably behind their male counterparts in rank; 38.5 percent of all enlisted women occupied the lowest Army rank of private compared to only 24.3 percent of all enlisted men. Enlisted men also had a far better proportional representation than female soldiers in succeeding Army grades, from private first class to master sergeant. WAC officers' possibilities for advancing through the ranks were limited as well by the legislation creating the corps which made the rank of colonel the highest any woman could attain, and then allowed only one, the WAC director. These factors in conjunction with Army regulations against women commanding male soldiers guaranteed that when men and women worked together it was usually men who occupied supervisory roles.[25] In addition, African-American servicewomen, were prohibited by Army policy from commanding their white counterparts. Conversely, white WAC officers were put in charge of African-American companies when there was a shortage of black female officers.[26]

Issues of gender, race, and class, moreover, were critical in the WAC caste system, a system parallel, but not identical, to that of the male Army. Like the male Army system, the WAC system divided enlisted women and officers into two separate groups. Traditionally, the officer caste in the male Army was composed of better-educated members of society with higher class status in the civilian world than their enlisted counterparts. Officers were "gentleman" given the responsibility of command and most entered Officer Candidate School (OCS) directly from the civilian sector. The enlisted caste was usually composed of men who functioned as laborers, the proletarians of the Army system, and the upper ranks of the enlisted grouping held positions analogous to foremen in a factory, interpreting and disseminating the orders of the officers to the other workers. Within the segregated Army system, while African-

American GIs held positions as noncommissioned officers within black units, many African-American units were officered by white men.[27]

On the surface, the WAC system was somewhat more egalitarian than the male Army's. With few exceptions WAC officers had to join the service as enlisted women first, and then be recommended for Officer Candidate School where they would go through training and be assigned as officers; thus, most female officers had served previously as privates.[28] In addition, the voluntary nature of the women's corps, and its higher education requirements than the Army for men, resulted in murkier divisions between enlisted women and WAC officers. Most African-American WAC units, moreover, were officered by black, not white, female officers. This was in part because of the small numbers of African-American women within the corps and the correspondingly greater number of black WAC officers available to lead African-American units.

Despite Colonel Hobby's arguments that moving up through the ranks of the women's corps to OCS was a democratic process based solely on merit, however, it remained, like the Army's selection process, largely a function of educational background and class status in civilian society. Review boards, for instance, looked for "good" and "bad" characteristics in officer candidates for the WAC. Listed under "bad" characteristics disqualifying a woman from an officer position were stereotypical middle-class descriptions of "lower-class" life, including a woman's origins in a "broken home," a "gratingly forceful" or "coarse" personality, or a "simple" background, while the "good" side of the ledger included a happy childhood, leadership ability, and "poise and culture." In addition, the question of whether the candidate was a "well-educated" and "well-rounded" person were crucial parts of the criteria for OCS.[29] Consequently, women from elite social backgrounds were more likely to be chosen for OCS than their counterparts from rural areas or those who had worked in factories. As one Army recruiting officer complained, it was only the "high society" types with the "social background" from Philadelphia who were selected for OCS in Pennsylvania.[30]

Enlisted women were further stratified through the Army rating system that designated "grades" for personnel based on their scores on the Army General Classification Test (AGCT). The higher the score, the higher the grade, with Grade I the highest and Grade V the lowest. These grades were used to determine the suitability of women for assignments and training schools and their eligibility for Officer Candidate School. Women in Grades I to III were usually assigned to office and clerical jobs while WAC officials often viewed unskilled women, located in Grades IV to V, as untrainable and consequently assigned them to more menial duties. Thus, a division between types of work was created, similar to that present in the civilian sector, with office jobs having higher status than service or factory work.[31]

African-American women's employment in the women's corps was predicated only in part on their skills and abilities and was usually circumscribed by their race and sex. Black women's opportunities were especially limited by the Army's segregation policies. Because many African-American women had been denied the same access to educational and civilian job opportunities as their white counterparts, they were often overrepresented in the lower two grades and thus likely to be assigned to service jobs. WAC policy on the employment of black female personnel, also dictated that requests for "colored" Wacs must come from Army commands and posts before African-American women would be assigned; all other requests for Wacs were treated as "white only," even if not specified. This system resulted in a large backlog of black servicewomen at Fort Des Moines and other training centers because of the lack of requests for their services. Hobby blamed this backlog on African-American women's lack of skills and education, making them "unemployable" in a number of areas in which the women's corps specialized.[32] The problem, however, was not that there were requisitions for black women and not enough skilled African-American Wacs to meet them, but rather that there were few requisitions in the first place.

Despite Hobby's assertion that black servicewomen were not skilled enough to fill available jobs, she clearly understood that the problem resulted from lack of requests. The director sent 1st Officer Harriet West, an African-American Wac and a member of her administrative staff, into the field to survey Army posts and persuade male commanding officers to employ black servicewomen.[33] West's efforts were undermined by the initial "replace a man for combat" framework for the employment of all enlisted women, which did not work for African-American women as their male counterparts were often racially typed into labor and service detachments whose duties were too heavy for women to assume.[34] The backlog problem was made more complex by the Army, which intensified segregation policies to avoid racial hostility and confrontation at its southern posts. Army leaders supported an informal policy of filling requests from these posts for "Negro Wacs" with southern, not northern black women. As one Army spokesman advised,

> If southern camps must be used for assigning Negro personnel, enrollees coming from the South should be assigned to these posts, since it is expected that these enrollees will understand and be better able to cope with the regulations existing in this section of the country than those from other sections.[35]

When Army commanders did request African-American servicewomen it was rarely for clerical duties and often for service work. Many of these requests stated explicitly that black women were not appropriate to fill the available administrative jobs and when recruits for high-skilled jobs were sought they were specified as requests for white women. "These Waacs will be performing clerical and administrative duties in the Chemical Warfare Service," one requisition order noted, "Negro Waacs are not suitable." Another reported "there are no duties which can be performed by Negro WAAC personnel." Conversely, requests for servicewomen to perform low-skill work often stipulated a desire for "Negro Wacs." A request for both black and white Wacs from Camp Murphy, Florida, for instance, asked for 104 white enlisted women to do administrative work and 38 "colored" enlisted women to perform service work. The request contained the caveat that "unless the 38 colored enrollees can be furnished no colored WAACs are desired."[36] Camp Murphy, in other words, had no positions for high-skilled African-American servicewomen.

The author of an Army report on the employment of black servicewomen noted that "some post commanders are at a loss to determine how Negro personnel can be used other than in laundries, mess units, or salvage and reclamations shops." WAC investigators at Fort McClellan reported that "Negro Wacs" were "being used as bus boys in the Negro and White Service Club and 4 were in the civilian dorm doing maid service."[37] African-American servicewomen's opportunities for overseas service were also initially curtailed when the only requisitions for their employment were in heavy types of service labor. WAC policies officially prohibited assigning women to this type of labor. As a result, black servicewomen did not make it overseas until November 1944.[38]

Male officers' initial uncertainty of how any women were to be assigned, as well as their lack of confidence in women's abilities to do jobs previously undertaken by male soldiers, curtailed full employment of servicewomen throughout the war. "One of the outstanding WAC problems," commented one Army historian, "was the frequent reluctance of COs to require full and responsible work from the WACs." The WAC Director also noticed this failure to fully utilize Wacs abilities and blamed such situations on some male officers who she characterized as too "fatherly and sympathetic," leading them to "waste(d) and hoard(ed)" personnel and refuse the transfer of women who had proved themselves qualified for specialized jobs. Some dissatisfied servicewomen complained that they did not have enough work to do, with one white Wac reporting that her work was usually done by 9:00 A.M. and she sat with nothing to do for the remainder of the day. She requested that she be released or reassigned to a job with more work. Both Colonel Hobby and unhappy Wacs argued that lack of sufficient work led to low morale and a number of women refused to reenlist in the WAC after conversion because the Army did not wholly use their abilities.[39]

Colonel Hobby fought the tendency of male personnel officers to assign servicewomen and officers according to gendered criteria throughout the war. She encouraged the Army to publish directives and create policies that would prohibit the use of women in unskilled, reproductive types of labor. Arguing that it would be almost impossible to recruit office workers as long as "the general public believed that women in the armed forces were used largely as cooks, waitresses, etc," the director convinced the War Department to establish and maintain a policy of using WAC personnel on food service assignments only "to the extent necessary to maintain WAC messes and make WAC units self-sustaining."[40]

Despite these policies, the requests for and employment of Wacs of all races in laundry and mess companies persisted. Several commands even requisitioned WAC companies to take over their entire mess units in permanent installations for men. Male officers felt that women would function well in these areas and pointed out the excellent work women did in WAC mess units and the success of such use of women in Great Britain: some even went so far as to suggest that WAC training be expanded in this direction.[41] Others requested WAC "laundry companies" to work with the Quartermaster corps. Many of these applications were specifically for black Wacs, indicating the resiliency of beliefs that the most appropriate duties for African-American women involved service work. Although most of these requests were also denied, some exceptions were made when an evaluation of the facilities demonstrated that they were clean and the equipment modern, thus requiring little heavy work. WAC headquarters made it clear that these requests would be evaluated individually and that the granting of such requisitions should not be construed as setting a precedent for the regular employment of servicewomen in this manner. In addition, Hobby ordered that both white and African-American companies should be considered for this work.[42]

Enlisted women as well as WAC officers were also occasionally assigned to jobs which reflected male officers' preconceptions of appropriate duties for women. At several posts problems arose involving the assignment of Wacs to "nonmilitary" duties, such as caring for dependents' children. At Fort Myer, a colonel even asked WAC headquarters to take action against a Euro-American WAC sergeant who would not sit with his baby. At another post, white enlisted women were assigned to a post commander's home to cook and act as personal servants to his wife. At Pasco and Los Alamos, both centers for the atomic bomb project, Euro-American enlisted women were often required to do baby-sitting and sometimes worked as barmaids, serving beer to civilian laborers. These difficulties were exacerbated when they took place on "secret installations" where no inspections were permitted; such exploitation of women was, therefore, not easily discovered or corrected.[43] Similar issues arose for WAC officers who were assigned and employed as aides to general officers and required to do routine stenographic and chauffeuring work normally performed by enlisted personnel. The use of WAC officers for secretarial functions and as "decorations" on high-ranking male officers' staffs was never explicitly prohibited by the War Department. On Colonel Hobby's recommendation, however, a memo was issued to all commands from the Chief of Staff, describing this type of employment of WAC officers as "inappropriate and inadvisable." The memo went on to note that General Marshall did not desire to make these instructions formal, but requested informally for generals to curb this practice in their commands. Still, in the European Theater of Operations, at the end of the war, 14 percent of all white WAC officers were working as personal assistants to ranking male officers.[44]

The employment of servicewomen on Kitchen Police, better known as KP, duty provides the clearest demonstration of how class, race, and gender intersected to determine the assignments of enlisted women. KP consisted of domestic-service type duties, and predominantly involved cleaning up the "mess" or kitchen area after each meal. This included cleaning the cooking and eating area, pots and pans, and trays and utensils for the entire company at least three times a day, sometimes more if alternate meals were served. KP was a duty assigned to both men and women and normally determined by roster rotation; enlisted men and women took turns performing these tasks when their name came up on the personnel roster. Exemptions from KP duty were determined in part by rank and Army custom, which dictated that neither commissioned nor noncommissioned officers (sergeant and above) would be employed in such work. This left most KP duties to the lower echelon of enlisted personnel, privates, privates first class, and corporals.[45]

Some male officers, however, believed that women's entrance into the military should mark an end to men's sentence in the Army kitchen. Because personnel officers expressed a clear need for skilled women's labor in other jobs, some also proposed making KP a full-time assignment for unskilled Wacs, thereby allowing skilled servicewomen freedom from KP duty as well.[46] WAC leaders opposed this practice arguing that, though understandable, it was unfair to women who volunteered for military service to give them permanent menial duties. On Colonel Hobby's recommendation, permanent KP was prohibited for enlisted women by WAC regulations in early 1944.[47] Nevertheless, the practice of assigning women to permanent KP continued and women who were untrained in office work and in the Grade IV to V categories were especially likely to be given these duties. On one post, a CO remarked that the work and conditions of KP were "comparable to those of like employment in civil life, and there will probably always be some women who will choose or be fitted for such work."[48]

Although some permanent KP workers were white, race in part determined whom would be "fitted for such work." When black and white women were stationed on the same post, permanent KP usually fell to women from the African-American detachment. At Camp Forrest, Tennessee, it was Mexican-American women who "volunteered" and were assigned these duties. The commander at Camp Forrest reported that the detachment "is very happy performing this job. Records show no aptitude or training suitable for other assignment. It is recommended permissions be granted to have these girls remain on their job."[49]

Despite Army and WAC policies which stipulated that personnel should be employed in jobs according to rank and skill, women had few opportunities to work in traditionally "masculine" fields in the Army. Although a significant minority of women entered the service with backgrounds in mechanical work or factory labor (17 percent in 1943 and 30 percent in 1945), these women were often retrained or used in service work; only 3–5 percent of servicewomen ever served in mechanical or trade jobs throughout the war.[50] On the one hand, Army planners argued that it was inefficient to employ women in this type of labor because there was a sufficient number of male personnel, many already trained in mechanical work, and that women on the whole possessed no aptitude for mechanical and maintenance jobs. On the other hand, some WAC instructors contended that women's low aptitude for mechanical work stemmed not from an inherent inability to do such work, but from lack of training and encouragement in mechanical fields because of their sex.[51] Regardless of women's potential in this area, patterns of women's employment remained fairly static throughout the war.

WAC leaders' overall attempts to portray servicewomen as generally feminine and respectable also steered the use of Wacs away from nontraditional jobs. Male officers and WAC Staff Directors were concerned that both the "masculine" clothing they would have to wear as mechanics and the "type of enlisted men" they would be working with would prove detrimental to the women and the corps. This latter objection reflected the understanding of

WAC officers that enlisted men were usually less educated than their female counterparts, and perhaps indicated a fear of the negative influence working-class men might have on women from higher-class backgrounds.[52] On several occasions male officers also refused to employ women with "unfeminine" skills in the duties for which they had been trained.

One of the most extreme examples of this occurred in the European Theater of Operations (ETO). In late 1944, 100 white Wacs trained as mechanics were sent to the ETO and were stationed at the Base Air Depot Area with the Air Service Command. They had been requisitioned from the United States specifically for work in technical jobs and were assigned to the maintenance division to work in the tool crib and the parachute rigging department. When a high-ranking male officer discovered that they wore trousers and shirts on the jobs, however, he reassigned them to jobs where they could be "dressed as women." Consequently, these Wacs were transferred to the Supply Division where they were given desk jobs for which they had no training.[53]

A summary of the employment of servicewomen in the ETO described this lack of flexibility in the utilization of Wacs and explained it in part by noting that "commanders considered the Wacs more as women then soldiers," and assigned them to jobs in which it would be possible for them to maintain a semblance of "femininity."[54]

The Army Air Force (AAF) was probably the most innovative in its employment of women, in part because as a newer branch of the Army it was not as locked into convention and Army custom. One account explained the greater acceptance of women in the AAF by noting that the "use of women soldiers was almost as revolutionary as the introduction of the airplane as a weapon of war." The commanding general of the AAF also thoroughly supported the full employment of women, including in nontraditional jobs.[55] As a result, the AAF experimented with women in a variety of occupations, including air traffic controller, tower radio operator, aircraft radio mechanic, and link trainer. Radio mechanics were trained in maintenance and operation techniques and were responsible for checking out aircraft radios on the flight line before they took off.[56] Women working as link trainer instructors tutored male student pilots in "instrument-only" or "blind flying" techniques to be used in low visibility weather and night flying. There was a need for women in such occupations because male pilots were needed for combat. While the AAF employed the majority of Wacs in clerical and office work, there were always larger numbers of women in nontraditional jobs in the AAF than in other branches and commands.[57]

Despite regulations to the contrary and WAC inspections of units to insure the proper utilization of female personnel, servicewomen faced difficulties throughout the war getting assigned to work for which they were trained. By 1944, 23 percent of Wacs had civilian skills needed by the Army that went unused, and 22 percent of women graduates from Army special training schools had been assigned duties unrelated to their schooling.[58] Regardless of the WAC response, Army policies and male officers' definitions of "women's work" as stratified by race and class shaped and limited the employment of all women within the Army.

The Army's employment of Wacs in predominantly women's jobs was also a product of its need to preserve distinctions between male and female soldiers. Army spokesmen often contended that enlisted men should learn how to fill military jobs, not perform tasks appropriate for women.[59] The Army's differentiation between "military jobs" to be done by enlisted men and "nonmilitary" jobs for which women would be responsible rested on the differentiation of combat from noncombat service. Defining all jobs that women performed within the military as noncombat served to preserve the Army's definition of "soldier" as male and having combat potential, regardless of the actual jobs performed by that soldier. A "woman soldier" or Wac, in contrast, had no potential for combat and was thus not eligible for the higher status that being a "warrior" conferred. Policies and practices that created a strictly sex-segregated labor force obscured the numbers of men also engaged in "women's jobs" as noncombatants and served to maintain the fiction that the Army was predominantly composed of "fighting" men.

Military distinctions between combatants and noncombatants also worked to circumscribe the position of African-American servicemen and marginalized their contributions as soldiers. By publicly acknowledging their reluctance to utilize black men in combat roles, for instance—a reluctance based on racial stereotypes—War Department and Army officials denied African-American men access to the status of "protector" and further reinforced black women's position as "unprotected."[60] Thus, the "warrior" aspect of the definition of "soldier" was defined not by the job performed or task assigned but by the sex and race of the person wearing the uniform. This paradigm allowed the Army to employ women of all races and African-American men while also maintaining the dichotomy between the white male "protector" and the white female "protected."[61]

The distinction between the noncombat service of all women and the potential and real combat service of predominantly white men was established in part by the legislation creating the corps. The bill prohibited the employment of women as combatants within the Army and was supported by succeeding Army regulations that prohibited the use of weapons or arms of any kind by members of the women's corps.[62] This differentiation between women's and men's service broke down on several occasions during the war, occasions which demonstrated both the practical flexibility of the line drawn between combat and noncombat service as well as the Army's desire to keep such flexibility concealed.

In the United States, the first breakdown involved the formation of an experimental antiaircraft (AAC) unit in the Washington, D.C. area staffed by Euro-American female and male personnel. The creation of this unit on January 1, 1943, was prompted by fears early in the war that the United States might be subjected to air raids and was modeled after the British government's successful use of women in fixed AAC gun installations in the British Isles. Within the framework of "total war," employing women in an antiaircraft combat unit within the United States was deemed acceptable by the Army because it involved a defense of the homefront, not an "aggressive" attack on an enemy abroad. The entire undertaking, however, was cloaked in secrecy lest the American public find out and object to even this limited employment of women in combat units. White WAC officers and auxiliaries, like their male counterparts, were given training and orientation in guns and fire control, automatic weapons, searchlights, radar, gun gunnery, automatic weapon gunnery, fire control methods against seen and unseen targets, and the employment of heavy antiaircraft weapons and searchlights in the defense of Washington, D.C.[63]

Despite women's training abstract gendered labels persisted, and men were designated as "combatants" and the women serving alongside them as "noncombatants." As the war progressed and it became clear that the United States would not come under attack, the companies were disbanded, but the Army described the experiment as a success and indicated that in the future an expanded utilization of women in these areas might be needed.[64]

The contradictions in the Army's practice designating servicewomen as noncombatants became most apparent, and the issue of whether Wacs should be employed as "women" or as "soldiers" most visible, overseas. In May 1943, a new War Department policy on the use of female civilians overseas prohibited their employment in "active combat areas" but noted that "Members of the WAAC, ANC and other female military organizations . . . are excepted."[65] Thus, a distinction was drawn between civilian women employees and female soldiers that allowed servicewomen to be utilized in "active combat areas" from which civilian women employees were restricted. This Army policy underlined the different status of the two groups, female civilians viewed as "women," and protected accordingly, and Wacs, employed as "soldiers" with many of the accompanying risks.

The employment of predominantly white servicewomen in combat areas was in part the result of the Army's integration of women into essential units in overseas theaters. Some male officers were opposed to bringing Wac units with them across the channel shortly after the D-Day invasion. They argued that Wacs would be in danger of being killed or captured and that "concern over the safety and security of American women would impair the efficiency of the fighting men." In contrast, proponents of employing military women in Normandy contended that Wacs were soldiers and should be utilized accordingly, and raised objections to the loss of productivity they feared would result in their units if Wacs were prohibited from moving to forward areas. As one observer reported "many officers in headquarters who had watched the Wacs take the buzz bombs as good soldiers did not underestimate their capability of working under hardships, and strongly objected to losing efficient personnel whom they considered essential to the success of operations." In this case it was deemed inefficient to indulge in employment policies which considered women's sex more important than their military status.[66]

In combat theaters, the differentiation between male soldiers as combatants and "female soldiers" as noncombatants was also undermined by the general blurring of combat and noncombat areas that began to occur during World War II. The distinctions between these "front" and "rear" areas deteriorated as advances in air warfare and longer range artillery made them less meaningful. Thus, despite the presumed danger on the front, Wacs overseas found themselves in rear areas under fire in the same manner as the civilian "noncombatants" around them.[67] White Wacs serving in Naples in early 1944 were subjected to nightly air raids and forced to move regularly from their barracks to the caves which housed the air raid shelters. Similarly, Euro-American Wacs who arrived in England in mid-1944, found that their presence coincided with the apearance of the new German V-2 rocket. The "buzz bomb" attacks occurred daily and Wacs grew accustomed to listening for the "put-put-put" which signaled their presence overhead, a noise one woman compared to a "motor on a boat back home." When the motor cut out the rocket would fall to the ground and detonate on impact.[68] Some Euro-American Wacs also served with the 5th Army in Italy in 1944 as part of an experimental unit to determine if it was possible to employ women with Army Ground Forces' tactical units. They followed the 5th Army for the entire

Italian campaign and lived in tents, wore enlisted men's wool shirts, trousers, and combat boots. They averaged two weeks in each location and were usually anywhere from twelve to thirty-five miles behind the front lines.[69]

Combat personnel were defined not by the designation of the area in which they were stationed or by whether or not they were subject to hostile fire, but by whether or not they could shoot back. The right to fire a weapon to kill in defense of country was a "privilege" accorded largely to white men in the Army, not to women, and only gradually to black men during World War II. Although white War Department and Army officials throughout the war were reluctant to use black male soldiers in combat, as the war progressed, increasing numbers of African-American soldiers were employed as combat troops, especially in the ETO. In contrast, women, regardless of their experiences, were always classified as noncombatants.

White Wacs who served in the southwest Pacific area in many ways faced the worst conditions and most dangerous situations. They were not employed in the area until May 1944, as most Army offices and commands relied on Australian civilians. Wacs were brought in because the Australian government felt it was too dangerous to send its civilian women outside of Australia and refused to allow them to be deployed along with U.S. troops.[70] Most of the Wacs who were stationed in this region moved from Australia to New Guinea and then on to the Philippines, often right behind male troops. The conditions women encountered were extremely harsh, largely due to the necessity of carving space for quarters and offices out of the jungle. It rained continually and Wacs found themselves mired knee-deep in mud and subject to constant air raids. They dressed like enlisted men, in fatigue pants and shirts, a move required by the medical department because of the greater danger of mosquito bites, and malaria, when women's legs were not fully covered by skirts.[71]

When the first Wacs arrived in Leyte in November 1944, the bombings and heavy artillery fire were still occurring, but the offices to which the women were attached were unable to operate if the Wacs were left behind, so they moved forward with their units. Servicewomen flying into Leyte were instructed to leave the plane as quickly as possible when it landed so there would not be time for a Japanese plane to fly in and open fire. When the first group landed, the alert siren sounded as they were deplaning and they dropped all their baggage and took cover in fox-holes as Japanese planes flew over strafing and bombing the airfield.[72] Despite the fact that Wacs served alongside male soldiers in forward areas, came under attack from Japanese snipers, were strafed on the beaches as they deplaned and found shelter in bunkers during the numerous air raids, they were not recognized as having been in combat because they were women.

While WAC noncombatants certainly did not face the same level of danger as male combatants, the fervor with which the Army denied women combat status even when they were in combat theaters and came under fire suggests a further purpose to these labels. One of the key reasons for the Army's maintenance of rigid ideological distinctions between men as potential combatants, and women as noncombatants was to uphold and reinforce gender hierarchies. "I have always resented the thought of a man being kept by a woman," wrote one male civilian, "but I never thought that we in America would come to the point where women would be placed in war theaters while our young, able-bodied men are kept home."[73] Women's presence in combat theaters when male GIs remained on the homefront suggested a crumbling of gender norms, particularly as concerned men and women's respective obligations during wartime. Thus, the paradox of women's military service during World War II and today is that by utilizing women and designating them as "noncombatants" the Army could preserve the roles of some men as "protectors/defenders" and some women as the "protected/defended," even as women's very presence within the military, and the nature of "modern war," threatened to undermine these absolutes.

While male antagonism was a factor influencing the experiences of all Wacs, it was often racial antagonism and individual prejudices that created the most difficult and dangerous situations for servicewomen. Ruth Freudenthal reported that while in basic training as a member of the 6th WAAC Company at Fort Devens, several non-Jewish auxiliaries constantly "jeered at her" and "taunted" her by "kicking up stones" while she was marching. The stones caused her to "become so nervous that I fell over one of the wooden upright markers in the field where the company was drilling." Freudenthal went on to comment that these enlisted women "objected to me because I was . . . Jewish" and several times other auxiliaries made statements in her presence that "We need Hitler to kill off the New York Jews. There are too many of them, especially in the Bronx." Freudenthal requested that these women not be punished but rather that "steps be taken" to eliminate this type of behavior as she did not think "Jewish enlisted women should have to listen to this type of talk. There are many Jewish girls who have had to listen to this and as a result have resigned."[74]

The experiences of African-American servicewomen were framed by the Army's segregation system, as well as the local racial policies and hostile attitudes of civilians in communities around posts where black Wacs were stationed. The Army did not intend to undermine conventional racial systems in its utilization of African-Americans, male or female, during the war. Instead its policies and responses to racial incidents served to reinforce these hierarchies. Despite Army claims that its segregation policies simply followed the racial laws and practices in local communities, most Army posts were segregated in states that had no such laws. Fort Des Moines, the site of the initial WAC Officer Candidate School (OCS) and training center, was segregated, though Iowa had a state law prohibiting segregation. African-American women arriving at Fort Des Moines for OCS were sent to "colored" barracks, directed to tables set aside in the mess hall topped with signs reading "Reserved C" (for "colored"), assigned seats in the classrooms based on race, and ordered to use the black, not white, service club.[75] Charity Adams, an African-American member of the first OCS class at Fort Des Moines, described her dismay when she found that black women were to be separated from white women from the outset.

> When we left the mess hall we were marched by twos to one of the stable buildings known as the Reception Center. We all sat down, but not for long. Almost immediately a young, red-haired second lieutenant stood in front of us and said, 'Will all the colored girls move over on this side.' He pointed to an isolated groups of seats. There was a moment of stunned silence, for even in the United States of the forties it did not occur to us that this could happen. . . . What made things worse was that after the 'colored girls' had been pushed to the side, all the rest of the women were called by name to join a group to be led to their quarters. Why could not the 'colored girls' be called by name to go to their quarters rather than be isolated by race?[76]

Segregation at Fort Des Moines and throughout the Army drew fire from the black press, as well as national African-American organizations, among them the National Council of Negro Women and its president, Mary McLeod Bethune.[77] Bethune was a vocal opponent of the Army's race policies and a tireless advocate for black servicewomen. Although strongly against segregation she also believed that service within the Army was a great opportunity for African-American women. Within this framework she worked to highlight African-American Wacs' contributions and bring to public attention the problems they faced.[78]

As a representative of the National Council of Negro Women, Bethune served several times as an informal adviser to the WAC but Colonel Hobby resisted her efforts to gain a permanent role with the women's corps. Instead

Bethune tried to improve the conditions of black servicewomen through letters to and semiregular meetings with WAC administrators. Bethune's protests against segregation were generally met with the standard WAC response claiming that the women's corps simply followed Army policy in this matter, a policy that would not change during the war. Bethune's recommendation that the Army should create an apparatus or procedure that would allow for regular inspections by African-American officers of posts on which black women were stationed was countered by Hobby's argument that the plan was impossible to implement due to a shortage of officers able to do general inspection work. Other proposals by Bethune were disregarded by Army and WAC leaders because they smacked of "special treatment" for African-American enlisted women and officers.[79]

Because of Bethune's visibility and her outspoken support of black servicewomen, she was often the recipient of letters of complaint and requests for investigations from African-American Wacs who felt that they would get a sympathetic hearing and quicker action from her than from their superiors. In May 1943, an anonymous black WAC officer sent a telegram to Bethune complaining of several demoralizing incidents at Fort Des Moines. This officer objected to an official memo which had been issued and affixed to the WAC information board instructing "colored personnel" to use only Service Club No. 2 and reserving Service Club No. 1 for "whites only." She also reported that white male Army officers at the downtown hotels, which housed some of the WAC officers, had made African-American officers in the dining room get up and move to another section so that black and white women would be seated separately. Bethune informed WAC headquarters of the contents of the telegram and requested an investigation. In response, Hobby sent 1st Officer Harriet West to evaluate the validity of the complaints.[80]

African-American women within the military were not always in agreement as to the most appropriate ways of surmounting the obstacles they faced. While some went outside military channels and reported the difficulties they encountered to the black press and prominent civilians, others worked within the Army to improve conditions. Harriet West was the only black woman on Colonel Hobby's staff and as a civilian had worked as Bethune's administrative assistant. She shared Bethune's opposition to segregation as well as her belief that military service offered great opportunities for black women. Unlike Bethune, however, West was part of the Army, not outside it. As the highest ranking black female officer (major) and a member of WAC headquarters she functioned as an official adviser on the conditions of African-American women's military service. At the same time Colonel Hobby used

West's presence on her staff to quiet critics of WAC racial policies, and as a reason to deny Bethune's repeated attempts to gain a formal role as an adviser to the WAC.[81]

West's function was not to dismiss complaints, but to find solutions consistent with Army policies, and to therefore minimize overt evidence of racial tensions while keeping the segregation policy intact. When she arrived at Fort Des Moines she met with most of the African-American women officers and cautioned them against going outside military channels with complaints. As her investigation continued she discovered that although most black women did not like the Army's segregation system, they could tolerate it when it was not constantly thrown in their faces. Many felt that the memo concerning the service clubs and the incidents at the Savoy hotel in Des Moines were unnecessary and intended to humiliate African-American women. West's recommendations in response to these grievances were that "all reference to white and colored personnel be completely eliminated." She argued that since quarters were assigned by race, all black women would automatically be in the same platoon and would consequently eat together and take classroom training together, and that there was no need for further mention of segregation policies. She concluded that if the Army adopted these suggestions, it would mean "less embarrassment to the colored personnel and a general feeling that a forward step has been made toward democracy."[82] Her recommendations fit within the Army system by not challenging segregation, but downplaying any direct mention of it.

The disagreement among African-American servicewomen and officers as to how best handle problems arising from racist attitudes and segregation policies was exemplified at Laurinburg-Maxton Army Air Base in November 1944. At this base the Army's segregation system was joined by racist hostile actions on the part of white civilians and Army personnel. One set of problems arose when white civilians employed in the Government Post Exchange refused to serve black Wacs; African-American women were also refused entrance to the only service club on the base. In the most serious incident, someone placed a smoke grenade in the women's barracks. While no one was injured, twenty-five members of the squadron were hospitalized overnight for shock and fright. The Army investigation into these incidents was prompted once again by Wacs going outside military channels for aid, this time through a letter to Eleanor Roosevelt detailing the situation on the base and asking for her help. Black enlisted women on the post felt that they were being humiliated by Army policies regarding the use of the service club, mistreated by civilians who worked on the base, and terrorized by incidents like the smoke grenade. They also believed that they were not supported by their commanding officer in their attempts to correct these situations. The African-American WAC command-ing officer, when interviewed by Army inspectors, claimed that she did all she could to address women's complaints concerning assignments and jobs but that she would not deal with "social issues" such as their lack of access to the service club. "I did not come into the Army to fight race problems," she argued, "I do not think that the Army is a place to settle these differences . . . I do feel that my girls think I am giving them a bad deal because I have not, as they think, stood up for them in general." The investigation yielded some gains; restrictions on black women's use of the service club were dropped and rigid policies on civilian interaction with African-American personnel were implemented. The Army's response to the smoke bomb, however, was merely to dismiss it as a "harmless prank" and blame the incident on "transient troops in the area," thus excusing the base from having to find and punish the perpe-trator.[83] The Army's segregation system both reinforced and was supported by similar racial policies in many civilian areas; black Wacs were forced to use the segregated civilian transportation system to get to and from posts in the South, thereby highlighting African-American women's second-class status within the United States and the Army. A female journalist for the *Philadelphia Afro-American*, who evaluated the conditions for black servicewomen at Fort McClellan, Anniston, Alabama, reported that the camp itself was fine,

> provided I could be dropped by plane into the post. Under no circum-stances would I wish to attempt to get to the post in any other manner. . . . Major Harriet West, also making a tour of the camps and I had come from Atlanta, Ga., to Anniston, Ala., . . . in a dirty, crowded segregated coach. She had been insulted by a white conductor whom she had asked to hand her baggage from the train. I had long ago abandoned bags, having sent mine back from Nashville when it seemed that I, and certainly not luggage, might not find room in the half coaches allotted to colored travelers.[84]

The presence of African-American women in uniform, like that of their male counterparts, often fueled the racial hostility of civilians in areas sur-rounding posts where black women were stationed. This hostility sometimes erupted into violence when African-American Wacs were perceived by civil-ians as refusing to conform with local race laws. On one occasion, two black Wacs stationed at Camp Sibert, Alabama, were arrested and beaten by white police when they would not surrender their seats to white people on a segregated bus. According to black newspaper accounts, the two women were seated in the rear of the bus, and ordered to stand by the bus driver as the bus began filling with white men and women. The Wacs refused to do so and the bus driver in turn refused to start the bus. One of the white passengers then left the bus and called a civilian police officer, who pulled one of the Wacs from her seat. The other Wac pushed the police officer and told him to contact an MP (military policeman) since civilian officers had no authority over military personnel. The civilian lawman refused the request and dragged both women from the bus, allegedly accompanied by chants of "kill'em, kill'em" from white men and women still on the bus. Both women were beaten several times before being turned over to the military authorities and one of them was hospitalized for a week. The Army's response to this incident was negotiations with the Mayor of Gadsden, Alabama (nearest town to Camp Sibert) to establish clear guidelines for civilian handling of military personnel. The agreement reached stipulated that no civilian police would interfere in matters involving military personnel, but instead would call MPs, and the bus company management agreed to issue directives to all drivers instructing them not to call the civilian police nor attempt to handle problems involving military personnel themselves. This type of settlement was established in several regions during the war but was sometimes abrogated by angry individuals and white civilian police.[85]

On several occasions the Army and its representatives not only failed to champion black Wacs who were assaulted by civilian police, but brought them up on military charges. Because the Army was intent on preserving, not challenging, race laws and hierarchies in the communities surrounding its posts, black personnel were sometimes sacrificed to maintain cordial relationships with local civilian populations. Three African-American Wacs, stationed at Fort Knox, Kentucky, were beaten by Kentucky law enforcement officials when they failed to move from the white to the crowded "colored" waiting room at a Greyhound bus station in Elizabethtown, Kentucky. The women were standing in the white waiting room when a Kentucky police officer ordered them to move. They told him there was no space in the "colored" waiting room and informed him that they were simply waiting for a bus. He responded "When white people down here tell n——s to they move!" and threatened to place them under arrest. According to the official Army investigation the officer then placed one of the women under arrest and all three of them started beating him, at which point he drew his blackjack to "protect" himself. In the interchange that followed, two of the Wacs were struck several times and one "either fell or was thrown to the floor."[86]

The black press served as a forum through which African-American servicemen and women could recount their experiences of racial terror. Accounts in the black press based on letters from the Fort Knox Wacs to their families, for instance, differed from the Army version and claimed that the women never hit the officer but rather were struck when they refused to enter the "colored" waiting room. These articles reported that when the women were finally returned to camp, the post commander ignored their need for medical attention and lectured them on obeying jim crow laws in the South. The Army's official response to the incident was to bring the women up on court-martial charges. Although they were later acquitted, the Army's reaction to the incident could hardly be interpreted as a defense of the African-American Wacs.[87] One anonymous Wac voiced her frustration in a letter to the *Afro-American*,

> Colored WACs in the South, as well as male soldiers, are subjected to Southern race prejudices and hate. One has to be a colored soldier stationed in the South to know what insults we receive—what segregation and prejudices are encountered. Some of us are of the opinion that perhaps we have been kept here because we get along and make no great protest, nor cause no undue racial friction. Meanwhile, we are being sacrificed. Must our ability to adapt ourselves to a bad situation keep us buried and subject to disagreeable circumstances for the duration?.[88]

While the racial climate in areas surrounding Army posts housing African-American personnel was at times more hostile than that they found within the Army itself, the situation was often reversed overseas. Members of the only black WAC unit to serve overseas reported favorably on the liberal racial policies they encountered in England and France. "The English are quite aware of our American color bar," one wrote, "and go miles out of their way to make one happy and contented."[89] Another African-American Wac recalled the thrills she experienced as a servicewoman in England compared to the fear she felt as a black woman based at Fort Oglethorpe, Georgia, noting that in England "we were treated like Kings and Queens" whereas at Fort Oglethorpe "we were just plain scared" to even venture off the post.[90]

The Army and the American Red Cross tried to institute segregation at the housing and recreational facilities for military personnel in Europe thus trying to recreate the social hierarchies that were broken down by the treatment of African-Americans in England and France. The American Red Cross (ARC) provided both recreation facilities and hotels in London for Wacs stationed in England who received passes into the city, and the African-American WAC unit initially used these services along with white Wacs, resulting in the integration of ARC facilities for Army women. The ARC, already highly criticized by black leaders for its policy of segregating its blood supply, responded to this situation by sending recreation equipment to the black WAC detachment so that they could stop using the ARC facilities where white Wacs gathered. Major Charity Adams, the commander of the black WAC unit, replied by sending the recreation equipment back to the ARC and allowing members of her unit to continue to frequent the ARC operation. ARC officials also approached Adams reporting that they had leased a special hotel especially for African-American Wacs. "We realize that your colored girls would be happier if they had a hotel all to themselves," the ARC London director explained, "so we have leased a hotel from the British government, and we are in the process of renovating and furnishing it now." Adams told the ARC that it wasn't necessary to "jim-crow" black women and refused to use the new facilities. She met with all the women of her unit and explained the situation, telling them that the ARC was "trying to create a segregated situation where previously an integrated one had existed" and asked them not to use the new hotel. According to Adams not one member of her unit ever did.[91]

The support given to black service men and women from African-American communities and the black press made racial tensions and African-American accomplishments in the Army a political issue. Consequently, black Wacs defiance of Army regulations and civilian race laws, whether perceived as a threat or a blow for racial justice, was much more visible than that of their white counterparts. African-American Wacs, for instance, launched the most effective letter writing campaign initiated by Army women after the War Department decided to dissolve WAC Band No. 2, the only black WAC band in the service. The order was issued as part of an Army-wide program which called for the discontinuance of a large number of bands. When the African-American band was dissolved its members dispatched messages objecting to the Army's action to their families, to national and local black organizations, and to the African-American press . This led to a flood of publicity in the black press and dozens of letters and phone calls to the War Department and WAC headquarters demanding that the Army either reactivate the band and reinstate its members or allow black Wacs to join the white band and continue their jobs as musicians. In light of these protests, WAC and Army leaders, unwilling to integrate the white unit, arranged for the reconstitution of the African-American band.[92]

One of the most visible and public episodes of resistance to Army authority occurred at Lovell Hospital, Fort Devens, Massachusetts, when six black Wacs launched a sit-down strike in early 1945 to protest their assignments and working conditions on the post. The situation at Lovell Hospital was created in part by a glut of trained medical technicians resulting in the assignment of black and white Wacs trained as medical technicians to service work as orderlies and ward clerks in Army hospitals throughout the United States. Army practices for the employment of black women, as well as the racial prejudice of hospital commanders and personnel officers, guaranteed that when African-American and white Wacs were stationed together it would be the black, not white, medical technicians who would be given the menial positions.

At Fort Devens, African-American Wacs with ratings as medical technicians were given jobs as hospital orderlies, work which included a great deal of heavy labor and tasks such as scrubbing the floors and windows of the wards. In addition, members of the African-American unit were ordered on several occasions to perform KP for the white WAC detachment. The employment of black Wacs in these duties was directed by the white commander of the hospital, Colonel Crandall. When the African-American Wacs met with him to air their complaints over the situation, Colonel Crandall made it clear that no black servicewomen at his posts would be "taking temperatures" or working with patients. He stated further that they were there to "do the dirty work," and on several occasions had been heard to remark that he didn't want any "nigger Wacs" around his hospital.[93]

In response to his remarks, most of the sixty black Wacs stationed at the hospital walked out of the meeting and the next morning they all refused to report to work. After Colonel Crandall ordered them to resume their duties, all but six returned to their jobs. At that point General Sherman Miles, commander of the 1st Service Command, stepped in and ordered the six once again to return to their posts. He further instructed a white WAC lieutenant to inform them all of the seriousness of refusing to obey a direct order during wartime, an action that could be punished by death according to military law. Two more returned to their posts, leaving four women who continued to refuse and who were then court-martialed.[94]

The black community was at first divided in its response to the women's actions. Throughout the war the NAACP and the African-American press supported black military personnel in their struggles against segregation, mistreatment, and exploitation, but stopped short of endorsing extralegal activism, fearing that such activities would hinder, not aid, the cause of racial justice. In keeping with this philosophy many black newspapers drew a line; they expressed sympathy for the situation which had prompted the strike, while not supporting the strike itself.[95] Bethune and the NCNW were more sympathetic to the predicament of the striking women, arguing that though the Wacs shouldn't have gone on strike during the war, their actions were understandable and justified given the terrible circumstances at Lovell Hospital. Bethune also tried to use the incident as leverage in her push for the formation of an investigating committee to visit all posts and camps where African-American women were stationed and which would function to identify problems and offer recommendations to improve the status of black Wacs.[96]

The local Boston chapter of the NAACP and its president, Julian Steele, were initially the least sympathetic to the women's plight. A statement issued by Steele, and signed by various black community leaders declared: "We deplore the action of colored Wacs in refusing to report for duty at Lovell General Hospital last week. We recognize that there is no right to strike in the armed service and that regular procedures have been established by the army for reporting grievances and securing their correction."[97] Steele went on to characterize the striking women as "misguided" and expressed his hope that "the splendid record which colored Wacs have made in this war will not be blemished by the . . . actions of these young women." He commented further that the Boston NAACP wished to "go on record" as opposing segregation but insisted that segregation was an "underlying but not immediate factor in this case." Despite his disapproval of their actions, at Steele's recommendation, the Boston NAACP provided counsel for the women's defense at their court-martial "because we feel that in spite of the misguided actions of these young women there are wide implications to this situation."[98]

The lukewarm support shown by the local NAACP for the Wacs' actions was replaced by a storm of protest when the court-martial verdict was announced and the women were given dishonorable discharges and sentenced to one year of hard labor. Although many individuals and organizations viewed the strike itself as wrong, they also felt the racial hostility of the commanding officer and the discriminatory policies affecting black women were factors that mediated against such a harsh sentence. The national NAACP, the ACLU, the NCNW, and African-American Congressman Adam Clayton Powell Jr., launched campaigns to appeal the court's decision, arguing that if the black women were guilty of disobeying an order so was Colonel Crandall, who disobeyed Army directives against racial discrimination. They petitioned the War Department to bring Colonel Crandall up on charges and exonerate the Wacs.[99] Their pleas were joined by letters from hundreds of individuals, white and black, who felt the women's sentences were wholly unjust. Many of these letters depicted the women as martyrs, striking a blow for the cause of racial justice. One white woman argued that the outcome of the trial would cause many African-

American men and women to have "grave doubts as to what their services and sacrifices are all about" and cause them to wonder "why so many thousands of young men are giving their lives in a war to wipe out Nazism when there are mounting evidences of its flourishing at home."[100]

The War Department responded to this flood of protest by quickly reviewing then reversing the verdict of the Army court; War Department officials reinstated the Wacs and had them transferred to a new post. In addition, orders were issued to stop assigning African-American Wacs at Lovell Hospital to menial duties and clearly delineated the types of jobs enlisted women were not required to perform, including scrubbing floors. Although the Army never mounted a full investigation of Colonel Crandall's role in provoking the strike, Army officials requested that the Surgeon General remove him from his command and retire him from service.[101]

While WAC leaders' opposed some of the more extreme gender and race stereotyping of job categories, their opposition focused predominantly on those situations in which Army officers assigned servicewomen to menial "women's work." Colonel Hobby believed that such assignments would undercut her organization's ability to attract "high-caliber" recruits for office work. In other words, WAC leaders generally approved of sex-segregation within the highest realm of "women's work," pink- collar jobs. Such employment of women allowed WAC officials to argue both that military women did not threaten gendered job structures and that these workers, as representatives of the white, middle-class, were "respectable."

The tightrope that WAC leaders walked between "equal" and "differential" treatment of servicewomen in terms of job assignments was part of what was being contested in some Wacs' resistance to job placements. In fact, the challenge to the Army's gender and race-segregated job structure mounted by some individuals and groups within the WAC undermined WAC leaders' construction of the women's corps as not questioning social order. The necessity of such a defensive construction was nowhere more evident than in the arena of sexuality, an area in which WAC leaders' insisted that differential treatment of servicewomen was critical to WAC legitimacy, public acceptance and, most importantly, the protection of individual Wacs and female officers from sexual exploitation.

5

Protecting Whom?
Regulating Sexuality in the World War II Army and the WAC

WAC leaders believed that asserting different moral standards for men and women was absolutely necessary to both protect the reputation of the WAC and offer protection to some individual servicewomen. While the corps' leadership wanted servicewomen to have access to jobs, for instance, based on their identities as "soldiers," they were unequivocal in their insistence that Wacs be treated as "women," not "soldiers," in the area of sexual regulation. The WAC sexual system was built on the premise that to "protect" individual servicewomen and female officers from sexual exploitation, victimization, and rumors of sexual immorality, it was imperative to gain legitimacy for the corps, a legitimacy WAC leaders characterized as based on the sexual restraint and chastity of female soldiers. By this logic, if the corps was considered respectable, then women within it would be also. The WAC system of protection in which the legitimacy of the corps was the overriding concern made clear that women who threatened this legitimacy through their "misbehavior" would be eliminated and thus characterized as unworthy of protection.

The WAC system of female protection was a mirage when viewed within the Army's larger regulatory framework governing both women's and men's sexuality. While the military's masculine culture encouraged men's heterosexual activity, manpower needs dictated that men should not be responsible for their sexual behavior. The resulting Army protective system shielded male GIs and officers from the consequences of their heterosexual behavior, including venereal disease and fatherhood, and blamed instead the women with whom they were involved. The protection the WAC system offered to individual servicewomen and female officers was, as a result, somewhat illusory. Because both the WAC and Army systems of protection reinforced and upheld sexual double standards for male and female soldiers, to behave, or misbehave, as male soldiers did, was to become "bad women," not men.

The question of whether to treat Wacs as "soldiers" or as "women" was most controversial in the arena of sexual regulation. Because the Army's approach to the issue of sexual regulation and control for male soldiers stressed health and combat readiness, not sexual abstinence, it served to reinforce public perceptions that women's entry into the military would encourage them to become sexually active. The Army expected and encouraged heterosexual activity among male soldiers and controlled male sexuality with regulations prohibiting homosexuality and sodomy and addressing the prevention and treatment of venereal diseases, as well as informal mechanisms upholding prohibitions on interracial relationships.[1] The creation of the women's corps forced the Army to reevaluate these policies and determine if they could be applied in the same manner to all soldiers, or if different applications were necessary to accommodate female personnel. The male military hierarchy's desire for uniformity collided with the female WAC director's firm belief in different moral standards for women, and her insistence that this difference be reflected in Army regulations.

The Army's venereal disease policies were premised on a sexual double standard that characterized servicemen's heterosexual activity as normal and expected, while defining women's sexual behavior as the "source of contagion" and "bad" women as the "cause" of venereal disease (VD).[2] Within this framework, Army officials sought to control women's sexuality as a means of protecting the health of male soldiers, especially after VD rates began to climb during wartime due to both social dislocation and the massive expansion of the military. The Army's scapegoating of women by defining female sexuality as a "danger" to the health of male soldiers was supported by civilian public health and social protection agencies. The subsequent national social protection campaign organized to meet this threat was developed by the Office of Community War Services (OCWS), the American Social Hygiene Association (ASHA), the U.S. Public Health Service (USPHS), and the military. This campaign named women's heterosexual promiscuity as "the problem" and moved to legislate women's sexual behavior in the guise of social protection.[3]

Blaming women for the rising rate of VD among male soldiers and officers grew out of shifts in social protection discourses in the 'teens and 1920s. Social and child protection programs after 1910, and especially during World War I, came increasingly to characterize women's sexual agency as the result of female sexual delinquency and attribute women's sexual victimization to this delinquency, not to male sexual crime. According to historian Linda Gordon, this shift was magnified during wartime when the problem was defined not as the need to "contain predatory males, but to control the girls." The emphasis on female sexual agents as sex delinquents, combined with the Army's protection of male soldiers from the consequences of their own sexual behavior, resulted in a focus on girls and women, especially those whose presence in "public and unrespectable places," made them suspect.[4] Within this wide-ranging social protection campaign, female prostitutes and other "promiscuous" civilian women were not only characterized as the "chief source of venereal disease among men in the armed forces," but were also the primary targets of both state regulation and criminal prosecution.[5]

The two major pieces of legislation addressing the problem of venereal disease in servicemen were solidly situated within this framework. The "8 Points Agreement," developed in May 1939, by the War and Navy departments in conjunction with the USPHS and state and local health departments, provided for a "broad, united attack on venereal disease by both the military authorities and civilian agencies to *protect the health* of the man in uniform and the industrial worker."[6] The "8 Points Agreement" was joined by the May Act, passed by Congress in July 1941. The May Act dictated that the focus of this "attack on venereal disease" would be female sexuality and made the practice of prostitution in specific zones around military or naval establishments a federal offense. This act could be invoked by the secretary of war or the navy in areas in which the local authorities were unable or unwilling to repress prostitution.[7]

A majority of the American public as well as individual military officers felt that the best and most appropriate way to decrease the rate of venereal disease among servicemen was to regulate, not repress, prostitution.[8] "Regulation" was defined as the establishment of segregated "houses of prostitution" which would be regularly inspected by medical officials to insure that women within them remained free of venereal disease. The support of regulation over repression was based on a definition of male sexuality that emphasized male sexual drives as unrelenting and the necessity of providing outlets for them. Although the Army officially supported repression many of its practices, issuing condoms to male soldiers and providing prophylaxis stations to be frequented after heterosexual intercourse, implicitly and explicitly condoned male sexual activity.[9] In fact, one provost marshal who disagreed with the Army's official espousal of repression sanctioned controlled prostitution by making bimonthly inspections of houses of prostitution.[10] Conceptualizing venereal disease as primarily an issue of "health" for men, not "morality," Army officials' attempted throughout the war to break down the stigma of venereal disease for servicemen in order to insure that male soldiers would seek treatment if they found themselves infected.[11]

The Army's framework for regulating male sexuality rested on the assumption that military men would be heterosexually active with "bad" women. Definitions of "bad" women were determined not only by their sexual behavior, but also by the race and class of the sexual actors. In this, contemporary racial stereotypes of the greater sexual immorality of African-Americans relative to white Americans supported constructions of black women as sexually promiscuous.[12] In several communities, fears that the repression of prostitution would create dangers for "good" women (white, middle-class) led community leaders to allow "Negro prostitution" to continue while mounting vigorous campaigns to repress commercial prostitution in general.[13] Although this practice violated national directives calling for the elimination of *all* commercial prostitution, it made clear the attitudes of some local officials who supported the sexual exploitation of black women to protect some white women's "virtue."[14]

To the degree that social protection agencies characterized their campaigns as protecting women, they did so not by focusing on women's health, and their potential contraction of venereal disease, but rather on good women's loss of sexual respectability once sexually active. Explicit within the public critique of repression were fears that shutting down all prostitution would lead to an increase in the rape and seduction of good women, heterosexual promiscuity in good women, or possibly greater instances of homosexuality in men.[15] Public concerns that the repression of prostitution would lead to an increase in heterosexual promiscuity among young women were exacerbated when efforts to eliminate commercial prostitution, though extremely successful, did not result in a dramatic decrease in the rate of venereal disease in the Army. By 1942 officials of the OCWS and the military claimed that the "new camp followers of the Army" were not "professional prostitutes" but thousands of young women who flocked to areas around military camps and stations looking for "excitement and adventure." "A high percentage of infections in the armed forces," one report noted, "has been traced to girls in their early teens."[16]

Given that discourses on sexual deviance often highlight popular fears of the consequences of "new sexual values," characterizing the "venereal disease problem" among servicemen as the responsibility of young girls, defined the female sexual agent as the most prominent symbol of sexual deviance.[17]

During World War II, young women who had sex with American servicemen and officers became the symbol of the breakdown of sexual standards and were dubbed "victory girls" by the wartime media. The label of "victory girl" referred in part to popular depictions of these young women's actions as intended to boost male morale and aid the war effort. The term, however, also invoked contemporary discourses on sexually delinquent girls that characterized their relationships with soldiers as irresponsible and dangerous and placed the blame for female sexual agency and victimization squarely on young women's shoulders.[18] Victory girls became the focus of an intensive social purity campaign aimed at controlling their sexuality and behavior. As historian Allan Brandt has observed, "The fact that controlling prostitution did not control sexuality forced many to confront the changes in American sexual mores" as the "harlot with the painted face was replaced by the girl next door."[19] During the war the Social Protection Division, OCWS, broadened the definition of prostitution to include any woman who was "sexually active despite the lack of sincere emotional content in the relationship," hoping to eliminate confusion like that voiced by one social protection officer who found it "difficult to draw a line between the girl who grants her favors for a certain sum of money and her sister who will indulge in identical activities for a T-bone steak."[20]

The Army's institutionalization of the dichotomy between "good" and "bad" women necessitated that WAC leaders define servicewomen as "good" and distinct from both male soldiers and "bad" women. Colonel Hobby's efforts to insure differential treatment for women, however, remained an area of struggle between the corps and the Army throughout the war. The question of whether servicewomen should be treated differently than their male counterparts in the arena of sexual regulation became the focus of heated debate and internal controversy over the subject of venereal disease control in the Army.

While the Army was trying to decrease the stigma of venereal disease for men in order to protect their health, Hobby's aim was to maintain the stigma for women with the aim of protecting their reputations. WAC leaders believed the Army's venereal disease program, premised on the assumption of heterosexual activity, would seriously damage the reputation of the corps if applied to women. To discuss the possibility of venereal disease as a problem among servicewomen was in Hobby's estimation a direct assault on Wacs' respectability, comparable to the slander campaign itself. The distribution of condoms and prophylactic information to unmarried women in the WAC, she argued, would be seen by the public and the families of servicewomen as both encouraging heterosexual promiscuity and subjecting enlisted women to sexual victimization at the hands of male officers.[21]

Nevertheless, Army surgeon general Norman T. Kirk, asserting his authority on public health issues, tried to set up a similar program for Wacs. In August 1942, without consulting Colonel Hobby or WAC Hq, Kirk called a meeting to discuss the details and scope of sex hygiene instruction for servicewomen. The result of this meeting was a series of recommendations proposing a thorough venereal disease control program for women, including a full course of instruction in sex education techniques for preventing venereal disease. Meeting participants also believed that the distribution of condoms to servicewomen was crucial, and since Wacs might be too modest to request them as men did, they suggested that condoms be dispensed from slot machines in WAC latrines.[22]

Colonel Hobby got support for her position from women in the War Department, as Emily Newell Blair, chief of the Women's Interests Section and a conference participant, sent a report on the proceedings to the WAC director. Blair's reaction supported Hobby's philosophy of differential treatment for women. Disagreeing with the conferees' definition of the WAC as simply a "feminine counterpart" of the Army, Blair outlined the major differences between Wacs and Army men that would demand distinctive regulatory programs. The major difference, she contended, was that Wacs were a "select" group who "may be expected to conform to higher set of standards" than a group selected only on the basis of age and health. Consequently, the conference members' expectations of a high rate of venereal disease within the WAC ignored the methods of recruiting auxiliaries, which should "provide a high type of women." Blair's connections between the civilian class backgrounds of servicewomen and their corresponding higher moral ideals paralleled those of the WAC director. Blair supported the imposition of "boarding school types of discipline on adult female personnel of the WAAC" criticized by the conference, and maintained that such rules were necessary for the "good of the group." "Speaking as a public relations specialist," she argued that the recommendations of the surgeon general's conference, if adopted, would "reflect an attitude towards sexual promiscuity that whatever the practice, is not held by the majority of Americans. The Army . . . is no place to propagandize new social attitudes."[23]

WAC leaders also struggled with the surgeon general and some Army medical officers over appropriate policies for infected servicewomen. There were two key questions involved in this struggle: should the WAC, like the Army, accept women into service who already had venereal disease; and should women who contracted the disease after joining the corps be discharged or treated and returned to duty. The surgeon general and several Army medical officers recommended that venereal disease be removed as a disqualifying defect from regulations addressing the WAC. They argued that there was a greater danger of public outcry if such women were sent back into the community than if they were accepted into the women's corps. WAC leaders disagreed and at no time during the war were women with venereal disease knowingly accepted into the WAC.[24] Hobby had less control over individual Army medical officers who, following the surgeon general's recommendations, arranged for the treatment of infected servicewomen and then returned them to duty. Although WAC regulations did not provide for the discharge of servicewomen who contracted the disease, many were removed from the corps under the Code of Conduct, and after conversion under the "traits of character" caveat in WAC Regulations, which provided for the undesirable discharge of women found guilty of "conduct unbecoming . . . or reflecting discredit on the Corps."[25] Some Army commanders and medical officers used the regulations covering men's heterosexual behavior and the corresponding medical approach to venereal disease to address similar issues within the women's corps. Evidence suggests that some Army officers even gave Wacs instruction on specific prophylactic measures to prevent venereal disease despite WAC polices and Army directives to the contrary.[26] One such lecture was brought to Colonel Hobby's attention when several white Wacs complained that they were instructed on sex hygiene and told by an Army officer at Camp Polk to carry their "own protection in [their] utility bag as the boys might not have any."[27]

One of the biggest problems generated by similar treatment of servicemen and women arose when at a number of Army posts medical officers performed monthly pelvic examinations on servicewomen in accordance with Army regulations requiring monthly exams to detect venereal disease. Within WAC leaders' moral framework, venereal disease exams, which presumed the heterosexual promiscuity of female soldiers, signified to many Wacs their unwarranted treatment as "bad" women. Despite the extremely low venereal disease rate among servicewomen throughout the war, many Army doctors refused to turn in a venereal disease report for the WAC unit on their posts unless they could perform pelvic exams on all servicewomen, since venereal disease in women could not be detected without such an exam.[28] Colonel Hobby and other WAC officers received hundreds of complaints from servicewomen who objected to this practice.[29] Most resented being examined for venereal disease at all, and were offended by the assumption of heterosexual promiscuity

behind such exams. One white Wac, Ruth Chambers, protested the "humiliating monthly physical exams, [required] before we could get our pay-
checks."[30] Others complained of "rough and painful" handling by "inexpert"
Army doctors. One white Wac wrote to her sister of the "pain and indignity"
accompanying the monthly inspection, alleging that for a week afterwards
"she hadn't been able to seat herself or arise again without pain."[31] Army directives ordering that pelvic examinations should not be done on a monthly basis
were passed and distributed throughout the war, but were not always followed
by Army doctors; these practices were never completely eliminated.[32]

"Bad" women in the corps did not have the potential for rehabilitation.
Women who engaged in behavior outside the bounds defined as appropriate
by the Code of Conduct and later regulations were under these rules liable
for discharge, but not "punishment." After the war Colonel Hobby discussed
this distinction, arguing that a "promiscuous WAC could be immediately discharged in the interest of unit spirit and welfare, but [she] could not legally
be punished." The director defined discharge not as a punitive measure but
as a protective one, "protecting" the group of women remaining within the
unit while also protecting the individual woman from further discipline
within the Army.[33]

Some Army commanders did not recognize or acknowledge WAC leaders'
paradigm of punishment and protection and invoked their own understanding of the sexual double standard to discipline Wacs by demoting them or
confining them to quarters for actions and behaviors that went unpunished in
male soldiers.[34] Moreover, despite Hobby's attempts to maintain the fiction
that sexual regulation of female soldiers was not punitive, women who were
absent without leave (AWOL) were routinely subjected to pelvic exams when
they were returned to their unit.[35] The assumption behind such an exam was
that servicewomen who went AWOL were going to be engaging in heterosexual intercourse and that their violation of Army regulations carried with it a
challenge to prescribed sexual norms and standards of morality. Pelvic examinations given under these circumstances were used to control and punish servicewomen's behavior.[36]

Pregnancy, along with venereal disease, was the most visible sign that a
woman had engaged in heterosexual intercourse. Illegitimate pregnancy was
an issue not only because it signaled heterosexual intercourse outside of marriage, but also because the pregnancy itself signaled the potential birth of an
"illegitimate" child. Further, illegitimate pregnancy within the WAC seemed
to confirm public fears that military service would either lead to the sexual vic-

timization of women or encourage them to choose to be sexually active. Although the WAC pregnancy rate was in reality quite low, rumors of the high numbers of pregnancies among servicewomen plagued the corps throughout the war. In fact, as WAC historian Mattie Treadwell observed, the WAC pregnancy rate "varied from 0 to 7 per 1,000 per month at different times . . . The final average of 4 per 1,000 per month or 48 per 1,000 per year was considerably less than the rate of 117 per 1,000 per year for civilian women in comparable age groups."[37]

Issues involving servicewomen's potential pregnancy, moreover, highlighted an enormously important difference between the consequences of male versus female soldiers' heterosexual activity. If concerns about men's sexual health were critically centered on issues of manpower, then women's ability to determine if they would become pregnant was critical to issues regarding womanpower. Pregnant women and mothers of young children were barred from the WAC and considered a drain on Army resources, as well as an embarrassment to the corps. The women's corps, however, included married as well as nonmarried women. If contraception was to be banned entirely, were married women then relegated to pregnancy if sexually active with their husbands? Did the Army have the right to tell married women that they could not use contraceptives? Both of these questions were addressed by an anonymous enlisted woman whom journalist John O'Donnell quoted in his second column. She argued:

> There will be times when I shall meet my husband . . . I wish to have the same rights of regulating my private life while in the WAACs that I enjoyed while we were just two civilians happily living together. This will only be possible if women, such as I, are able while in the army to have available those essentials which, at least officially, are banned.[38]

Birth control advocate Margaret Sanger also argued in an article in *Time* that the Army should give contraceptive information to all servicewomen so they could make their own decisions.[39]

Some Army medical officers shaped their own replies to these questions by including information about contraception within their lectures on health and hygiene, despite directives to the contrary. At Santa Ana Army Air Base a male Army captain gave a lecture on birth control. In the ensuing investigation, a white WAC officer, Edna L. Johnson, reported that while the captain stated that his talk was aimed "primarily at married women," he also made it clear that "any one of us was privileged to take advantage of the facilities offered by the Army." The male officer also allegedly remarked that it was the

Army's wish "to avoid as many pregnancies as possible." Johnson testified that in the course of his discussion he stressed the use of diaphragms as a contraceptive measure, passed around a model to demonstrate how to insert a diaphragm, and suggested that any member who wished to do so "could be fitted for a diaphragm at the infirmary." While Johnson's testimony was used to condemn such practice she supported the captain and his motives, suggesting that at least some servicewomen felt they had a right to such knowledge and services.[40]

The WAC's official approach to pregnancy and contraception, like venereal disease, was focused on encouraging sexual abstinence, not on providing information about contraception or contraceptives themselves. WAC policies were articulated and enforced through three major overlapping mechanisms: the WAC Sexual Hygiene Pamphlet, the Code of Conduct, and discharge regulations pertaining to pregnancy. The WAC Sexual Hygiene Manual, distributed just prior to O'Donnell's controversial article, described illegitimate pregnancy as "a personal tragedy as well as a loss in womanpower." The pamphlet was silent on the issue of contraception, containing no information on how to use birth control devices or where they might be obtained.[41] In addition, Colonel Hobby, in meetings with Army personnel and in statements to the press, repeatedly denied that the corps condoned the distribution of contraceptives to servicewomen, and insisted that the issue of contraceptives had "never been discussed at any meeting to her knowledge."[42] Instead, she used the formal regulations within the Code of Conduct to stress the "high moral standards" of the corps and to impress on servicewomen the need to comply with these standards if they wished to remain in the WAC. The Code of Conduct was used in conjunction with WAC and Army regulations providing for the discharge of all women who became pregnant.[43]

In keeping with this emphasis on sexual abstinence, the first WAC regulations dealing with pregnancy made a distinction between "legitimate" and "illegitimate" pregnancy, and provided for the honorable discharge of all *married* pregnant women and the "summary" or undesirable discharge of all *unmarried* pregnant women.[44] One problem with this differentiation was that the issuance of a discharge "other than honorable" was predicated on the presence of a violation of military or civil law. As long as women had not violated other military or civil laws, the fact that they were unmarried and pregnant was not a legal infraction and therefore could not be punished as such.[45] Colonel Hobby was aware of this difficulty and successfully recommended alterations that gave blanket "honorable" discharges to all pregnant servicewomen in December 1942. She immediately faced opposition to this policy change from married members of the corps and ranking male officers who objected to an honorable discharge for unmarried pregnant women. This opposition dissolved, however, when Hobby asked if these critics were going to require "legal proof that the married woman's husband was the father of the child."[46]

Although subsequent WAC regulations provided for the honorable discharge of all pregnant women regardless of marital status, some unmarried pregnant servicewomen nonetheless continued to be undesirably discharged. The new regulation provided that an honorable discharge was available only if there was no "violation of the Code of Conduct" involved. If the Code of Conduct were breached, then an undesirable discharge would be issued because of violation of the code, *not* because the servicewoman was pregnant.[47] The practical application of this new regulation in many commands insured that unmarried pregnant women would continue to be given undesirable discharges under the Code of Conduct. Thus, the reference to the Code of Conduct in the new discharge regulation functioned to maintain the distinction between "legitimate" and "illegitimate" pregnancy.[48] This practice did not stop until after conversion when the WAC became subject to regular Army rules. After conversion the discharge procedures for pregnancy did not include a reference to the Code of Conduct and provided only for honorable discharge in all cases.[49]

Colonel Hobby's major aim in changing the WAC regulations on "illegitimate" pregnancy was not only to correct previously illegal procedures, but to protect the corps from unfavorable publicity. She believed that giving women discharges "other than honorable" simply because they were unmarried and pregnant would only increase public hostility and criticism focused on the Army's "victimization" of servicewomen.[50] As I will discuss in WAC leaders' approach to discharging lesbians, removing women under the Code of Conduct proved sufficient to excise the so-defined bad women from the corps swiftly and without calling public attention to the specific reasons for doing so.[51]

The mandatory discharge of pregnant Wacs raised the related issue of whether servicewomen who attempted to halt their pregnancy through abortion should be discharged. As with illegitimate pregnancy, Hobby claimed that her major concerns were to protect the rights and health of individual women while also "preserving the right of the Corps to choose the type of members it desired." Within this paradigm, WAC leaders worked to find some legal means of requiring discharges for women suspected of having abortions so that this "type" of woman would not find a home in the corps. At the same time Hobby also attempted to protect the rights of individual Wacs, and the reputation of the corps, by insuring that such discharges would be honorable.[52] Because women who had abortions were not generally subject to criminal prosecution, there were few civil or criminal statutes that could be used to support any type of discharge for abortion, honorable or otherwise. WAC officers investigating options for discharging women also noted that they had considerable difficulty in obtaining proof that abortions had occurred: "It is impossible for a medical officer to furnish a certificate that an abortion has been performed or that any obvious miscarriage was due to an abortion unless there was a witness to the operation," reported one WAC medical officer, "In illegal abortions proof would be practically impossible."[53]

Colonel Hobby discovered that the other women's military services were facing a similar dilemma. The WAVES had also found no legal basis for discharging women suspected of having abortions. The solution adopted by the SPARS (Coast Guard) was the creation of a regulation requiring a woman to report her possible pregnancy as soon as possible. Thus, within the SPARS' convoluted system, if a woman failed to report her pregnancy and the pregnancy was terminated through abortion (spontaneous or intentional) or miscarriage, she was given an undesirable discharge for violation of the regulation to report, not for the termination itself.[54] Hobby was dissuaded from adopting this plan for the WAC after consultation with the Office of the Surgeon General and several female medical officers, who argued that this strategy would discourage women from reporting any problems arising from abortions and would unfairly punish married women whose pregnancy ended in miscarriage.[55]

The result of these difficulties was that the WAC during World War II never adopted a standard policy on abortion. Instead a hodgepodge of formal regulations and rules of conduct were used to address the issue. First, the WAC discharge regulation on pregnancy was altered and a line was added indicating that "pregnancy *and the direct complications and sequelae thereof*" would be grounds for discharge with "no misconduct involved." Second, if the medical officer could *prove* that an "illegal abortion" had occurred, the woman's action was regarded as "misconduct" and she would be given a "blue" (undesirable) discharge under WAC regulations providing for undesirable discharges for women guilty of "conduct unbecoming a member of the Corps, conduct prejudicial to the service, or reflecting discredit on the Corps."[56]

This informal means of handling abortion created several problems. It placed the power of determining the "guilt" and subsequent "punishment" of a Wac suspected of terminating her pregnancy in individual male commanding officers and WAC unit commanders. This situation led to differential interpretations and enforcement of applicable regulations and resulted in some commands giving dishonorable discharges to enlisted women suspected of obtaining abortions while others were retained in service. Moreover, WAC leaders and some male Army officers feared that the lack of an explicit policy on abortion, combined with the regulation requiring mandatory discharge for pregnancy, would encourage women to have abortions. Hobby also feared that if the public discovered that the WAC had no regulation prohibiting abortion it would lead to negative publicity for the corps and would be interpreted as the Army rewarding women who sought abortion by allowing them to remain in the WAC.[57]

WAC leaders' characterization of illegitimate pregnancy, abortion, and sexual activity as associated with a few so-called bad women who slipped into the corps was critical to their ability to convince the public that the WAC would protect good" women and provide them with a safe, healthy and controlled environment. Despite this emphasis, sending these women back to their communities pregnant, unmarried, and sometimes with undesirable discharges raised the possibility that the public, especially families, would view women as victims and their conditions as symbolic of the Army and WAC's failure to protect members of the Corps. To offset this prospect WAC leaders' attempts to limit Wacs' sexual behavior and regulate their sexuality were joined by an increasing acknowledgment of the responsibility borne by the Army and the WAC for servicewomen's circumstances. This latter strategy manifested itself as the war progressed and was represented in part by Hobby's efforts to develop and implement maternity care programs for pregnant Wacs, married and unmarried.

Colonel Hobby was aware that, to many, the WAC's treatment of women who became pregnant while under WAC protection was roughly equivalent to that of a cruel male lover. Undesirable discharges carried with them not only disgrace and shame, but also denial of material benefits especially important to unmarried mothers. The net effect of WAC policies regarding unmarried pregnant servicewomen was to disavow them, stigmatize them, and propel them toward poverty by denying them military benefits available only to honorable discharged soldiers. As a result, Hobby considered various suggestions concerning possible maternity programs for the WAC. All discussion of these proposed plans was framed with two concerns: the health and well-being of pregnant servicewomen; and the negative publicity that might arise from the discharge of pregnant servicewomen who would most likely have "no means of support, no opportunity for securing medical care" and who were "likely to become indigent." As WAC historian Mattie Treadwell notes, such a situation was "undesirable not only for humane reasons, but for the prestige of the Army and the Women's Army Corps," particularly if such a woman "did her wandering" in search of the support of various social institutions and charities "in uniform."[58]

The ideas for a WAC maternity program were of two types. The first advised using Army hospitals to provide care similar to those available to enlisted men's wives. This system would require that women be retained in the WAC on inactive duty status until delivery and then discharged.[59] Colonel Hobby rejected this plan, contending that keeping unmarried pregnant women within the corps until after delivery would result in serious damage to the discipline, morale, and reputation of the WAC. She helped author an alternative maternity policy that would keep the mandatory discharge requirement for pregnancy and would work through the Veterans Administration (VA) and their hospitals in providing care for pregnant ex-Wacs.[60]

Unfortunately, Hobby encountered problems in her efforts to implement this program when the VA refused to consider pregnancy as a medical ailment, and claimed it was merely a "normal condition." As a result, the VA denied Wacs access to veterans' facilities for maternity care and delivery.[61] The War Department refused to intercede with the VA on Hobby's behalf for fear that any "attention to the problem might lead the public to exaggerate the numbers involved."[62] The fears of both WAC leaders and the War Department concerning the negative publicity that might arise from either the process of creating a system of care for pregnant Wacs, or from the implementation of such a plan, guaranteed that pregnant servicewomen would have to wait until the end of the war to have access to any governmental sanctioned maternity program.[63]

The difficulty of establishing a military maternity plan for Wacs prompted Hobby to seek alternatives for providing such care within the private sector. The most logical organization to help with such care was the American Red Cross (ARC). The ARC had a long history of working with the Army as a private welfare agency; it provided services for male GIs and their families and sponsored programs in Army hospitals for military personnel. In addition, the ARC had been designated by military authorities as the "sole nonmilitary agency" to provide welfare and recreation services to the U.S. expeditionary forces overseas.[64] The WAC Director asked the American Red Cross (ARC) to work as a mediating agency to counsel servicewomen discharged for pregnancy.[65] As early as 1942, ARC representatives demonstrated a willingness to help support Wacs discharged for pregnancy, agreeing with Colonel Hobby that: "The act of sending any woman back into her community without being sure she has a place to go; a means of earning her living; or some provision being made for her support until she can become self-supporting; might bring much unfavorable comment on the Army as well as on the Red Cross for permitting such conditions to exist."[66]

The WAC plan, developed in cooperation with the ARC, directed that after a diagnosis of pregnancy was made, the WAC unit commander would apprise the woman awaiting discharge of her veterans rights and benefits and inform her of the services which the ARC offered. If the woman desired to avail herself of this assistance, the unit commander would immediately contact the ARC and arrange a conference between a ARC representative and the servicewoman. After this initial meeting, the details of planning for the woman's welfare following discharge were referred to caseworkers at the local ARC office in the community to which the woman would be moving. In theory this phase of the plan allowed Wacs to choose a place of residence other than their home community in which to complete their pregnancy. In addition, caseworkers made inquiries as to local employment opportunities, child placement if necessary, medical care, and social services. On the basis of these investigations, the Wac was then able to make final decisions and the arrangements she desired. Last, the ARC established financial assistance plans for Wacs and encouraged them to register with the United States Employment Service so they would be eligible for unemployment compensation under the GI Bill of Rights when they were unable to work.[67]

The early 1940s marked a transition point in state and professional policies toward and treatment of unmarried pregnant women. The evangelical rescue and private maternity homes of the 1920s and 1930s, for example, were in the 1940s supplanted by institutions with a more secular outlook staffed by social work professionals trained in psychological theory. Moreover, the 1930s emphasis on unmarried women keeping their babies was in the 1940s being replaced by a new race-specific discourse that defined unwed mothers as inherently unfit and encouraged white women to give their babies up for adoption. The emerging psychological discourse on "illegitimacy" defined white unmarried women who chose to mother as immature and mentally deficient. Within this medicalized framework, the illegitimate pregnancy of black women was attributed to biological factors, in particular the inherent hypersexuality of their race. As feminist scholar Rickie Solinger puts it, while white women were "shamed," black women were "blamed."[68]

The shift from a focus on unmarried white women keeping their babies to an emphasis on adoption as the most efficacious solution to these women's

dilemma was in progress but not complete during World War II. The relaxation of state adoption laws, making it easier for agencies to assist unwed
mothers in giving up and placing their babies, occurred for the most part in
the postwar period.[69] As a result, the American Red Cross encountered several difficulties in carrying out its plan of assistance to pregnant servicewomen. In many areas housing for pregnant ex-servicewomen was scarce or
unavailable. This was in part due to the fact that many private maternity
homes refused to accept women who were not residents of their state. Since
many unmarried ex-Wacs wished to complete their pregnancies in a location
removed from their home community, this shortage of housing became especially severe. Varying state laws concerning adoption also hampered the abilities of ARC representatives to assist ex-servicewomen who wished to place
their children up for adoption. Some states, for example, required that the
alleged father be contacted and give written consent to the adoption before it
could be legalized. In many instances the putative father had been contacted
and refused any assistance, but in other cases the woman had not been in
touch with him. In all situations these laws made it difficult for a servicewoman to make her own decision as to the welfare of herself and her child.
Instead they placed the power to make such decisions in the hands of a man
who had either denied responsibility for her pregnancy, or whom she wanted
to have no part in her planning.[70]

Although the WAC assumed some measure of responsibility, as well as a
great deal of control over pregnant servicewomen, Army and WAC officers
sometimes undercut efforts to ensure that servicewomen who became pregnant while in the corps would have access to benefits upon discharge. On several occasions the Army and specifically WAC officers failed to fulfill their
obligations to inform pregnant Wacs of their rights and benefits as veterans.
This information was especially crucial to the financial situation of ex-Wacs.
Servicewomen who received an honorable discharge were eligible for 52
weeks of unemployment compensation under the GI Bill of Rights. In order
to qualify for this benefit, they had to register with the U.S. Employment
Service (USES) immediately after discharge. If they were subsequently
unable to take a job because of their pregnancy, they were still able to collect
unemployment if they had previously registered with the USES. Because
some women were not informed of these procedures upon discharge, they lost
eligibility for these benefits and for the critical financial assistance they could
provide.[71] Further, many pregnant servicewomen who were returned from
overseas for discharge had been greatly misinformed as to the Army's system
of dealing with pregnancy. Some were told by Army medical officers and

WAC commanders that they could remain in service until delivery and for a period of three months thereafter; they expected to receive full Army pay and housing during this time. Others had been informed that if they wanted to place their baby up for adoption, the Army would facilitate this procedure and they could remain in service afterwards.[72] Instead, pregnant Wacs returned to the states only to find that they were to be discharged immediately, leading a number of women to feel as if the Army had "tossed them out" and rejected them.[73] Moreover, the failure of confidentiality accorded some women's case files resulted in public discussion of their conditions within their units and among personnel in the Army hospitals where they stayed prior to discharge. Such discussions and the open contempt shown by hospital staffers amounted to public humiliations for a number of Wacs.[74]

Once out of service, most single, pregnant, servicewomen grappled with the questions of what to tell their families and whether or not to keep their children. Because the state (in the form of the military institution) would not assume familial responsibilities for Wacs, the options remaining to servicewomen were to rely on private organizations or to move back into a family setting, choices that were in part dependent on their race and class status. Given the shortage of housing and the unavailability of maternity homes as a viable option for most unmarried, pregnant ex-Wacs, ARC caseworkers often encouraged women of all races to return to their families, believing that returning women to a private family setting was the best solution to the problems and limited choices faced by unmarried pregnant servicewomen.[75] This option had been and continued to be the most viable for Black women who were excluded from many private maternity institutions in the 30's and 40's and whose home communities typically did not require the expulsion of "unmarried pregnant daughters" as white families and communities did.[76]

It is important to point out that while some servicewomen believed returning to their families was their best option, by offering a reconstituted family structure as the "solution" to pregnant Wacs' dilemmas Red Cross policies and rhetoric significantly obscured both the severe economic hardship and social ostracism most unmarried, pregnant, ex-Wacs faced, and the Army's responsibility for exacerbating their difficulties.

The most difficult decision faced by servicewomen was whether to keep or give up their babies. In making this decision some women, especially those who were white and middle class, faced pressures to give up their babies for adoption. Those women who wished to return to their families, for instance, believed that having their babies away from their home communities and then giving them up for adoption would enable them to do so.[77] On the other hand, ex-Wacs who wanted to keep their babies sometimes found themselves encouraged to give them up. An ARC report observed that on occasion "officers' wives and others who were eager to obtain infants" brought "great pressure . . . to bear on the ex-servicewoman, hospital workers, and chapter workers." Despite the postwar emphasis on white women placing their babies up for adoption, evidence suggests that ARC caseworkers during World War II were often quite supportive of and sympathetic toward white women who wished to keep their children. As one ARC report noted, when freed from "all of the emotional pressures from individuals to obtain possession of the infant," many servicewomen decided to keep their babies.[78]

Financial constraints also influenced Wacs' choices. Such constraints on occasion left women open to exploitation by unscrupulous hospitals and private agencies. In one extreme case a ranking WAC officer discovered that in New York City, hospitals were bargaining with ex-servicewomen to give them care and perhaps place infants in return for these women's entire separation pay of $100 to $200, thereby leaving them completely destitute.[79] Lack of money also contributed to some women opting to "join forces" with other servicewomen in similar situations by sharing living arrangements, expenses, and emotional support. This last option was heartily disapproved by WAC officers, namely Lt. Colonel Katharine Goodwin, who felt that such strategies were "opportunistic" and argued that "constructive long-term plans" were necessary.[80] While women shared their lives and resources in the WAC, in other words, such an arrangement was inappropriate for civilian mothers who were instead encouraged to either attach themselves to a proper "family," give up their children, or tough it out alone.

In the end servicewomen made a variety of different decisions about their lives. Some kept their babies while others chose to give them up. Some opted to return to their families while others resolved to make it on their own. Of those who determined not to return to their families some eventually married the fathers of their children, while others married male friends or relatives of the alleged fathers.

The Army's unwillingness to assume any responsibility for pregnancy among Wacs was reflective of a larger paradigm of military sexual regulation. The Army's policies in the arena of sexual regulation were predicated on upholding racial hierarchies and encouraging male heterosexual activity while discouraging male responsibility for their sexual activity or its consequences. Male responsibility was limited to venereal disease programs, and aimed at protecting the health of servicemen; the rights of their female sexual partners, however, were routinely abrogated if they proved a burden or nuisance to the Army or individual servicemen. Within this framework women with whom male soldiers had pre- and extramarital sex were defined as "bad," unworthy of respect and undeserving of the protection such respect demanded. The cases that follow are representative of the situations of those women whose GI lovers failed to take responsibility for their sexual actions, or were prevented from doing so by Army officials, and make clear the priorities of the Army's "protective" system.

The Army's sexual paradigm became most clear in overseas theaters where local women bore sole responsibility for pregnancies resulting from sexual relationships with U.S. servicemen and male officers. Marriage and financial assistance were the two major ways male GIs and officers could share the responsibility of pregnancy with their sexual partners. Army regulations concerning both discouraged male soldiers' assumption of any such responsibility, even if they desired to provide support or marry the women who were to bear their children. In general, the commanders of specific overseas theaters formulated their own rules concerning marriage, but the overall Army policy on the marriages of servicemen and officers to foreign nationals stressed "the many difficulties and complications arising from such marriages, in the hope that such warning would act as a deterrent to overseas marriages with foreign persons."[81]

While even intraracial marriages with non-U.S. citizens were discouraged, interracial marriages were made virtually impossible and in some theaters were expressly forbidden. The War Department invoked both state laws prohibiting interracial marriages and federal U.S. policies which restricted the immigration of certain groups, specifically "nonwhite" persons, as a rationale for its policies.[82]

Overseas theater commanders' restrictions on marriage, though designed predominantly to discourage American GIs and male officers from marrying foreign women, also prevented all Wacs from marrying U.S. servicemen. These prohibitions were joined by other theater directives which required the separation of Wacs from their military husbands. General Eisenhower's policy in the European Theater was that: "Persons in military service will not . . . be permitted to establish homes and families in this active theater . . . and will be stationed widely separate or one or the other removed from the theater."[83]

This regulatory framework was counter to the wishes of Director Hobby, who believed that such constraints acted as deterrents to "responsible" and "respectable" behavior. Her fears were substantiated when Eisenhower's policies in the ETO resulted in "undesirable consequences." Several Army chaplains reported to WAC leaders that military men and women who preferred to be married but did not want to be separated from one another instead "shacked up" together.[84] In addition, marriage restrictions in the China-Burma-India theater, initially developed to discourage white GIs and officers from marrying Asian women, prompted several white Wacs to get pregnant intentionally as the only means of persuading theater authorities to let them marry their military boyfriends.[85] Finally, constraints on overseas marriages between female and male U.S. military personnel were sometimes blamed by pregnant unmarried Wacs for their subsequent conditions and the dilemmas they faced upon their return to the United States.[86]

Army regulations restricting marriage, together with War Department policies addressing paternity claims, affected both civilian women and Wacs who found themselves pregnant by American servicemen or officers. The Army considered both civilian and military women's requests for support or services contingent upon a serviceman or officer's willingness to acknowledge paternity and his subsequent provision of or application for financial assistance. The only monetary relief available to civilian women, other than the minimal amounts that came out of the servicemen's pockets, was that provided by the Army's program of allotments for the "dependents" of male GIs and officers. These monies were procurable only for the child, not the mother, as Army policy did not allow a soldier to claim dependency allotments for what they termed a "common-law wife." As a result, even when a soldier acknowledged paternity, no financial help was available for the pregnant woman as the allotment was contingent upon the birth of the child.[87]

Wacs, unlike civilian women, were able to tap into the maternity programs, counseling services, and financial assistance formally offered to them by the American Red Cross. Like their civilian counterparts, however, servicewomen also found the Army extremely unwilling to force individual servicemen to assume any responsibility for their pregnancy. In one case a white ex-Wac wrote to Hobby asking her help in contacting the alleged father. She had not informed her family of her predicament and maintained that as a single mother she was having trouble supporting herself and her child on her salary. The Army's investigation of her petition for support ended when they contacted the man in question and he denied that the child was his. She contended that the Army's investigation of her claim was "inadequate and biased," and that the Army was more interested in protecting the officer who was the alleged father than in helping her. She closed her letter with the observation: "A person could be dead before they [the Army] would lift their finger [to help]."[88] The response from WAC Headquarters followed Army guidelines. Major Kathryn Johnson, writing on behalf of Hobby, informed the woman that "every investigation had been made," and that her only option was to try and seek a judgment through civil courts, since "questions of paternity and support . . . are legal questions which are covered by civil, and not military law. Action in regard to these matters would necessarily come under civil courts."[89]

The Army's policies and procedures available to civilian women petitioners and Wacs failed to provide mechanisms through which American servicemen and officers could be held responsible for their heterosexual behavior. These policies offered much more in terms of "protection" for men than they did for women. The Army's concern with protecting servicemen from civilian women's paternity allegations was made clear when, after the war, the War Department requested that the ARC discontinue its aid to unmarried mothers in overseas theaters. As a result, the ARC agreed to eliminate its communications services between these women and American GIs and officers. The ARC supported its action by arguing that ARC service was for servicemen, veterans, and their dependents only, and that an unmarried mother "cannot be so classified no matter how meritorious her claim appears." In addition, a letter of notification to field offices noted that "in a high percentage of the cases, the men are married, and some broken homes may result if the ARC attempts to follow up after the man returns home."[90]

The Army's regulation of servicewomen's heterosexual behavior was framed by two intersecting paradigms of protection. The first encouraged male soldiers' heterosexual escapades as a sign of virility.[91] This paradigm stressed the protection of male soldiers' health, and discouraged male responsibility for the health or well-being of either the women with whom they were sexually active or the children they fathered in such relationships. This approach implicitly defined women with whom soldiers had pre- and extramarital sex as "other"—that is, "bad" women who were undeserving of the protection or respect supposedly granted "good" American women back home, whom soldiers were fighting to protect. The second paradigm, created by WAC female leaders and in constant tension with the first, stressed unmarried servicewomen's sexual abstinence and chastity as a mode of "protecting" servicewomen from the dangers associated with heterosexual behavior.

WAC leaders' agenda of protecting the reputation of both the women's corps as well as the women within it rested on their construction of "female soldiers" as "good" women, a definition which ostensibly demanded that servicemen and male officers be responsible to military women for their sexual behavior. Once servicewomen engaged in sexual activity, however, the illusion of protection vanished. By defining these "female soldiers" as "bad" women and dismissing them from the corps, WAC policy reinforced the presumption that women who engaged in sexual relations with male soldiers were dangerous and parasitic, a source of "moral contagion" to both men and women in the military.

While the portrayal of the WAC as an organization of exclusively good women was critical to Colonel Hobby's legitimization of women's entrance into the military, and deflected fears that military women would challenge gender, racial, and sexual hierarchies, servicewomen nonetheless resisted and manipulated these frameworks throughout the war. Female soldiers understood the risks of stigma and dismissal should they be discovered in heterosexual activity outside of marriage, activities that were encouraged in their male counterparts. Becoming a soldier did not give Wacs rights comparable to those of male GIs. It did, however, give them economic independence and freedom from familial control, conditions that were also encouraging many civilian women to take sexual risks during World War II.

6

"I Want a Man!"
Pleasure and Danger in the Women's Corps

The fears about women's sexual agency and/or victimization expressed after the creation of the WAC prompted several questions. Was there a reason for public concern? Were women who entered the Army consciously attempting to challenge gender and sexual norms? Were women likely to be victimized by "unscrupulous male officers" or GIs? What were the choices enlisted women and WAC officers faced? Were their opportunities for "pleasure" circumscribed by the presence of "danger"?[1]

The possibility of military service for women during World War II *did* represent a shift in women's abilities to function outside traditional networks of control and protection. Some servicewomen and female officers used all the new possible space created to engage in heterosexual activity. These women *did* have greater opportunities for such activity away from their home communities and families, despite WAC leaders' attempts to assign the Army and the WAC as guardians/controllers of their decisions and behavior. Such opportunities were joined by new pressures and choices facing young women. Like other young women outside the military, Wacs were part of a larger generation of women who, while free from some of the constraints of past models of sexual control and protection, also faced risks by becoming sexually active. As historians John D'Emilio and Estelle Freedman have argued, the decline of traditional frameworks for understanding women's sexuality meant that "the dilemma young women face of how far to go differed from their mothers and grandmothers who confronted norms that drew a sharp line against any sexual expression before marriage."[2] Historian Karen Anderson has also demonstrated that during World War II, it was difficult for young women to "heed proscriptions on sexual behavior when many men made their attention contingent upon women's sexual cooperation."[3] While women might be punished by their own families and the larger society if they *were* sexually active, they might be punished by individual men if they were not.[4] Many servicewomen nonetheless saw their own self-interest in upholding the regulatory framework that WAC leaders propounded because it provided protection for some white women at the same time as it limited their sexual choices.

Women's heterosexual agency within the WAC illuminates the shifts in women's heterosexual behavior occurring during the war. Individual servicewomen and female officers negotiated the different pressures and dangers and made choices to be or not be sexually intimate with men. Women's choices were shaped not only by the formal systems of sexual control discussed previously, but also by informal mechanisms such as Army customs prohibiting social interactions between officers and enlisted personnel, peer pressure within the WAC itself, and changes in contemporary discourses on women's sexuality. This chapter explores each of these factors, focusing in particular on the ways in which servicewomen and female officers interacted with and manipulated Army rules and sexual ideologies. In addition, I address the issue of sexual danger and violence, from sexual harassment to rape, as it affected military women's daily lives and decisions about their sexual activity.

In April 1944, Colonel Hobby received a letter from two pseudonymous soldiers who reported their alleged sexual interactions with a white WAC officer. These men, calling themselves "Jack" and "Bill," criticized the WAC for paying too little attention to the "mental, moral, and emotional health" of servicewomen. At the heart of Jack and Bill's complaint was their story of a "sexually promiscuous" WAC officer, Lieutenant Irma Jones,* whom both had dated, and with whom each had sexual intercourse. Their concern was not with their own behavior, which they viewed as "normal" and acceptable, but with that of the WAC officer. They gave a detailed account of their encounters with Lieutenant Jones and invoked their credentials as "amateur psychiatrists," based on their enrollment in several college courses in elementary psychology, to diagnose Jones as "mentally and emotionally unstable." They recommended that she get immediate psychiatric help. Jack and Bill did not blame Irma Jones for her heterosexual promiscuity, but instead declared her a victim of the social disorder attendant in wartime mobilization. They

---

*All names contained in the unpublished case studies I discuss in this chapter, other than those of female and male military administrators, are ethnically matching pseudonyms.

asserted that "away from the restraining and uplifting forces of normal living" she was "just as much a tragic casualty of this war as a soldier who has faced the enemy and gone to pieces under the stress and strain of modern battle."[5]

While invoking contemporary psychological theories to "diagnose" Lieutenant Jones' problems, Jack and Bill concurrently utilized a "moral" discourse to discuss the situation. They expressed their dismay, for example, at the possibility that a woman would choose to move away from her "finer more sensitive nature" in order to take advantage of the "selfish and masculine enjoyment of the sensual and emotional and animal delights of war." They claimed that this action, if followed by all women, would make them "unworthy of the respect and love of man" and they would become "used and abused and despised as men often use, abuse, and despise each other." Although Jack and Bill perceived Irma Jones as a victim of war, they viewed her actions as hurtful not only to herself, but also to the WAC, society at large, and, in particular, to the "men she gives herself so carelessly to."

> When women believe that happiness for themselves can be achieved without self-respect or the respect of men by participating equally with men in man's seeming and foolish freedom from morals and by participating equally with man in all his lowest and worst characteristics and activities, then society will be taking a great backward step away from human happiness and welfare and away from mankind's noble destiny of decency and fine living.[6]

The aspect of Jones' behavior that seemed to be most threatening to Jack and Bill was both her choice to be sexual and her obvious enjoyment of and passion during sexual intercourse. They described her as holding on "to the pleasures of sex with all the frenzy and desperation with which a drowning man reaches for a straw and attempts to gulp one last breath of air," and noted that Bill was "frankly taken back by her violence." Their way of meeting this threat was to reinterpret their sexual encounters with Lieutenant Jones and redefine her not as an agent but as a victim. Jack and Bill preferred to feel that they victimized Irma Jones, rather than that she chose to have sex with them, enjoyed it, and was not apologizing for it. In closing they asked Colonel Hobby to use the "evidence" they had collected about Lieutenant Jones to get her some psychiatric help. They argued that she was not a "hard, bad, vulgar, cheap, wicked, evil woman" but rather a "little girl emotionally—frightened, lonely, sick at heart, lost and engulfed in the difficulties of a world for which she was not prepared and which she does not understand."[7]

Jack and Bill's letter in part reflects the shifts and contemporary confusion in ideological paradigms used to analyze women's sexuality apparent in the mid-twentieth century. Their reference to themselves as "amateur psychiatrists," for example, and their recommendation that Jones get psychiatric help, were indicative of the growing influence of the fields of psychiatry and psychology in defining normative and deviant sexual behavior in women. This medicalization of the discourse on women's sexuality did not tear down the sexual double standard, but rather reformulated it in the language of "scientific objectivity." Historian Barbara Hobson has argued that these reformulations were more "insidious" than earlier paradigms of "fallen women" because they pretended to have their roots in empirical studies, not in cultural standards of morality.[8]

Despite psychiatry's movement away from explicit references to "immorality" in discussions of women's sexual behavior, the clinical categories of "maladjustment" and "mental instability" which replaced that of "bad/fallen woman" remained rooted in moral judgments and were defined by women's deviation from norms of "appropriate sexual behavior."[9] These norms of "appropriate sexual behavior," while allowing for the presence of active sexual desire in women, continued to rest on the idea that men had a greater sex drive than women and characterized women as having a special responsibility to "curb male lust."[10] Sexual behavior deemed "appropriate" by psychiatrists took place only within heterosexual marriage. Within this framework, "maladjusted" women were those who engaged in homosexuality, heterosexual behavior outside of marriage, or like Lieutenant Jones, desired sex too much. Thus, during World War II, when "controlling the sexual behavior of women was seen as the key to regaining control over sexual norms and behavior in general,"[11] these psychiatric theories and practices could be and were used to restrict the sexual and social freedom of women.[12]

The medical reformulation of the sexual double standard did not completely replace the good vs. bad/fallen woman paradigm. "Society . . . was not ready to assign the psychiatrist responsibility for the management of such [moral] problems," noted an article in the psychiatric journal *Mental Hygiene*. "Society regarded them not as medical problems, but rather as problems for the educator, judge and clergyman."[13] Thus, the categories of "bad" and "good" woman continued to distinguish women whose sexual behavior deviated from accepted cultural norms from those whose behavior conformed to such norms. These categories remained rooted not only in the behavior of an individual woman but also in her class, race, and educational background. Jack and Bill's speculation as to the reasons for Irma Jones' alleged promiscuity are illustrative of the resiliency of these archetypes. They characterized Jones as a "victim of circumstance," a confused "little girl" who was unable to handle the social disruptions caused by war. Yet, despite her alleged promiscuity, they made a clear distinction between Lieutenant Jones, a woman whose race (white), class status, and educational background (represented in her position as a WAC officer) would ordinarily qualify her for admittance to the category of "good" woman, and other "bad . . . vulgar . . . cheap" women, whose sexual promiscuity was to be expected.[14] Their differentiation between these two types of women enabled them to support a double standard that condemned Lieutenant Jones' behavior but also allowed her the possibility of reclaiming her good woman status once she submitted to the control of psychiatrists. Contrasting her explicitly with bad women, who presumably were beyond help, her status as a "child-like" victim paved the way for her redemption.

WAC songs, authored by enlisted women, were a means of exploring servicewomen's own expectations of military service, responding to public perceptions of themselves and the corps, and elaborating on topics defined as dangerous by the WAC administration. WAC melodies that dealt with sexuality often had a playful tone and provided a mechanism for "female soldiers" to enter the public debate concerning their sexual behavior and offer their own appraisal of the issues without changing their positions as subjects of that discussion.

I Want a Man
I want a man . . . I want a man . . .
I want a mansion in the sky
I feel like hell . . . I feel like hell
I feel like helping some poor guy

And when the dam . . . dam . . . dam . . .
Damage is done
I'm going to have my child . . . child . . . child . . .
Childish fun
I want a mansion in the sky.

I want to neck . . . I want to neck
I want a necklace made of pearls
I want to pet . . . I want to pet
I want a petty book of curls.

And when the dam . . . dam . . . dam . . .
Damage is done
I'm going to have my child . . . child . . . child . . .
Childish fun
I want a mansion in the sky.[15]

The tongue-in-cheek song "I Want a Man!" reflected some servicewomen's recognition of the shaky terrain on which they navigated and negotiated their sexual choices. The lyrics above illustrated servicewomen's mediation between public concerns with the heterosexual promiscuity of Wacs and WAC leaders' attempt to present them as nonsexual. On the surface "I want a man" seems a breakthrough of heterosexual passion which is then replaced by something entirely nonsexual, domestic, and thus respectable, " I want a *man*sion in the sky." To "want a man," to "pet," or to "neck" were by themselves not legitimate desires, but require cloaking in an "acceptable" explanation, the boosting of male morale or desire for domesticity. The singers are singing most about their difficult negotiations, the dissemblance necessary to both get what they want, yet couch it in terms the public will accept.

Some servicewomen certainly understood the necessity for women to explain their sexual choices with reasons other than explicit references to female desire. Moreover, the chorus can be read as an acknowledgment of the dangers inherent in heterosexual activity with pregnancy, referred to as the "damage done" and a result of the "childish fun" in which the singers engaged. Thus, the text was both an affirmation of women's heterosexual desire and an acknowledgment of the potential "danger" for women who acted on such desire.

Major Margaret Craighill, the medical consultant for Army women's health and welfare, acknowledged that the sexual standards of some Wacs changed during their military service. Craighill, like civilian psychiatrists and medical practitioners of the time, described such changes as a product of women's removal from traditional networks of protection and control, namely their families and home communities.[16] In doing so, she generated a picture of Wacs who, away from all things familiar, made poor choices in terms of their sexual activity because they were unprepared for the situations they faced. Her portrayal of sexually active Wacs as "victims of circumstance" was similar to the manner in which Jack and Bill described the plight of Lieutenant Jones.

Craighill focused on women's greater opportunities for dating and socializing with men within the military as one of the major factors contributing to the "decline" in military women's standards of conduct. She contended that the "social pressure" on women because of their scarcity, especially overseas, created situations in which men "frequently long separated from any women, and always outnumbering them, competed for their attentions."[17] She argued that the skewed male to female sex ratio combined with the temporary nature of most Army assignments created situations in which female soldiers had fewer opportunities to "truly know" the men with whom they were involved. These conditions resulted in "casual associations" between servicemen and women, which encouraged a "lack of [sexual] restraint."[18] Her opinion was vigorously seconded by Major Albert Preston, the Army psychiatrist assigned to the WAC Training Center at Fort Des Moines, who remarked that women, especially those going overseas, should have been prepared, not for "combat first aid or map reading, but for the peculiar social environment of a woman overseas; the certainty of an exaggerated popularity and the danger of an overemphasis on social life." Preston believed that these factors contributed to the "maladjustment" of individual Wacs.[19]

The skewed sex ratio at many Army posts in the United States and overseas did result in some problems and difficulties for enlisted women and WAC officers. The greater opportunities for social and sexual interactions with male military personnel often led Wacs overseas to complain that they suffered from "burn-out" in their attempts to keep up with the barrage of requests for dates from male soldiers.[20] In some overseas theaters such situations resulted in servicewomen's demands for separate "women's only" areas where they could get away from the men for awhile, relax, and enjoy "feminine companionship."[21]

On the other hand, the greater numbers of men also created situations in which servicewomen could and did dictate the terms of the heterosocial engagements they decided to accept. Similar to the "treating" behavior that historian Kathy Peiss described in young working-class women's heterosexual relationships, some Wacs exchanged their service as social companions to male soldiers and officers for material goods for themselves and their units. Both in the United States and overseas some servicewomen made their acceptance of male offers conditional on men's ability to provide supplies for their barracks and food and clothing that were otherwise unavailable.[22] "Every GI outfit vied with its neighbor in thinking up attractions to lure the WACs to parties," remembered one white Wac. "Food was the most successful. But many a luxury was obtained by 'moonlight requisition'—a broom for our tent . . . an Australian iron, air mattress, or GI comforter, extra trousers or shirts, or a jar of pickles or canned turkey from the Navy."[23]

Wacs addressed issues of heterosexual activity and sexual choices, and the skewed sex ratio and plethora of male dates available to servicewomen through several WAC songs. A WAC song entitled "Real Camp Abbott Girl," for example, challenged the notion that women's relationships with men should be monogamous and asserted servicewomen's right to "play the field," declaring:

> She's got a private in the Service Company
> She's got a T/5 at the Motor Pool
> She dates a corporal in Demolitions
> And her sergeant, he's a jewel
> And from Company B of the 52d,
> He's the one who has her in a whirl
> Though she swears that she loves them all the same
> For she's a typical Camp Abbott girl.[24]

The song "Real Camp Abbott Girl" might have reflected the choices some servicewomen were making during the war. One white corporal, Nancy Blumfeld, stationed at Fort Benning, dated several different men at the same time during her tenure in the WAC. Her actions were investigated when one of her boyfriends complained about her behavior to WAC Headquarters. Evidently, civilian James Fisher had known Nancy Blumfeld for over two years and dated her occasionally within that time period. Fisher's dissatisfaction with Blumfeld's decisions to go out with other men and the lack of total commitment to him that such actions implied led to his attempts to discredit her. After Corporal Blumfeld married, Fisher tried to get her thrown out of the WAC and recover the various presents and money he had given her during their relationship. Fisher claimed that Corporal Blumfeld had agreed to marry him and then reneged on her promise and that the gifts she received from him were taken under false pretenses.[25]

The matter was investigated by Army and WAC officials with the result that Nancy Blumfeld was reduced in rank to private. Fisher, however, was informed that the issue of monies and presents did not fall under the jurisdiction of the government and should be taken up as a private matter. Although the Army inspector characterized James Fisher as a "frustrated suitor" and concluded that the relationship between Nancy Blumfeld and James Fisher was a personal matter, his recommendation that Corporal Blumfeld be "busted" to private also indicated the degree to which the military was willing to punish women whose behavior did not conform to gender and sexual norms. The Army's willingness to take James Fisher's letters of complaint seriously also demonstrated the power individual military men continued to hold in their relationships with women.[26]

A discussion of WAC sexual agency would be incomplete without also examining the many servicewomen who supported WAC officials' standards of sexual morality. While some Wacs undercut the "sexual agent as victim" paradigm and embraced the expanded opportunities they found within the service for sexual and social heterosexual interactions, others articulated a view of women's sexuality consistent with WAC regulatory policies. One white Wac stationed at Fort Devens wrote an article, for instance, berating other Wacs for "misbehaving" in uniform. "I'm so proud of my uniform that I sizzle when girls behave like low-brows and cheapen our corps," she exclaimed. She demanded that all Wacs remember that they were "ladies" and work at being "ladylike and feminine."[27] Her viewpoint was echoed by an African-American Wac private, who wrote disparagingly of several women in her unit who acted like "sex-crazy females" and "literally pick[ed] up men."[28]

These warnings to other Wacs about the dangers of discarding standards of feminine chastity in wartime were incorporated by the WAC administration into formal efforts to influence the sexual behavior of all servicewomen. In the ETO (European Theater of Operations) white WAC officers were given several letters written by members of the corps who supported the WAC regulatory system and were asked to distribute them among their units. One such letter implored Wacs serving overseas to refrain from doing "anything you may regret later or which will bring you as a changed person back home when the war is ended." The writer went on to assure Wacs that all servicewomen feel the pressure to engage in different types of behavior than they would "back home," and that everyone is tempted by the "setting and the freedoms." To withstand such "temptations," she asked women to think of their service overseas as just a "crazy interlude . . . it isn't real life"; rather servicewomen's men back home, special dates, and husbands are the *real* thing. "Don't do anything that will change you," the letter concluded, or "you'll miss your chances to return to the good life."[29] The sympathetic tone of this letter is countered by the underlining admonition that if servicewomen did not "behave" they risked losing their respectability and their place in the community when they returned to the United States.

Within Major Craighill's framework, the letters and articles above represented a form of "group disapproval" of "loose sexual relationships." She argued that such "group disapproval" was one of the greatest deterrents to Wacs contemplating such relationships, and represented the efforts of servicewomen to warn their "sister Wacs" who "went off the beam" to cease such behavior lest it "bring discredit to the others." She argued further that the lack of privacy in the military encouraged conformity to group standards of behavior.   [30]

Certainly the influence of peer pressure cannot be underestimated, particularly within the small and self-contained environment of most WAC units. Peer pressure could, however, work to encourage individual Wacs to engage in sexual or social behavior they might have refrained from had they not had group support, or pressure, to do so. Even the WAC officer who authored the advisory letter used in the ETO recognized that such peer pressure did not always work against women's choices to engage in behaviors considered inappropriate and unseemly by Hobby and the WAC Code of Conduct. This officer urged servicewomen to *resist* peer pressure to "join the party" overseas by *refusing* to engage in extramarital sexual relationships.[31] The WAC administration certainly feared that peer pressure would encourage sexual risk taking. On several occasions, officers investigating allegations of servicewomen's so-called loose behavior determined that servicewomen's misconduct stemmed from their membership in social cliques within their units that promoted and supported extramarital sex.[32]

Similarly, although the lack of privacy in military life made it difficult for servicewomen to behave in ways deemed unacceptable by the Code of Conduct, or similar WAC policies, it did not completely prevent such behavior. Some women worked within the system of allowable privileges to date and/or be sexual with their boyfriends. One white Wac, Auxiliary Agnes M. Ellard, was charged with "immoral conduct" after she obtained overnight passes from her commanding officer. In order to get the passes she had informed her CO that she wished to visit her husband, William Ellard, whom she claimed was being shipped overseas. Instead, she spent the weekend at a hotel with her boyfriend. Because they were discovered at the hotel, she was charged and courtmartialed. Despite her wish to remain in the WAC, she was discharged "because of conduct" and the discharge was "other than honorable."[33]

Besides allowing for the less-than-honorable discharge of those who were caught having extramarital sex, the WAC administration developed informal procedures that promoted supervision and the use of chaperones as techniques for limiting possibilities for both heterosexual activity as well as sexual exploitation. This manner of addressing and regulating women's sexual behavior was similar to that espoused by the deans of women's colleges and those agencies running homes for wage-earning women in urban areas. Although not mandated by formal regulations, WAC Hq recommended that servicewomen bring their soldier dates to the dayrooms (recreational and reading rooms) and recreational facilities provided on Army posts. Colonel Hobby believed that this would allow for informal surveillance and decrease the opportunities for sexual relations between male and female GIs.[34]

Servicewomen also had to cope with the scrutiny of Military Police (MPs) and civilian detectives when they stayed at hotels in surrounding areas on overnight passes. Civilian detectives, for instance, routinely made rounds of hotel rooms in towns and cities near military posts as part of antiprostitution efforts. Wacs were sometimes caught in these sweeps as hotel detectives with MPs entered their rooms unannounced to insure that there was no misconduct occurring.[35]

Wacs were expected to follow informal rules of behavior when socializing with servicemen at city hotels; if Wacs and male soldiers were in the same room the door had to be left open.[36] Because servicewomen had to deal constantly with assumptions that they were having sex with military men, they were forced to enter into and engage with the developing discourse on female soldiers' sexuality and in many ways were required to take action and make affirmative choices about their sexual behavior.[37]

The key issue for WAC administrators was not whether a Wac had actually engaged in heterosexual intercourse with a male soldier but rather whether there was an "appearance" of impropriety generated by the actions of a Wac and her soldier date. The assumption that Wacs engaged in inappropriate behavior only in hotel rooms with the doors closed and locked was obviously flawed. Wacs could and did engage in nonsexual interactions with male soldiers in their hotel rooms at the same time that other Wacs engaged in sexual interactions with male GIs outside such confines. One white Wac, for instance, was found in her hotel room with a white male soldier and was turned over to her commanding officer by the MPs. The MPs reported that the woman's shirt tail was out and her hair was messy when they entered the room. They assumed that these conditions were caused by her having engaged in sexual relations with the male soldier present. The Wac herself claimed that she had recently retired to her room and was getting ready for bed. She had untucked her shirt and was putting her hair up in rollers when her soldier date reappeared at her door and she let him in for a few minutes. Immediately after she let her date into her room the MPs entered. Although the subsequent investigation proved no wrongdoing on her part, she was reprimanded and confined to quarters for not thinking about how her actions might look to others.[38]

In a different setting, another white Wac worked around the rule of "no closed doors" by making out with her soldier date in the hallway outside her hotel room. When approached by MPs she told them the soldier had come to her room to say goodnight. She went on to explain that in accordance with WAC rules she had not allowed him to come into her room but had gone out into the hall with him to say goodnight and therefore was not guilty of any improper behavior.[39]

The question of whether Wacs should be treated the same as male soldiers in terms of Army policies arose repeatedly in connection with Army customs regulating the social interactions of male soldiers and officers. These informal fraternization policies, though not official regulations, forbade any social interaction or contact between enlisted personnel and officers. Restrictions on fraternization between officers and enlisted men were aimed at maintaining a rigid separation between different classes of male personnel, and were intended to discourage potential favoritism on the part of officers holding power over enlisted men. Most commanders contended that there was too much of a chance that an officer's "objective" judgment would be impaired if he socialized with enlisted men off-duty. In addition, many Army officers believed that even if they were able to remain objective, other soldiers would interpret the situation as bias if the "favored" enlisted man was promoted or given an overnight pass.[40]

The presence of women in the Army created doubts in the minds of some male Army administrators and Colonel Hobby about the legitimacy of this custom and the wisdom of extending its application to male/female relationships. The discussion of this issue returned to the question of whether Wacs should be treated like all other (male) soldiers or if allowances should be made for male/female interactions across the caste lines established by the military. Many enlisted women and female officers strongly resisted Army attempts to place restrictions on their choices of social companions and some Wacs who had pre-enlistment involvements with officers were extremely vocal in their resentment of what they perceived as Army policies dictating whom they should or should not date.[41] "Many of us have husbands, brothers, fathers, and friends who are officers serving in the armed forces," complained one white Wac, "and we feel that we have the right to choose our friends as we did in civilian life."[42] Army nurses echoed the concerns of Wacs by challenging the stipulation that they could not socialize with male orderlies. One nurse remarked that the fraternization policies did nothing so much as create impossible situations for heterosexual nurses who, without being able to date enlisted men, were faced with the choice of dating married officers. "Which is the less of two evils," she asked, "to fraternize with good, respectable privates or travel around with a married man just because he is an officer?"[43]

Colonel Hobby and some other WAC administrators agreed with military women that fraternization customs should not be extended to male/female interactions and worked unsuccessfully throughout the war to obtain a formal policy change that would allow off-duty associations between enlisted women and male officers.[44] The WAC Director's major concern was that such restrictions on women's choice of heterosexual partners would hurt recruiting, particularly since women entering the WAVES faced no such constraints. Some

WAC leaders held that men of class background comparable to most enlisted women were likely to be officers. To restrict Wacs' interaction with Army men was therefore tantamount to downward mobility in their dating behavior. As WAC historian Mattie Treadwell noted in her description of the situation for servicewomen, "Inasmuch as over half of the enlisted women in the theater, were eligible for OCS it was impossible to hope that 'natural social level' would cause them to prefer enlisted men."[45]

The possible competition between enlisted men and male officers for "rights" to servicewomen was one of the underlying reasons behind the Army's resistance to any formal change in these policies. While Hobby's aim in relaxing Army customs prohibiting the association of enlisted and officer personnel was to improve the morale of enlisted women, some Army commanders were equally concerned with the impact such a change might have on enlisted men. Male enlisted personnel were outspoken in their resentment of any alterations in Army fraternization policies that would allow enlisted women to date male officers, and some enlisted men even argued that male officers who dated Wacs were usurping their pool of women.[46] This attitude suggests that some enlisted men were under the impression that part of the function of WAC units was to "boost their morale" with individual Wacs acting as their social companions. Army leaders occasionally supported this interpretation of servicewomen's role. The adjutant general of the American Expeditionary Forces, for example, recommended that the social policy prohibiting the association of officer and enlisted personnel should not be relaxed for Wacs until "our enlisted male personnel have become more adjusted and accustomed to their restricted social surroundings in Germany with respect to female companionship."[47]

Overseas some male soldiers tried to limit women's choices of whom they would interact with socially and/or sexually. While in general enlisted men made clear their resentment of officers dating "their" pool of women, white male soldiers also worked to obstruct white women's choices to date African-American soldiers. White soldiers in the ETO, for example, refused to associate with British and French women who dated black soldiers and spread racist rumors about the violent personalities and sexual habits of African-American men.[48] In England, moreover, while white male soldiers boycotted white British women who dated black GIs, white Army officers characterized such women as "too low" to even worry about.[49]

While the black press made efforts to assure its readership that for the most part African-American servicemen and women were only interested in one another, some black soldiers and Wacs regularly socialized with "foreign"

women and men.[50] The presumption of some male African-American soldiers, however, was that black servicewomen should not socialize with white
men. "Our Negro soldiers in the area . . . didn't care much for our hobnob-
bing with the whites," recalled one African-American Wac stationed in
France. "One of them was so incensed over it that he slapped a WAC one
night when he saw her going out with a white civilian."[51] On another occasion
she described her anger when several black soldiers tried to "separate" her and
her friends from the company of a white French sailor with whom they were
having coffee. She noted that when the soldiers were unsuccessful in these
efforts they "became belligerent, followed us out and everywhere we went."[52]

Servicemen of all races exerted similar pressures on Wacs to discourage
them from dating "foreign" men while stationed overseas. Army reports noted
frequently that U.S. servicemen thought it "nothing less than a crime for any
Wac to cast more than a pleasant glance at a foreigner"—especially when there
were "so many Americans in Europe who preferred American women."[53] A
white Wac, Dorothy Bjornsen, who married a Danish man when with the
Army of Occupation in Europe, remembered being "looked down on" by GIs
for going out with her future husband, despite the fact that these same GIs
often "went out with and some even lived with foreign women."[54]

Some enlisted men also accused male officers who dated Wacs of favoritism in handing out ratings (promotions) and privileges such as passes.[55] When
asked to comment on the issue of fraternization specifically in terms of
male/female relationships, many Army officers raised similar concerns. They
worried that such interactions might result in the "boss and the stenographer
situation, the colonel and the corporal," situations that most felt would
undermine command effectiveness and lead to a breakdown in discipline.[56]

Some enlisted men's proprietary claiming of enlisted women as well as
their accusations of favoritism represented one way in which male objections
to women's presence in the Army could be expressed. In the first case the issue
of *women's* choices of whom they would date were rendered unimportant and
invisible. Servicewomen were treated as a scarce resource, to be alloted to particular groups of male soldiers for morale-boosting purposes. In the second
scenario, women who made the decision to date officers, whether such
actions were permitted or not, were vulnerable to allegations that they "slept
their way" to promotions and other privileges. Collectively, these attitudes
undercut Wacs' capabilities and threatened to undermine servicewomen's
effectiveness and identities as soldiers. In addition, these perspectives reinforced public and Army opinions of the inability of women to function in the
military in anything but a sexual capacity.

While Colonel Hobby worked for the relaxation of Army fraternization policies, she was also aware of the potential dangers such situations posed to enlisted women when they dated men with substantial power to disrupt or control their lives. To offset some of these hazards WAC leaders tried to insure that even in areas where fraternization was allowed, the "common sense" rules of the civilian business world prevailed. The only prohibition on enlisted/officer dating that she supported was that Wacs should not date their immediate superiors, a restriction similar to the "taboo on social association between an employer or supervisor and his immediate subordinate in civil life."[57] Unfortunately, Hobby's failure to get the War Department to make fraternization rules consistent was paralleled by her failure to insure that her recommendations on enlisted women dating their immediate male superiors were followed.[58]

Public concerns with the potential sexual victimization of servicewomen were in part raised by these issues of male command authority over enlisted women within a rigidly hierarchical structure. The possibility of sexual exploitation in such relationships was realized early in the corps' existence. At several WAC training camps, for example, white male Army officers, because of the initial scarcity of WAC officers, were placed in charge of entire units of enlisted women. An investigation of Army officers' behavior toward white Wacs at the Daytona Beach training center yielded the following report;

> Army officers in highly responsible positions were drinking and misconducting themselves with Waacs and were promoting to positions of leadership only those who offered them favors in return. Members of the Army staff, when written statements were taken, officially accused each other of 'running around' and "carrying on" with Waacs, and of using force on enlisted women while drunk.[59]

There is also some evidence to suggest that male officers on the staff of Army commands in which Wacs were stationed sometimes encouraged enlisted women to break particular WAC rules of conduct and then protected them from punishment, thereby effectively subverting the WAC internal command structure.[60] Several other incidents revealed that some male officers who were soon to be shipped overseas adopted "high pressure" tactics with the Auxiliaries.[61] "I was leaving the Post to go to the overseas unit and I made a reservation at a hotel with a friend, and some male officers invited us into their room for a drink," explained one white Wac. "They were frank about it and told us that the gals they entertained were expected to sleep with them as they were going overseas and didn't give a darn, so we left."[62]

While enlisted women were particularly vulnerable to sexual harassment at the hands of male officers, the Army ranking system also put female officers at risk with male commanders, most of whom outranked them. An Army investigation of one such situation at the Wilmington (N.C.) Air Defense Regional Office reported Colonel Woodward, the white commanding officer (CO) of the Norfolk Air Defense Wing, repeatedly sexually harassed several white WAC officers. This harassment involved both his issuance of orders for these women to come to his hotel room late at night as well as his punishment of several officers who failed to obey his requests. The orders of male officers, despite the obvious dangers women sometimes perceived in following them, could not be overtly refused unless the Wac could prove ill intent. The difficulty of doing so is illustrated in the situation at Wilmington. Colonel Woodward requested the presence of WAC officers from two different units ostensibly to "observe the organization and functions" under his command. When the first group of officers arrived, the colonel met them at the railroad station and escorted them to their hotel where he had already made reservations for them. He insisted on personally conducting their off-duty entertainment and accompanied them on all of their official observations of the operations under his command. At the end of their stay, he paid their hotel bill in full.[63]

When they were ordered to return for an additional visit the colonel showed a particular interest in Third Officer Peggy Crane, and ordered her to report to his hotel room the evening of her arrival. She sought the advice of other female officers and a male Air Force medical officer and they advised her to comply with the request as it was a verbal order. She subsequently went to the colonel's room and though he made no "improper advances," the entire situation made her extremely uneasy. On yet another visit Third Officer Crane went out with friends and upon her return to her hotel was given the message to report to the colonel's hotel room as he had been "trying to locate her all evening." She ignored this order because of the lateness of the hour and returned to Norfolk early the next morning. The investigation noted that "Third Officer [Crane] is naturally very nervous and unhappy over the possibility of continued repetition of such orders."[64]

Although Crane was not reprimanded, the second group of female officers to arrive in Wilmington were punished for failing to engage in Colonel Woodward's "evening of entertainment." This group obtained permission from the regional commander (Colonel Woodward's superior) to travel by bus instead of train, and were ordered by the regional commander to report to Colonel Woodward the following morning. When they arrived in Norfolk, they checked into the hotel that Woodward had reserved for them, and then contacted friends and went out for the evening. Upon their return, they found a bottle of whiskey and a note from the Colonel Woodward indicating that he had expected them to arrive by train and stating that their earlier bus trip was in violation of orders. The note ordered them to contact him immediately, which they did. Despite their explanation of the circumstances, he told them that they had been AWOL, and ordered them to accompany him to the Norfolk Air Defense offices where he made them work until 2:30 A.M. as punishment for their "disobedience." For the remainder of their stay in Norfolk Colonel Woodward completely ignored them and when they checked out of their hotel their bill had not been paid.[65]

It is clear from these events that Colonel Woodward was interested in social, and probably sexual, relationships with one or several of the WAC officers under his command. In pursuing such contacts he used his authority over these women to force them to accompany him socially and to order them to his hotel room on several occasions outside of normal duty hours. This sexual harassment was repeated several times with different groups of female officers and was also marked by inappropriate punishments for those officers who failed to accede to his requests. The decisions of these women to report the colonel's activities to WAC Headquarters helped them extricate themselves from this predicament. The WAC administration, however, was unable to obtain any punishment or censure of the colonel.

WAC leaders did not or could not challenge either military men's sexual exploitation of servicewomen, or the ranked hierarchy of the military itself; they instead promoted the "protection" of Wacs through the sexual control of servicewomen and officers. The sexual victimization of Wacs and WAC officers threatened not only individual women directly, but also Colonel Hobby's construction of the corps as a safe haven for young women and as a guardian of their welfare and morals. Even those women who were clearly exploited, harassed, and unwilling to engage in sexual activities were viewed as "the problem" in a military structure that encouraged and expected men's heterosexual activity.

Male responsibility was not part of this system of protection and control. Within this structure any negative consequences that resulted from Wacs' social or sexual interactions with servicemen and male officers were disproportionately assigned to female soldiers. When Wacs and male soldiers or officers were caught together in hotel rooms, for instance, they were turned over to their respective commanding officers. The sexual double standard institutionalized within WAC and Army procedures insured that at most male military personnel might receive a reprimand, but guaranteed that servicemen's behavior would be dismissed with a "boys will be boys" philosophy. In contrast, similar behavior for servicewomen, even the appearance of impropriety, could and many times did lead to "other than honorable" discharges.[66]

This disparity between male and female Army personnel in terms of responsibility and punishment for similar actions was also apparent in the enforcement (or lack thereof) of fraternization customs. In practice, the social interaction of male officers and female enlisted personnel, and vice-versa, varied from post to post and over different theaters. The practical consequences were that women were far more likely to be punished for infractions of fraternization customs than men, even though informal Army rules held that the officer involved should be held accountable.[67] The problem was that most commands did not punish male officers for an infraction of fraternization rules when it involved women. In many cases the WAC detachment commander was given responsibility for meting out discipline and since she could only punish Wacs, and not military men, the officer often went free.[68] The applications of these policies indicated that it was servicewomen's responsibility to say "no" to these encounters.

The most extreme example of Army efforts to control Wacs' behavior in the guise of "protection," occurred in the Southwest Pacific Area (SWPA). The Army invoked characterizations of the male sex drive as all powerful and unstoppable to restrict white Wacs arriving in New Guinea in 1944. The SWPA Hq directed that in view of the great number of white male troops in the area, "some of whom allegedly had not seen a nurse or other white woman in 18 months," Wacs would be locked within their barbed wire compound at all times except when escorted to work or to approved group recreation by armed guards. No leaves, or passes, or one-couple dates were allowed at any time. Many Wacs found these restrictions unbearable and patronizing, and complained that they were being treated as criminals and children. The mounting complaints from women to WAC Hq and rumors of plummeting morale moved Colonel Hobby to protest to the War Department and ask for a discontinuation of what many Wacs referred to as the "concentration camp system."[69]

In response War Department officials changed their explanation and invoked sexualized racial stereotypes of African-American men to justify the policies, noting that theater authorities insisted that the system was required "to prevent rape of Wacs by Negro troops in New Guinea."[70] Societal stereotypes of African-American men in particular as rapists, and male sexuality in general as dangerous for women, were used to defend the extremely restrictive policies of the military toward Wacs in the SWPA. In this situation the

Army stepped in as the surrogate white male protector defending white military women's honor and virtue by creating a repressive environment designed to insure a maximum of protection and supervision.

The Army's system of protection of servicewomen from male aggression and its corresponding practice of assigning responsibility for "misconduct" was rooted in racial and class as well as gender ideologies. Within this framework black women were less likely to be protected than white women and African-American men were more likely to be held responsible and punished than white men for reported sexual misconduct, particularly if their alleged misconduct was with white women. As feminist theorists have argued, the myth of the black male rapist and the black female prostitute, two sides of the same coin, insured that violence against African-American women would be "legitimated and condoned," while racist depictions of black men as "sexually charged beasts who desired white women," would provide ideological justification for violence against black men.[71]

Although the Army was often unwilling to respond to the complaints of white servicewomen who were faced with sexual harassment, they were less willing to do so for black Wacs who encountered the same problems. On numerous posts white and black Wacs reported difficulties with male soldiers who tried to enter the WAC barracks at night after bed check. The Army's response to some of these incidents consisted of using war dogs and MPs to patrol at night and erecting high wire fences around WAC areas.[72] On several occasions, however, African-American Wacs' complaints were dealt with differently. According to a reporter for the Philadelphia *Afro-American*, black Wacs stationed at Fort Benning were given nightsticks after men "invaded" their barracks and told to "use their judgment on any man they saw in their area."[73]

One African-American Wac at Camp Claiborne (La.) related that her unit was continuously assailed by Peeping Toms, white servicemen who would "sneak over to our barracks and peep through our windows." Although they reported the difficulty to the administration, no action was taken to address the problem. The harassment continued and finally the women of the unit organized: "We put out all the lights and armed ourselves with shoes, brushes, and with shoes combs, and cooking utensils. The Peeping Toms showed up and we converged on them, beating them unmercifully. Of course when it was reported to the administration we denied everything."[74]

Male soldiers' harassment of servicewomen in this manner was most likely a product of their resentment of women's presence within the military as well as the contradictory messages generated by the Army about the function of servicewomen as "morale boosters." Such messages encouraged enlisted men to believe that Wacs were present to provide them with dates and entertainment and that Wacs were "fair game" for this type of behavior. While most Wacs viewed this male mistreatment as annoying and frightening, for some the stress generated by the harassment led to hospitalization and occasionally discharge.[75]

Although the Army took action aimed at preventing this type of abuse, servicemen who engaged in such behavior were rarely punished. The one exception to this practice was if black men were alleged to have harassed white Wacs. At Columbus Army Air Base, for instance, an African-American soldier entered the WAC barracks at night. He was reported by members of the white WAC unit and subsequently tried by a court-martial board and sentenced to ten years hard labor.[76] This particular example was consistent with the fact that during World War II a much higher proportion of black men were accused, tried, and convicted of sex-related crimes than their white counterparts. The racial stereotypes of black men as rapists, particularly of white women, fueled white fears before, during, and after the war and underlay the differential punishment system constructed by the military.[77]

This racial system was not only imposed from above by the Army administration, but was accepted and reinforced by some white servicewomen. On several occasions white Wacs invoked racial fears to try and make gains for themselves within the organization. One white Wac stationed in New Guinea wrote to Clare Booth Luce of the "dangers" of going out of the WAC area even with an armed escort. She claimed that "colored troops sneak up on the couples and stab the fellows and then try to rape the girl." The servicewoman wanted to be transferred away from New Guinea and used the "threat" of African-American troops in the area to make her case.[78] Another white Wac, stationed at Madigan Hospital, Fort Lewis, Washington, wished to be discharged because her son had been recently released from service. To accomplish this she wrote a letter to her senator, Wayne Morse, alleging that "many of the WAC barracks are situated close to a large company of negro soldiers and these Wacs do not dare to venture out alone after dark less they be molested by some of these colored men."[79] White WAC officials' response to these queries seemed to indicate their own sympathy with these fears. In her reply to Senator Morse, the second WAC director, Colonel Westray Boyce, reported that there was a "negro staging area" at Fort Lewis, about one and a half miles from the WAC barracks and that there were some "negro" patients in the hospital. She went on to note that "this is unavoidable and MP escorts are provided for WAC personnel returning to the post late at night."[80] Boyce's response did not call into question racial stereotypes concerning the alleged dangers black men posed to white women; rather, she pointed out the steps the Army had taken to meet these "threats."

The Army's general reluctance to convict most soldiers and officers on charges of rape is supported by the fact that during the war there were only 971 total rape convictions of members of the U.S. Army. This figure is fairly astounding given that over 12 million men served in the Army during the war. Further, only 273 of these convictions came before V-E Day, indicating that the majority took place after most of the fighting in Europe had ceased and the U.S. Army had become an occupying force.[81]

These figures do not by any means indicate the frequency with which rape occurred or was attempted. Male sexual violence toward Army servicewomen spanned a continuum moving from the kinds of sexual harassment documented previously to rape. White ex-Wac Florence Holmes reported that white servicemen's efforts to illegally enter WAC barracks at her post also often involved attempts to rape enlisted women they found inside. She went on to describe the situation of one woman in her unit, a "nice girl" who was "not the type to fool around," who was badly beaten and raped by a male soldier. The Army responded to these attacks at her post in the same manner as they did to Peeping Toms. The male Army commander stationed MPs outside the WAC area but failed to prosecute the woman's attacker.[82] It is equally likely that many perpetrators were never brought to trial, or that they were charged but not convicted.[83] A white servicewoman serving with a WAC Hq company in Wilmington, North Carolina, was forced into a car and raped by two white officers from nearby Camp Davis. The officers were tried but not convicted of rape and the Wac victim was transferred to another post.[84] "Incidents" like this one did not find their way into Army statistics on rape.

The definitions of rape utilized in some Army lectures tended to either trivialize rape or blame the female victim for the assault. During an Army inquiry one auxiliary testified that women were told to carry "preventives" (condoms) in their purse so that if "a soldier should attempt rape there would be no danger of venereal disease."[85] In another lecture focusing on sexual assault, the white Army officer in charge told servicewomen a short story he had "read in a magazine" to illustrate the definition of rape and what he considered the optimal manner in which the matter should be handled:

> Behind the cases of rape which reach the courts is the implication or accusation that the girl was forced against her will. When such a case is tried before him, one wise old Magistrate once handed down the decision that the defendant must either marry his accuser or pay a sizable fine. The

young man decided that he would prefer to pay the fine, and the girl walked out of the courtroom with the money in her possession. "And now," said the Judge, "follow that girl—take your money by force." Amazed, the young man obeyed, but the girl defended herself so energetically that he could not secure the money. When he was informed of this episode, the Magistrate called the two before him and ordered the fine returned. "Had you defended your chastity," he explained to the girl, "as well as you defended your money, it could not have been taken away from you. Dismissed."[86]

Behind this story is the clear implication that women can protect themselves if they choose and that those who do not, those who claim they have been raped, must not have resisted sufficiently and therefore are guilty of not protecting their chastity. The issue of "consent" as defined by the Army often hinged on whether or not servicewomen had "casual associations" with enlisted men and officers prior to the alleged attack. In other words, women's actions as sexual agents, their choices to date and interact socially or sexually with men, made it impossible for them to claim status as victims, to call on the Army or the WAC administration to protect them, or to seek redress within the military legal system. Thus, it was impossible for women both to *want* sexual activity and at the same time *not* want to be raped.

Servicewomen's allegations of rape were given little credence if they had a previous history (established either by fact or innuendo) of sexual interactions with men. In July 1943, a white auxiliary, Bernice P. Hackett, stationed at Camp Edwards, Massachusetts, accused a white soldier, Private John Harkey, of sexual assault. After a brief investigation the commanding officer, Colonel Howard S. Patterson, decided that a court-martial was not warranted and referred Auxiliary Hackett to her female CO for "possible disciplinary action." Army investigators dismissed Auxiliary Hackett's testimony as not credible in part because they believed she did not show sufficient resistance—there was "no evidence of a struggle." They also noted in the official Army report that her husband had divorced her in 1936 on the grounds of adultery. Most damning to the investigators, however, was information given by several members of her unit who reported that she was "boy crazy" and had gotten "quickly chummy" with Private Harkey, holding hands with him in the Service Club and walking out with him arm in arm.[87]

The issue of "consent" was also key in the case of Private Nancy Edwards, a white Wac who accused a white soldier of rape. The physical evidence that she had been attacked included bruises, abrasions, and blood on her legs and underwear, and the Army physician on duty at the hospital testified that her condition was consistent with someone who had been assaulted. Despite these facts, no action was taken against the alleged perpetrator because a condom had been used and to Army investigators such an object implied consent. The final report noted:

> In order to prove this charge [rape] it is necessary to show that the accused had carnal knowledge of the female and that the act was done without her consent. Force and want of consent are indispensable in rape. Mere verbal protestations and a pretense of resistance are not sufficient to show want of consent and where a woman fails to take such measures to frustrate the execution of man's design as she is able to, and are called for by the circumstances, the inference may be drawn that she did in fact consent . . . Any tribunal before which this case might come for trial would place considerable weight on the fact that a contraceptive (condom) was used in this relationship. In a situation where a woman is resisting and struggling to the utmost of her ability it is decidedly [sic] unusual for the man to cease his attempted attack to secure and adjust the device. Further, it is unlikely that a condom could be adjusted and at the same time a struggling woman be prevented from fleeing.

Army officials rejected Private Edwards' claims that her assailant had one hand on her throat, threatened her life, and that she was too terrified to move or struggle, as not credible.[88]

Private Edwards case would have ended at this point if she had not related her difficulties to her brother, the Reverend Victor Edwards. The construction of rape as a violation not only of the woman involved but also, and perhaps more importantly, to the men in her family (husband, brother, father), was apparent in Reverend Edwards' success in demanding that the investigation be reopened.[89] After characterizing the first Army inquiry as "careless" and indicative of "gross neglect," he wrote and called the War Department, his congressional representatives, WAC Headquarters, and the commanding officer at Keesler Field, insisting that they reexamine his sister's allegations. In response to Edwards' letters and calls, the Army did carry out a second, more thorough investigation. Midway through the second inquiry, however, Private Edwards dropped all charges, stating she could no longer deal with the stress and turmoil created by the ongoing investigation. The military took such an action as a tacit acknowledgment of complicity on Nancy Edwards' part.[90]

The centrality of an aggrieved white man was also apparent in the case of three African-American soldiers accused, convicted, and sentenced to death for the rape of a white woman. Mary White worked as a waitress at Camp Claiborn, Louisiana, where the three men were stationed. The soldiers, who were MPs, testified that while on a routine patrol of the camp they came upon

White asleep under a blanket with a white man, Private Frank Kohler. They took the two into the jeep and returned Private Kohler to camp, then went back out with Mary White. The soldiers claimed that they gave her $2 to have sex with them and then returned her to her tent. Her roommate testified that she did not seem disturbed and went to work as usual the next day. The charges of rape were initiated not by Mary White, but by Private Kohler, the white man she was with when the MPs found her, and she agreed to support his allegations. A physical examination found no "evidence" of a struggle or an attack, but did turn up a chronic case of gonorrhea. It is apparent that in this case, compared to that involving Auxiliary Hackett or Private Edwards, very different criteria were used to judge the credibility of the accuser, as evidence of Mary White's previous sexual involvement with men was disregarded, or seen as unrelated to the decisions to order a court-martial and to convict the black soldiers.[91]

The major factor determining a guilty verdict in this case was that a white woman was accusing a black man of rape, a clear threat to racial hierarchies in the military as only white men were assumed to have "access" to white women. Sexually active white women who accused white men of rape were dismissed as unworthy of "protection" as they overtly challenged the corps' system of sexual regulation that accorded women protection only if they could claim sexual purity and were submissive to systems of sexual control. Black men, on the other hand, were expected to refrain entirely from interacting sexually with white women. This same racial paradigm forces us to ask the question of whether Mary White went along with the charges because that was the only way she could "save face" within a culture that did not recognize the possibility of consensual relationships between white women and Black men. The fact that her white "date" initiated the charges highlights the aggrievement as that of white men acting to "protect" their own rights of sexual access to white women by denying the same to men of color. The sentence of death handed down by the court-martial board, and changed to a prison sentence after the intercession of the NAACP, was far harsher than any that might have been accorded a white man accused of rape. Black men accused by white women of rape were far more likely to be prosecuted and convicted than white men who were accused of rape by white or black women[92]

The social construction of rape as defined by the military and servicewomen's experience overall did not result in punishment or increased male responsibility for sexual assault. Instead it was used to control the actions of African-American men and all women. In this context the mythic cultural paradigm of the rape of white women by black men served to both obscure the reality of the rape of black women by white men and foreclose the possibility that relationships between black men and white women, would be perceived as anything other than coercive. White Wacs' decisions to have relationships with black men were made in negotiation with this framework. Thus, white women who chose to have sexual relationships with black men often had such interactions reinterpreted as coercive, not consensual, reinterpretations that both reinforced racial hierarchies and negated white women's sexual agency.

Auxiliary Mildred Collins, a white woman stationed in Charleston, South Carolina, was having a sexual relationship with Sergeant Charles Hemstead, a black man. The two were discovered together by civilian police officers on a routine patrol of the area. The white officers found them in the woods naked where, according to their report, Mildred Collins was "accepting fondling, caressing, and kisses" from Sergeant Hemstead. Hemstead and Collins were arrested by the officers and brought to the Charleston police headquarters for questioning. They were joined there by the mayor of Charleston, city and county legal officials, city and county police officials, and the provost marshall of the Charleston Military Police district. The Charleston officials, especially the mayor, were eager to impose a definition of "rape" on the encounter despite Hemstead's testimony that he and Collins had been on a date. They were prevented from doing so because Auxiliary Mildred Collins insisted that she had sought out and enjoyed the "attentions" of Sergeant Hemstead. She claimed that the purpose of the date "was to have been a normal, natural sexual intercourse" that was interrupted by the arrival of the police officers. As a result, no civilian charges were brought against either of them and the two were eventually turned over to their commanding officer. As they were leaving the police station the mayor of Charleston told Hemstead, "You know they lynch negroes here in the South for things like this."[93]

The mayor's parting remark indicated that interracial sexual liaisons would be constructed as "rape" regardless of the testimony of those involved. Army officials supported the aims, if not the method, of the mayor and defined the encounter between Collins and Hemstead as a "racial incident," while indicating the need to prevent any further similar types of interactions.[94] Collins' choice to have sex with Hemstead interrupted the negotiation between groups of men over their respective rights of sexual access to certain groups of women.

Despite formal regulations and informal customs intended to control their behavior, Wacs and female officers, like Auxiliary Collins, nonetheless persisted in engaging in heterosexual activities that threatened racial and gender hierarchies. Like Collins, other servicewomen insisted on taking advantage of opportunities to engage in behaviors that might have been impossible in their hometowns or under the close supervision of their families. For all Wacs, there were risks in engaging in such behavior. Yet, there also proved little protection for women in the military. Even those women who chose to stay within the closely circumscribed sphere created by the corps' policies could do little against threats of harassment or assault. For many servicewomen, choosing to move beyond its boundaries and to engage in sexual behavior was one of the great advantages to military service, and its attendant risks were not sufficient to offset new-found pleasures.

Wacs who engaged in homosexual behavior made similar assessments of risk and pleasure. Although women's heterosexual activities were circumscribed and stigmatized by the Army, WAC, and larger culture, lesbians were deemed a far more serious threat to gender and sexual hierarchies. Mere suspicion that one was a lesbian could warrant discharge and dishonor. No military men, moreover, were benefiting from lesbians' greater willingness to engage in sexual activities. The presence of lesbians in the corps threatened sexual and gender hierarchy to perhaps a greater degree than did heterosexual women's activity, and thereby threatened the legitimacy of the auxiliary and the WAC as well. Yet lesbians also found that wartime military service created conditions conducive to their taking risks. Like their heterosexual counterparts, they were away from their families and communities and able to make new choices. Unlike heterosexual servicewomen who took advantage of living and working with many men, lesbian Wacs concentrated on the all-female subculture of the women's corps itself as opportunity for the exploration of sexual desire.

7
The "Lesbian Threat"

Attempts to develop frameworks for understanding lesbians historically have tended to be distinguished by their emphasis or lack thereof on the connections between gender and sexuality. In a recent essay, historian Donna Penn argues that much of the historical work on lesbians has been of two types, either a "gendered history that is desexualized or a sexual history that is degendered," the former generated by scholars within the field of women's history, the latter by historians of homosexuality.[1] As Penn contends, historians of women have often rejected sexual activity as a "primary criterion for determining who was and who wasn't a lesbian."[2] At the same time, historians of homosexuality have focused predominantly on the proliferation of legal and medical models generated in the early twentieth century to explain male homosexuality. Using paradigms that for the most part discount gendered understandings of female sexuality these studies are somewhat limited in their ability to describe and explain the experiences of lesbians in the past.[3] While we can learn much from both sets of scholars, their collective unwillingness to utilize gender and sexuality weakens our ability to understand the construction of lesbianism and the lesbian subject historically.

To fully understand and explain the emergence of a lesbian identity in the twentieth century requires that historians place lesbian existence and struggles within a larger discussion of female sexuality historically. Studies that address lesbians within the context of the development of a male homosexual identity for the most part privilege a model of male homosexuality over a discussion of how female sexuality was constructed during a given historical period.[4] Allan Berube's social history of "gay GIs" during World War II is the most recent example of this tendency. Berube's work is significant because he uses oral histories to create a larger sense of gay men's experience in the military, and balances those experiences against contemporary institutional interpretations of homosexual identity. His study has in many ways set the standard for scholarship on the construction of gay identity historically. Yet, by subsuming lesbians in the Women's Army Corps under a larger paradigm for addressing issues of homosexuality in the military, Berube fails to account for the specific circumstances of lesbians as *women* entering a preeminently male institution or as female sexual agents.

Male GIs and servicewomen were subject to differential regulatory systems and public scrutiny for sexual behavior, including homosexual and heterosexual behavior. The broader WAC program for regulating women's sexuality was concerned overwhelmingly with the suppression of all sexual behavior among servicewomen, based as it was on the belief that only chaste women could retain public legitimacy for the corps. While historians have analyzed the respective challenges gay men and lesbians posed to the military, they have not addressed the precarious position of women within the Army, either as a group or as individuals. Gay men were perceived as a threat to the military because they were homosexual, but their presence did not endanger *men's* position within the military generally; joining the military reinforced men's claim to a masculine identity that was presumed to be a heterosexual one as well. In contrast, accusations of lesbianism within the WAC were the apotheosis of cultural anxieties over women's entrance into the military, the seeming renunciation of feminine values for the embrace of the masculine. Articulated fears of the kind of woman who might flourish in a martial environment, regardless of suspicion of particular sexual behaviors, were rife with allusions to lesbianism, and threatened the legitimacy of all female soldiers.

WAC leaders created a framework in which masculine appearance and behavior, not only sexual acts between women, were the key criteria for defining the "lesbian threat" within the corps. Laws addressing gender disguise and women's adoption of male dress are far more relevant in analyzing the cultural construction of lesbianism historically than are sodomy laws.[5] The latter have been connected by historians of homosexuality to the emergence of a gay male identity, and are especially pertinent to discussions of male homosexuality within the military. Because such laws were rarely used to prosecute lesbians or lesbian sexual acts, historians of homosexuality have generally concluded that criminal law overlooked lesbians. Historians have characterized this "lack" of legislation concerning lesbianism as a "history of invisibility" and contended that because military officials issued no explicit policies or procedures for screening out lesbians during World War II this invisibility continued in the WAC.[6] Yet, while lesbian civilians were rarely prosecuted for sexual acts, those who adopted male dress were subject to criminal charges under urban morals codes for cross-dressing. Moreover, legal categories addressing gender disguise and cross-dressing represented independent lines in legal doctrine within the realm of family law.[7] Within the WAC the issue of female masculinity or mannishness became one of the major frameworks under which issues of lesbianism were addressed.

The nonoverlapping categories of "woman" and "soldier" informed popular connections between lesbianism and women's entrance into the military. Cultural associations between masculine women and female homosexuality formed the basis for suspicions that at least some female soldiers would be lesbian. As historian John D'Emilio has observed, the theories of Sigmund Freud, Havelock Ellis and Kraft-Ebbing all linked "proper sexual development" to conventional definitions of "femininity" and "masculinity" and described women's deviations from prescribed "feminine" gender norms as one possible sign of female homosexuality.[8] Within this framework a woman's entrance into the WAC and her donning of a masculine style of dress seemed a clear example of cross-gender behavior and therefore a possible indication of lesbianism. Although historian George Chauncey has argued that sexual object choice replaced gender inversion in the early twentieth century as the primary psychiatric criterion for diagnosing homosexuality, it seems clear that this was more true for gay men than lesbians.[9] Thus, although contemporary psychiatric wisdom was slowly moving away from connections between "mannishness" in women and homosexuality, prevailing popular attitudes still linked the two and the "mannish" woman became the public symbol of the social/sexual category "lesbian."[10]

Discussions of mannish women were not limited to women's participation in the WAC but were also generated from larger cultural concerns with female sexual agency. The image of the mannish woman was not simply imposed by the medical establishment, but was also in part embraced — and recreated — by lesbians as a means to assert an explicitly sexual identity. Historian Esther Newton has characterized some female homosexuals' adoption of male images in the early twentieth century as a mode of breaking through nineteenth-century assumptions about the sexless nature of women and offering an alternative, sexual, vision of women's relationships with one another.[11] Further, in Madeline Davis and Liz Kennedy's study of working-class lesbian communities in the mid-twentieth century, they suggest that by manipulating the hierarchical distinction between male and female and masculinity and femininity, butch women and their femme partners found a way of challenging heterosexual hegemony and publicly expressing their love for one another.[12] Within this context "mannish" or butch women and butch/femme dyadic relationships within the WAC were distinct targets of hostility, accusations, and discharge proceedings, and formed the foundation of visible lesbian communities in the women's corps.

Not all lesbians were considered equally threatening; class and cultural divisions made some same-sex female relationships more acceptable than others. While butch/femme couples were the most recognizable lesbians during the 1940s, historian Leila Rupp has argued that their culture defined only one tier of a class system of relationships between women that existed in the twentieth century. Rupp suggests that while butch/femme was a largely working-class phenomenon, it was paralleled by the continuation of traditions of "romantic friendships" between white middle-class and upper-class women.[13]

Cultural perceptions of butch/femme women and their less visible middle-class and upper-class counterparts helped define both the spectrum of lesbian relationships during the 1940s and the limits of public tolerance of same-sex female affiliations. The use of degeneration theory by Kraft-Ebbing and Havelock Ellis to describe different categories of homosexuals formed the basis for some of these judgments. Both Kraft-Ebbing and Ellis labeled "masculine" women as the most degenerate lesbians, while Ellis went on to develop a continuum marking female "romantic friendships" as the least degenerative.[14] As historian George Chauncey contends, degeneration theory in particular embodied white, middle-class assumptions concerning the class nature of sexual morality.[15] Thus, though female "romantic friendships" came under stricter scrutiny throughout the twentieth century, many white middle- and upper-class women forming same-sex relationships were perceived as sexually respectable.[16] They were able to do so largely because they structured their relationships in relation to contemporary standards of white, middle-class, sexual morality, including their de-emphasis of explicitly sexual components in their ties to other women. At the same time, butch working-class lesbians were the subject of hostility and criminal charges. The differential treatment of butch/femme women vis-à-vis those women involved in "romantic friendships" paralleled assumptions as to the class-based nature of heterosexual behaviors. Contemporary Euro-American middle- and upper-class cultural attitudes toward working-class people ascribed to them a more vulgar and obvious sexuality, and assumed their greater sexual immorality. Both the greater visibility and assumptions about sexual aggressiveness contributed to the general hostility toward butch women. In the same manner assumptions as to the inherent sexual respectability of white middle- and upper-class women were part of the greater tolerance shown their relationships with one another.

The formal and informal procedures for dealing with "suspected" lesbians within the WAC were consistent with this larger framework and supported Corps leaders' overall emphasis on the recruitment of white middle-class women. "Romantic friendships" were often "tolerated," although not encouraged; so long as they remained invisible to the public they were not considered a threat to the larger aims of the WAC sexual regulatory system which defined threats to the public legitimacy of the corps as the primary criterion for punishing sexual misbehavior. Rooting out lesbians who maintained their "femininity," and did not call attention to themselves, would have made the "lesbian problem" more visible to the public than the WAC leadership desired.

WAC and Army strategies for regulating the sexuality of female soldiers created a "hierarchy of perversity" that prioritized threats to the women's corps based on the class, race, and sexuality of the sexual actors. This was not a fixed system, but rather a fluid, shifting set of male Army and WAC priorities, depending on particular contexts and the degree of public knowledge and scrutiny of specific sexual practices. Officially, servicewomen were not expected or allowed to engage in any sexual relations. Yet Army and WAC administrators were often more concerned about certain kinds of relationships than others, and therefore encouraged types of sexual behavior they believed less threatening. They often encouraged intraracial heterosexual relationships between servicemen and women, for instance, in order to deflect public fears of homosexuality and discourage interracial heterosexual liaisons. In other contexts, they tolerated homosexual behavior when they believed the alternative to be relationships between black men and white women. "Butch" women, however, who were believed to be more aggressive sexually, and dangerous to other Wacs, were usually treated more harshly than those women who were characterized as "passive victims" of their attentions. Both heterosexual and lesbian servicewomen acted within this system to protect and increase their own space vis-à-vis other women, working sometimes to reinforce and other times to challenge the sexual boundaries set in place by the WAC administration, the Army, their peers, and themselves.

Understanding the regulation of female homosexuality within the WAC during World War II requires analysis of the tensions between masculinity and femininity that shaped the construction of the "lesbian threat" and lesbian communities within the corps. In other words one must address the relation-ship between gender and sexuality contained within the public connections between female soldiers, mannish Wacs, and lesbians. In a culture increas-ingly anxious about women's sexuality in general, and homosexuality in par-ticular, the formation of a sex-segregated women's unit within an otherwise wholly male institution sparked a storm of public speculation as to the poten-tial breakdown of heterosexual norms and sexual morality. These concerns focused on the potentially "masculinizing" effect the Army might have on women, and especially on the disruptive influence the WAC would have on sexual standards. Servicewomen's position within these debates can be viewed through the metaphor of the "cross-dresser," a "woman" assuming a "mascu-line" identity, by embracing the role of "soldier" and the male garb that went with it. But unlike the cross-dresser, who might "pass" without being discov-ered, GI Jane's secret was "out" and Wacs, whether heterosexual or homosex-ual, were forced to negotiate within cultural and medical frameworks that viewed their desires to enter the Army and their role within the WAC as pos-sible evidence of lesbianism.

Public fears that female soldiers would become masculinized or that a women's corps would attract mannish women were in part supported by the military's acceptance of contemporary psychiatric theories naming gender inversion as one of the major criteria for distinguishing lesbians. WAC psychi-atrist Major Albert Preston, for instance, contended that women's desire to enter the military was in itself proof of their masculine identification.[17] Psychiatrists like Preston linked cross-gender behavior in women, including their aspirations to male occupations and/or adoption of male dress with "sex-ual confusion," a code word for rejection of femininity and heterosexuality. As a result the "mannish woman" came to signify the "lesbian" because her behav-ior, job, and/or appearance manifested elements designated as exclusively mas-culine.[18] Within this framework military women's masculine appearance, as defined by the uniforms they wore, and their movement into an institution that defined American manhood, seemed clear cause for alarm.[19]

Wac appearance played a crucial role in public accusations of lesbianism and informed the responses of the WAC administration to allegations that the military "masculinized" women. In particular, the WAC uniform was the focus of constant public criticism during the war. Public opinion surveys addressing the WAC made it clear that many civilians felt that the WAC uni-form was the most "unfeminine" and "unattractive" of all the services.[20]

The masculine appearance of the WAC uniforms was due in large part to the fact that the Philadelphia Quartermaster's Depot for most of the war based its patterns and sizes for women's attire on male models. Consequently, the WAC uniforms simply could not compete with the tailored WAVES uniforms, which were available at women's clothing stores. Navy women could purchase their uniforms and be individually fitted for them as opposed to their Army counterparts, who were issued military garments based on regulation sizes.[21]

In a 1944 segment of the popular military camp comic strip "Male Call," the strip's creator, Milton Caniff, explored the interaction between his femme fatale protagonist, Miss Lace, and a WAC private. The segment's title, "Know Which Arm You're In," aptly described this cartoon's four-frame content as Miss Lace awakens from an evening's sexual encounter and is startled by the sound of a female voice in bed beside her. Somewhat shocked she stares at the uniform hanging on the chair next to the bed as the WAC private in bed with her asks her what's wrong. Lace replies, "They should have more distinctive insignia on those WAC uniforms!"[22]

Although this particular segment was censored by the Army and therefore not distributed to military camp newspapers, it suggests in a humorous fashion the correlations between masculine appearance and female homosexuality, in particular the explicit connections between women in uniform and lesbianism. The predicament of Miss Lace arises from a case of mistaken identity— her assumption that Army uniforms are worn only by men. Caniff's cartoon suggests that Wacs wearing Army uniforms were "passing" in a very concrete sense, if they can be mistaken for men by Miss Lace, a perennial male GI favorite. Moreover, Caniff's casual treatment of the lesbian Wac also implies that the presence of lesbians within the women's corps was well known.

Throughout the war the WAC administration made attempts to create a feminine look for female soldiers. Brightly colored accessories, including scarves and gloves, were added to the women's uniform and off-duty dresses were designed, all in an effort to make Wacs look less masculine.[23] The WAC director and her staff also encouraged the creation of informal policies that cautioned against the adoption of "mannish hairstyles," while simultaneously advocating the development of a feminine WAC pompadour courtesy of Elizabeth Arden salons.[24]

The controversy surrounding the issuance of trousers to female soldiers exemplified the connections between male attire and male power, and between mannishness and lesbianism. "Wearing the pants," like "wearing the uniform," was a symbol of women's usurpation of the types of power and status conventionally associated with men, and servicewomen donning trousers generated anxieties among male military personnel as to their own positions and authority. In the ETO (European Theater of Operations) trousers never became an official part of the field uniform. Pants were suggested as part of the WAC uniform in Europe because they were warmer and were superior to skirts in preserving servicewomen's health during European winters. They were rejected, however, because of the adverse reactions of male military personnel and commanders. Enlisted men and male officers complained that the experimental "trouser outfits" initially issued to Wacs were "bulky . . . unbecoming . . . and could not be tailored to the female figure," making it difficult to distinguish between male and female soldiers.[25] One civilian woman urged the WAC to adopt trousers as part of the official WAC uniform, but also suggested that they be distinguished from those worn by men by a "slightly different shade of color." She believed this would "help ease the mental anguish and embarrassment of men," by assuring a distinction between female and male soldiers that she feared would otherwise be perceptible only by "looking at their hair." She concluded that "properly handled the WAC members could eliminate any feeling on the part of the male officers and men that they [women] were trying to wear the pants."[26]

The sight of female soldiers in trousers also highlighted the problem of female masculinity. Wacs in New Guinea adopted makeshift trousered uniforms and wore them throughout the war because they provided much better protection than skirts against heat rash and insect bites endemic to the area. In June 1945, however, Hobby issued orders requiring Wacs serving in New Guinea to wear skirts, though most enlisted women opposed the plan.[27] Throughout the war the WAC director went on record against the adoption of slacks, saying that she preferred women to wear skirts "to avoid rough or masculine appearance which would cause unfavorable public comment."[28] After her visit with the New Zealand women's army corps, one WAC officer reported:

> The wisdom of the Director's emphasis on maintaining femininity was certainly stressed. Apparently nothing has been done along that line and the masculine characteristics of some of their leaders, added to the natural tendency of regimentation, probably have influenced the women to adopt mannish haircuts, long strides, etc. It . . . has been responsible, I think, for many of the depreciating comments I heard made by some of the civilians I met.[29]

The "depreciating comments" that Hobby feared were those that linked the masculine aspects of some women within the WAC to the presence of lesbians. The efforts of Colonel Hobby and her staff to femininize the appearance of female soldiers, including the prohibition of mannish hairstyles and pants, were aimed at subverting these connections and in effect created one set of parameters for identifying and eliminating lesbians from the women's corps.

Most WAC policies that affected lesbians were not specifically addressed toward female homosexuals but fell within the larger WAC regulatory system addressing female sexuality in general. The predominant concern of this design, based in the Code of Conduct, was to portray women within the corps as sexually respectable and to eliminate those whose behavior or appearance undermined this goal. Within this paradigm, sexual agency in general was defined as a threat to the legitimacy of the women's corps, no matter *who* was the object choice of the female sexual actor. Wacs who acted on their sexual desires were violating both gender and sexual norms as the potentially masculinizing effect of the military on women was not only defined as women's taking on male characteristics, appearance, and power, but also as women adopting an aggressive, independent, and masculine sexuality. Throughout the war, Hobby's efforts to address the problem of female masculinity were aimed at women whose dress, demeanor, and/or behavior linked them with the popular cultural stereotype of the mannish lesbian who was by definition a sexual agent. Both of these frameworks had an affect on lesbians within the corps.[30]

The procedures developed by WAC officials for evaluating applicants to the corps did not specifically address lesbians until the war was near an end. Because the WAC was a volunteer organization whose requirements for enlistment were much higher than those used by the Army to rate men, military leaders and psychiatrists affiliated with the women's corps believed that the process of self-selection would be sufficient for screening out "undesirables."[31] Yet, while no formal system for identifying lesbians existed, the WAC *did* develop and use screening procedures that were partially aimed at detecting and rejecting lesbian applicants to the corps. This informal setup focused on class background, education, personality, and behavior, and worked to eliminate women who demonstrated characteristics culturally associated with female homosexuality. WAC policies for selecting women for the first officer candidate class and for subsequent officer training included criteria for the exclusion of women whose manner was "rough or coarse," whose build was "stocky or shapeless," and whose demeanor, including dress and "voice type," was "masculine." While these policies did not name *lesbians* as persons to be refused admission to the corps, WAC leaders' efforts to eliminate "masculine" women from the corps most likely resulted in some female homosexuals being denied entrance.[32]

Policies that explicitly identified lesbians as persons to be rejected developed slowly over the course of the war and were usually part of broader strategies aimed at rejecting any woman whose behavior suggested sexual deviance. In November 1942, the director's office issued a memo to the adjutant general that addressed the "enrollment of auxiliaries . . . of doubtful reputation" and called for increased emphasis on the "examination of enrollees" in order to "keep out those individuals who are known to have very bad traits and habits."[33] The "questionable moral standards" of the enrollees described within subsequent reports to the adjutant general were defined in large part by references to heterosexual promiscuity and homosexuality. In response to Hobby's request the adjutant general issued confidential instructions to all service commands ordering them to revise their recruiting procedures to include inquiries into the applicants' "local reputations." These instructions also listed nine "undesirable habits and traits of character" that recruiting officers should look for when interviewing applicants, including "promiscuous association with men" and "homosexual tendencies."[34]

The adjutant general's "confidential instructions" to Army commanders within the United States were the first to contain explicit references to homosexuals as individuals who should be excluded from the corps. Numerous euphemistic references to "lesbians," however, were used as benchmarks by WAC recruiters in screening applicants during the same period. WAC recruiters, for example, were asked to intensify their inquiries into applicants' motivations for joining the women's corps, in order to "get under the patriotic motive." One question recruiters were encouraged to ask was if part of the applicant's motivation was to "be with other girls?" This question was aimed at "catching" women of "questionable" character, in particular lesbians.[35] Simultaneously, representatives of the WAC's civilian advertising agency recommended changes in the WAC recruiting pamphlet that would serve to deemphasize the all-female aspects of the WAC environment.[36]

Subsequent screening procedures that addressed female homosexuals were the result of Hobby's struggles to institute stricter screening measures in the wake of the "slander campaign" waged against the WAC through the latter half of 1943 and early 1944. She received needed support for her efforts when the surgeon general appointed Major Margaret Craighill to oversee the health and welfare of the women's corps. Craighill, a psychiatrist, believed strongly that a psychiatric examination of prospective Wacs was necessary to determine women's fitness for admission to the corps. Their combined efforts resulted in a WAC Selection Conference held July 27–29, 1944, with the intent to improve screening procedures. The conference yielded a new WAC Selection Policy that required recruiting officers to reject applicants when there was evidence of "promiscuity or behavior difficulties" and included provisions for Army or WAC psychiatrists' evaluations of recruiters' reports before a candidate was enlisted.[37]

The most explicit antilesbian policy of the war came on the heels of this conference when the War Department issued specific instructions to guide military psychiatrists in their evaluation of prospective recruits. This manual (TB MED 100), entitled "WAC Recruiting Stations Neuropsychiatric Examination," gave medical examiners general background on the difficulties servicewomen might encounter and provided a list of specific criteria for rejection. A section defining the "object of neuropsychiatric examination" warned psychiatrists to "be on guard against the homosexual who may see in the WAC an opportunity to indulge her sexual perversity . . . and cause no end of difficulty." Although offering no specific criteria for identifying lesbians, the authors did suggest that an applicant's appearance was key to such a diagnosis, noting that "homosexuals are quickly detected in the WAC" and "they should be excluded at the time of examination."[38]

WAC policies addressing homosexuality within the corps, like the screening procedures, were fashioned as part of general measures for handling sexual agency of any kind. These informal procedures were described in the sex hygiene course created by Major Margaret Craighill. The lectures and pamphlet that defined this course were intended to instruct officers in the proper modes of handling cases of venereal disease, pregnancy, heterosexual sexual relationships, and homosexuality as they arose in their commands. The entire program was designed to discourage actions that might bring negative publicity to the WAC. Officers were told to deal with issues of homosexuality in much the same manner as heterosexual promiscuity, advocating guidance and informal measures to control servicewomen's behavior, with discharge used only as a last recourse.[39] The pamphlet explained that WAC officers should expect some degree of homosexuality within their commands but advised them to handle such occurrences with "fairness and tolerance." They were further informed that, "if there is any likelihood of doubt, it is better to be generous in your outlook, and to assume that everyone is innocent until definitely proved otherwise."[40]

While this model suggests an extremely tolerant attitude toward homosexuality within the WAC, the behavior, appearance, and class background of

individual lesbian actors were often used as criteria for determining which lesbians would be deemed threatening to the corps. WAC policies encouraging
tolerance for same-sex relationships were aimed at those associations that
stayed within the nonsexual rubric of female "romantic friendships"; relationships between middle-class, feminine, women that, even if erotic, were
not visibly sexual.[41] Suggestions for addressing such relationships included
directing servicewomen's attentions toward appropriate forms of companionship, specifically with men, and encouraging a woman with "homosexual tendencies" to substitute "hero worship" of a WAC officer: "If she is deserving of
the admiration of those under her command, the officer may be enabled, by
the strength of her influence, to bring out in the woman who had previously
exhibited homosexual tendencies, a definite type of leadership which can
then be guided into normal fields of expression, making her a valued member
of the corps."[42]

Although the information distributed to WAC officers on how to identify
homosexuals within their units was full of contradictions, it is clear that mannish appearance and behavior were used as criteria for identifying female
homosexuals in the corps. The creators of the sex hygiene course, for instance,
cautioned against conflating mannishness and homosexuality, explaining that
"many homosexuals are indeed the very opposite in appearance of masculinity." Yet, they also described female homosexuals in ways that explicitly linked
the appearance of "latent masculine characteristics" in women with lesbianism and continued to refer to lesbians as women who "attempt to take on characteristics of the opposite sex."[43]

The basis for the WAC's "tolerant" framework for dealing with homosexuality lay in WAC leaders' concerns with the image of the corps. Colonel
Hobby felt that the adverse publicity generated by investigations and court-
martials of lesbians within the WAC could only hurt the corps. Thus, while
Army regulations provided for the undesirable discharge of homosexuals, discharge proceedings specifically on the grounds of homosexuality were rarely
initiated against lesbians in the WAC. In fact, WAC officers were warned to
consider this action only in the most extreme of situations. Hobby felt that
such proceedings would only result in intensive public scrutiny and disapproval of the women's corps. Instead, WAC leaders suggested that officers use
informal methods of control, including shifting personnel and room assignments and transferring individuals to different posts. On several posts informal
WAC policies prohibited women from dancing in couples in public.[44]

WAC directives encouraging less public methods for dealing with lesbians
were joined by explicit prohibitions against "witchhunting." Prohibitions

against witchhunting should not be interpreted as reflective of sympathy or understanding of lesbians. Because lesbianism was so visible a threat to the legitimacy of the corps, witchhunting was in itself understood to undermine the WAC publicly to a greater degree than the persistence of lesbian practices among some individuals. Officers were warned of the adverse effect rumor and innuendo might have on the reputation of the corps and the morale of the women involved, and were thereby ordered to have "definite evidence" before proceeding against any "suspected homosexual."[45] Officers, however, sometimes acted on suspicion only, caught between instructions to seek the "prompt removal" of "active homosexuals" who were "addicted to the practice" and the knowledge that sufficient evidence to accomplish this was often very hard to obtain.[46]

Some heterosexual Wacs themselves, moreover, entered the Army with sufficient fears of masculine women and lesbians to contribute significantly to the explosiveness of public accusations. The information given to officers concerning the appropriate means of addressing homosexuality was not passed on to enlisted women who occasionally acted on their own suspicions concerning their peers. "Any girl with marked masculine tendencies, any two girls with close friendships," observed WAC psychiatrist Margaret Craighill, "were under suspicion and were practically convicted by a whispering campaign, with little opportunity to defend themselves." Craighill felt that the tendency of some Wacs to spread false rumors that might lead to witchhunts was frequently a worse problem than the actual presence of lesbians.[47]

Given the difficulty of obtaining "definite evidence" of a servicewoman's lesbianism, suspicion based on gossip and rumor was sometimes enough to eliminate enlisted women and officers from the WAC. Because of the many strictures on servicewomen's behavior, lesbian soldiers, unlike their gay male counterparts, were vulnerable to charges more easily proved than homosexuality, such as "drinking to excess" or being drunk in public. Thus, in the women's corps, where female soldiers' conduct was the subject of constant scrutiny and comment, Wacs whose homosexual tendencies or masculine appearance might be insufficient to convict them in a court-martial proceeding could find themselves discharged for other socially deviant behaviors.

In the case of white Wac Lieutenant Martha B. Hayes,* "suspicion of homosexuality" was a sufficient reason for her superiors to "encourage" her to resign her commission, although the investigating officer reported that there was "not sufficient evidence to support disciplinary action." WAC officials' attempts to

---

*All names used in the case studies in this chapter, other than those of male and female military administrators, are ethnically matching pseudonyms.

"punish" Lieutenant Hayes for her lesbian desire went beyond pressuring her to leave the service; WAC and Army officials tried to insure that Hayes would receive a dishonorable discharge though there was insufficient proof of her homosexuality to guarantee such an outcome in a formal hearing. To accomplish this, WAC investigators asked Lieutenant Hayes to resign her commission "for the good of the service." Officers who tendered their resignations with this condition were released from the WAC but their discharge was "other than honorable." The dishonorable circumstances of their discharge would become a part of their permanent record, affecting future employment opportunities and making them ineligible for veterans benefits. Lieutenant Hayes resisted this attempt to penalize her behavior; although she agreed to resign her commission, she refused to qualify her request and accede to a dishonorable discharge. While some WAC and male Army officials recommended refusing her resignation for this reason, the decision of WAC Headquarters was that the need to remove her from the WAC "without delay" was the chief priority; she was separated from service under honorable conditions.[48]

In other situations, WAC officials found ways to oust enlisted women suspected of lesbianism when there was not sufficient evidence to eliminate them for "sexual misconduct." In the case of Technical Sergeant Julie Farrell, rumors that she was a homosexual followed her from her post at Daytona Beach to the Army Administration School (AAS) in Richmond, Kentucky. Speculation concerning Farrell's sexuality was started by Lieutenant Alexander, one of the WAC officers at the Army school who had served with Farrell at Daytona Beach. Alexander informed other officers and enlisted women on the post that Farrell was a trouble maker and was possibly a homosexual. Several of Alexander's officer colleagues later noted that Farrell's appearance, especially her mannish haircut and behavior, seemed to confirm these suspicions. While Farrell's homosexuality was the subject of much discussion on the post, there was no definite evidence to support such allegations. Thus, when WAC officials took action against her it was for public drunkenness and insubordination, not for lesbianism. Although the issue of homosexuality was addressed during Farrell's court-martial proceeding, she was discharged for "evidence of habitual drinking of alcoholic liquors" and for behaving with "disrespect toward her superior officers." She was given an honorable discharge with the notation that she was not recommended for enlistment in the Women's Army Corps after conversion.[49]

Colonel Hobby's desire to portray female soldiers and officers as sexually respectable resulted in the creation of a "hierarchy of perversity" in the women's corps within which she and other WAC officials addressed female sexual agency, both heterosexual and homosexual. In New Guinea the efforts of Army and WAC officials to control the sexuality of male and female military personnel illuminated this hierarchy. As I discussed above, white servicewomen stationed in New Guinea found their freedom of movement severely restricted. These constraints, placed on Wacs ostensibly to "protect" them from black male lust, resulted in a series of rumors emerging in late 1944 claiming that there was widespread homosexuality among Wacs in New Guinea. Originating in letters of complaint from several Wacs, the specific allegations were that restrictive theater policies created an ideal habitat for some women to express and explore their "abnormal sexual tendencies."[50] Simultaneously, there was a reported increase in the number of incidences of homosexuality among African-American men who were prohibited from dating white Wacs in the area.[51] In this situation, the "lack" of opportunities for heterosexual relationships for both black GIs and white Wacs was defined as "causal" in the reported increase in homosexuality in each group.

Colonel Hobby, with the cooperation of the War Department, sent a WAC officer to the theater to explore the allegations pertaining to female personnel. After her investigation Lieutenant Colonel Mary Agnes Brown, the WAC staff director, reported that while homosexuality was certainly not widespread, several incidents had occurred. She believed that the situation was accentuated by the rigid camp security system to which Wacs were subjected. Her suggestions were to increase the opportunity for heterosexual recreational activity for Wacs "with a view of maintaining the normal relationships between men and women that exist at home and avoid the creation of abnormal conditions which otherwise are bound to arise."[52]

When faced with a choice of protecting women from men or protecting them from lesbian relationships, Brown's recommendation was to protect Wacs from the possibility of homosexuality, prioritizing it as more dangerous than heterosexual liaisons between white men and women. Yet the threat of interracial heterosexual relationships was deemed more dangerous than black male homosexuality. The Army did not lift the proscription on interracial dating, for example, indicating that Army officials preferred black men have sex with one another than run the risk that they might form sexual relationships with white servicewomen. Thus, in New Guinea, the treatment of heterosexual and homosexual agency depended on the race as well as the sex of the sexual actor. In constructing the parameters for the sexual agency of African-American men, Army officials implicitly characterized interracial sexual relationships as a greater danger than intraracial homosexual relationships. At the same time WAC officials constructed women's intraracial heterosexual sexual agency as less of a hazard than the possibility of women's involvement in homosexual relationships.

Military service provided arenas that offered women both economic autonomy and a social space away from the constraining environments of their home communities, in which they felt freer to explore their sexuality and sexual desires.[53] Some women discovered their sexual attraction for women during their wartime military service. Others joined the women's corps to be with other women, already certain of the direction of their desires. Still others chose to act as heterosexuals. Women joining the WAC formed their own attitudes toward homosexuality and acted on their sexual choices. In doing so they were all forced to negotiate within the regulatory framework created by Hobby and the WAC administration, a framework that, while condemning women's sexual agency generally, also continued to characterize homosexuality as the most sexually deviant behavior for women.

Although servicewomen, unlike their male counterparts, did not have to deal with explicit questions about homosexuality in the screening process, many found themselves nonetheless grappling with issues of homosexuality raised by the "rumors" surrounding the corps and the presence of lesbians in their units.[54] "When we knew of it [homosexuality], it was talked about but quietly." Ex-Wac Martha Ward recalled that "For many of us it was our first knowledge of it." "I didn't know what the word [homosexual] meant until I went in the service," commented another former enlisted white woman.[55] For some women this "new" awareness generated questions about their own sexuality or led to a "tolerant" attitude toward sexual diversity. For others it gave them a language of heterosexual privilege with which to expand their own authority within the confines of the women's corp.

While some historians have argued that even servicewomen who were not lesbians tended to treat homosexuality with a "who cares" attitude, in fact heterosexual Wacs' response to lesbianism fell along a continuum ranging from condemnation to acceptance.[56] Certainly there were heterosexual servicewomen who were sympathetic or supportive of lesbian friends. Remembering with regret the undesirable discharge of a lesbian friend, white ex-Wac Bessie Weaver recalled, "a secretarial friend who came and cried on my shoulder after having to serve as court reporter at a court-martial for a woman we had known and liked so much."[57] Some Wacs claimed that "no one really cared" whether a woman was homosexual. Other servicewomen, however, attest to a general atmosphere of distrust at some posts, in which even a rumor about alleged lesbianism was assumed to threaten the status of the WAC unit as a whole, thereby encouraging harsh control or condemnation of suspected lesbians. "Homosexuality was a problem whenever it was believed to exist," claimed former Lieutenant Colonel Anne Clark. "The members of a unit were shamed by even a rumor of it within their unit and very conscious of public rumors about service women's characters."[58]

Heterosexual officers and enlisted women who were hostile toward lesbians sometimes used the greater power given them through their rank within the military hierarchy to control other servicewomen's sexual behavior and diminish what they perceived as the "homosexual problem." Ex-WAC Staff Sergeant Catharine Thompson remembered "pulling rank" on a lesbian in her unit and threatening to report her unless she "stayed away from another girl." Former Lieutenant Colonel Bee Charles, stationed at Fort Des Moines through most of the war, felt that homosexuality was a "very big issue" in the corps and declared that as a result she had "many people discharged."[59]

Because homosexuality was such an explosive issue for the WAC, some heterosexual women manipulated fears of lesbianism to enhance their own power. For some, like Jane Williams, this involved alleging that her CO (commanding officer) and 1st sergeant were lesbians as revenge for being demoted and later discharged when it was discovered she had a dependent.[60] Others used such accusations to expand their opportunities for heterosexual activity. In this latter circumstance heterosexual women's actions, though reinforcing homophobia, also functioned as an assertion of their autonomy and right to find their own means of sexual expression within the authoritarian structure of the Army.

In February 1944, white Wac Captain Delores Smith was ordered to report for duty as the CO of the Army Air Force WAC detachment at Fort Worth, Texas. As a new CO, Captain Smith sought the help and advice of her officer staff in familiarizing herself with the company and environment. Receiving little support from them, she turned for advice to the ranking enlisted woman, Sergeant Norma Crandall. Shortly after her arrival Smith reprimanded several of her company officers for allowing enlisted men to frequent the WAC barracks and mess hall and cautioned these officers on their fraternization with male enlisted personnel. Two weeks later these officers brought charges of homosexuality against Captain Smith. They cited her restrictions on male/female interactions on post, her "dislike" of socializing with servicemen, and her "close association" with the enlisted woman, Sergeant Crandall, as evidence of her "abnormal tendencies." Despite the lack of concrete documentation to support these accusations, Colonel Hobby and the Board of Inquiry felt that to allow Captain Smith to continue as a WAC officer would only damage the reputation of the corps, and she was forced to resign from service.[61]

Captain Smith's case exemplifies the workings of the "hierarchy of perversity" within the WAC. Although the WAC investigation uncovered evidence indicating heterosexual sexual "misconduct" was widespread on the post, the possibility that the WAC commanding officer was a lesbian was deemed a much greater problem.[62] The disposition of this case suggests that female officers who enforced Army regulations against fraternization of male and female officers and enlisted personnel ran the risk of being seen as "antimale," or of being accused of discouraging "normal" heterosexual interactions. The heterosexual WAC officers at Fort Worth were angered by what they perceived as the imposition of unfair restrictions on their social lives by Captain Smith. They responded by invoking public concerns about the potential homosexuality of female soldiers. In doing so they acted to defend their right to choose how and with whom they would socialize, and simultaneously reinforced social taboos and Army proscriptions against lesbianism, thereby using the "lesbian threat" as a language of protest to force authorities to broaden their heterosexual privilege.

Within these parameters lesbians in the WAC developed their own culture and identity, though the risks of discovery and exposure remained. Evidence suggests that "finding" other lesbians within the corps was facilitated by the visibility of butch women. As such, masculine appearance and demeanor, were not only criteria used by WAC officials to "flag" homosexuals but were also ways in which some lesbians identified one another. Ex-Wac Pat Bond realized her first commanding officer was a lesbian because she had a "man's haircut" and demeanor—"the whole thing," as Bond called it. Her "masculine" appearance, Bond remembered, created some problems in the barracks at night because "the women would scream—they thought a man was loose."[63]

Technical Sergeant Julie Farrell dropped clues concerning masculine appearance and used covert questions in trying to discover the sexual orientation of a WAC officer at her post. Farrell approached Lieutenant O'Riley one evening to discuss what she characterized as the Army's efforts to make her "suppress her individuality," including criticisms and reprimands for her "mannish hairstyle" and "masculine behavior." Receiving a sympathetic response, Farrell went on to ask O'Riley if she understood "double talk" and if she had ever been to San Francisco. Farrell used these questions to determine if it was safe to discuss issues of homosexuality with O'Riley. When the lieutenant answered in the affirmative to her queries, Farrell proceeded to speak explicitly of the "natural desires" of women that the military attempted to suppress. She ended with what O'Riley later termed a "humiliating suggestion." Farrell was surprised by O'Riley's insistence that she had "no interest in such things," remarking, "Well, when you first came on this campus we thought that maybe you were one of us in the way you walked."[64] Lesbians like Farrell were careful to speak only indirectly about their homosexuality or to use coded language that presumably only other lesbians would understand and respond to accordingly.[65]

Army investigations into allegations of homosexuality at Fort Oglethorpe also found that lesbians there had "certain signals" they used by which they recognized one other and that they used specific terms to describe themselves. Such signals included women whistling the "Hawaiian War Chant," alluding to social encounters as a "gay time," and referring to one another as "dyke" or "queer."[66] Historian Allan Berube found that "working-class lesbian slang" was used by many lesbian servicewomen during the war, including referring to the masculine partner in a relationship as the " 'kyke,' the 'lesbian' the 'butch' or among Black servicewomen the 'dagger.' The feminine partner was the butch's 'lady,' 'girl,' or 'girlfriend.' "[67]

The means lesbian servicewomen used to recognize one another and to protect their communities could also be used to support military officials' actions against them. In fact, the very visibility of butches left them vulnerable to investigation as lesbians. In Julie Farrell's case it was clear that as a woman exhibiting "masculine" mannerisms and traits, she was more recognizable as homosexual to military authorities.[68] During the Army's investigation at Fort Oglethorpe, masculine appearance and behavior became the key criteria for naming women as "sex perverts." Military authorities deemed any woman effecting "mannish appearance," defined by her "haircut . . . manner of wearing clothing . . . posture . . . or stride" as most likely homosexual and any woman acting as the "male partner" in a relationship with another woman suspect. Authorities especially condemned women who deviated from gender norms by behaving as the active partner in erotic same-sex relationships. Thus, seeking to "date other girls such as a man would," paying "all the bills," or otherwise conducting oneself as "normally a man would with a woman" were seen as clear proof of a woman's homosexuality.[69] The assumption behind these criteria was that women looking or acting "like men" with other women in public spaces were also likely to interact with other women sexually, as men would, in private spaces.

Regardless of the risks, Army lesbians developed spaces in which to socialize together. Many lesbians used the service clubs present on most military posts for this purpose. Service clubs were designed by the Army to furnish male and female personnel with supervised recreational opportunities, providing drinks, a jukebox for dancing and tables for talking and socializing. At Fort Olgethorpe the Wac service club became a place where lesbians could meet and talk together, sometimes even dancing with one another. Allan Berube has demonstrated that service clubs also provided an arena in which lesbians identified other "dykes" and "cruised" one another.[70] For Pat Bond the service club was the setting of the "girl's night home," held once a week, a time when she and gay women from her social group danced, drank, met other lesbians, and "fell in and out of love."[71]

"Getting together" at the service club was supplemented by nights out "on the town," as groups of lesbian military personnel tried to find or construct space for themselves within the civilian sector. Although urban areas during the war provided the setting for the creation of a public gay nightlife and culture, opportunities for lesbian servicewomen to associate at civilian establishments were more limited than those available to their gay male counterparts. Civilian vice laws intended to discourage heterosexual promiscuity and repress prostitution made it difficult for women to enter taverns without a male escort. As a result there were few all-female bars in cities, though all-male bars were fairly common. In addition, due to the segregated nature of military life, civilian entertainments for African-American lesbians often developed separately from those of their white counterparts.[72]

Bars that catered exclusively to lesbians, as well as men's bars in which lesbians carved out their own spaces, provided what Allan Berube has termed a "temporary refuge" for lesbian soldiers during the war. The importance of such havens was underscored by ex-Wac Pat Bond, who fondly recalled the lesbian club Mona's in San Francisco. Mona's was one of the only bars catering exclusively to lesbians during the war. Bond described the nightly entertainment, male impersonators, as "gorgeous women with silver hair at the temples and tuxes." She also portrayed the bar as a "community" made up of "civilian dykes" and a few, like herself, "military out of uniform." To a young Pat Bond, San Francisco in the 1940s was a place in which you could get drunk and flirt with other women but most importantly a place that developed her sense of belonging. As she noted, "It was a sense of being somewhere finally where everybody was gay, not just you."[73] This "sense of belonging" was important for lesbians in their struggles to overcome negative cultural attitudes toward homosexuality.[74] Ex-Wac Johnnie Phelps claimed that she "fought not to be a lesbian for many years after I knew I was one" because "I knew it was 'wrong.' "[75]

Yet many gay and lesbian soldiers during the war also resisted such characterizations. They built communities with others "like themselves" and struggled toward a positive sense of identity based on their shared experiences, including military service.[76] Although lesbian communities in the WAC were often embattled, they nonetheless provided an arena within which women could fall in love and have sexual relationships. Ex-Wac Johnnie Phelps remembered having her first "real, down deep, hope-to-die-and-go-to-hell love affair" with a woman she met while stationed at an Army school.[77] While falling in love was exciting, finding a private space to express that love was extremely difficult. Sometimes lesbian soldiers sought moments together in the hallways, latrines, and barracks. Heterosexual ex-Wac Nellie Gruber, for instance, claimed that when she arrived at her new post most women in the barracks were "sleeping together." Remarking that she wanted to *sleep*, she said she dragged her cot into the hallway.[78]

Despite this example, the WAC barracks were not usually a comfortable place for women to make love to one another. Lesbian servicewomen most likely used overnight passes to secure private hotel rooms in surrounding towns in order to spend a night alone with their lovers. Due to the scrutiny of servicewomen's behavior, especially in hotels, however, such spaces were more limited for lesbians than for their gay male counterparts and women who might already be "suspected" as homosexuals could find their behavior monitored even in civilian arenas. At Sergeant Julie Farrell's court-martial several female officers testified that they had been requested to "observe" her behavior at her hotel with the purpose of confirming or refuting "malicious gossip" concerning her homosexuality.[79] It is also possible that this scrutiny, because it was generally aimed at preventing heterosexual liaisons, might have worked in some situations to increase the space for lesbians to be together.[80]

The difficulties of maintaining lesbian relationships in the corps were exacerbated by the personnel policies of the Army and WAC. Women who began relationships during basic training might be stationed at different posts upon its completion. Others serving in the same location might find themselves or their lovers transferred to another assignment in a different area of the country or shipped overseas. While married servicewomen could petition for passes and leaves to visit their husbands, this option was obviously not available to lesbian soldiers who desired to continue their relationships. The situations of lesbians who were separated from their lovers was probably made more difficult because they often had to deal with their pain alone, unlike the millions of separated heterosexual lovers to whom wartime songs and culture expressed unending sympathy.

The greatest challenges to lesbians' relationships and positions within the corps were presented by Army and WAC investigations of suspected homosexuals. These inquiries, both formal and informal, produced some of the most trying situations for lesbian soldiers. During these investigations, Army and WAC officials used a variety of coercive methods to obtain "proof" of suspects' homosexuality. One of the most effective means employed by WAC officials was to pressure enlisted women to "inform" authorities about other lesbians in their unit.

In May 1943, white Wac Lieutenant Georgia Joyce began an informal investigation of suspected homosexuals at the WAC installation, Daytona Beach, Florida. According to two WAC 1st sergeants who were undesirably discharged as a result of Joyce's inquiries, the lieutenant had approached them several times and asked if they would help her substantiate some rumors and gossip concerning the involvement of officers and noncoms in homosexual activities. The sergeants, Joan Pound and Norma Chambers, claimed that they were "embarrassed and surprised" by Joyce's questions but thought that she had singled them out because they were familiar with both past and present personnel at Daytona Beach. Sergeant Pound also contended that when she asked Lieutenant Joyce why she wanted such "gossip" and if she was going to "use it against someone," Joyce became angry and defensive and said that she wanted to know for her own "personal information and to satisfy her own curiosity." Pound said that Joyce asked them to disregard her higher rank and frequently sought them out for ostensibly social reasons. During these encounters Joyce "continually and persistently approached the subject at every opportunity." Obviously, Lieutenant Joyce attempted to "befriend" the sergeants in order to gain their trust with the intent of encouraging them to incriminate other women at Daytona Beach.[81]

At this point in her informal investigation Joyce took the evidence she had gathered to Army regimental headquarters and was given official sanction for her activities. Once Lieutenant Joyce received this authority she brought four women up on charges of homosexuality, including Sergeants Pound and Chambers. The sergeants claimed that their arrest was due to their involvement in a "framed trap" with two female officers. After their arrest they were confined in separate hotels for eleven days and not allowed to speak to anyone except the investigating officer. They felt this situation deprived them of the opportunity to vindicate themselves while giving Joyce the chance to "strengthen her case." Both women believed that Lieutenant Joyce had violated their rights and argued that her sole motive in the investigation was personal gain.[82]

While it is impossible to ascertain Lieutenant Joyce's motives for launching this investigation, the results are clear. Joyce was promoted and transferred to a prestigious posting in the inspector general's office; Sergeants Pound and Chambers were undesirably discharged for "habits and traits of character that serve to render their retention in the service undesirable." Yet, Pound and Chambers clearly believed that they were entitled to better treatment by the WAC and deserved more than disgrace and dismissal. They wrote their congressman, outlined their situation, and asked him to pressure the Army into reopening the investigation. In defending themselves, the sergeants incorporated the WAC discourse of toleration, arguing that the situation at Daytona Beach lent itself to abnormal relationships and false allegations "because of the inactivity and lack of normal social contact." They also claimed that they "could have implicated a lot of people in protecting their character and reputation but chose to uphold the Corps." Despite their efforts their case was not reopened, and evidence suggests that officials from the WAC and adjutant general's office did not reexamine the information given during the court-martial, fearing to stir up unnecessary publicity concerning homosexuality in the women's corps. As a result, Pound and Chambers' desire for reconsideration was denied, while Lieutenant Joyce received a letter from the adjutant general's office complimenting her on "carrying out an undesirable and disagreeable assignment which aided in unearthing an unwholesome situation involving a group of members of the Women's Army Corps."[83]

In a similar situation African-American servicewoman Frankie Casey wrote to Colonel Hobby, requesting that the director reopen the case that had resulted in Casey's undesirable discharge. Casey, like Sergeants Pound and Chambers, felt that her treatment by the military, especially by WAC officers, was unfair and that she had a right to demand redress. She claimed that while stationed at Fort Bragg she and several other women in her company were ordered by their African-American WAC CO to see the post's psychiatrist. His questions indicated to Casey that they had been sent to him "so that he could determine if we were or were not homosexual cases." Several days later Casey was presented with hearing orders and subsequently discharged for homosexuality. According to Casey, her CO, Captain Harriet White, regularly called WAC enlisted women into her quarters and promised them compensation in return for giving her information about other women's homosexuality. Casey also claimed that White forced servicewomen to sign incriminating statements and that during her court-martial one of her friends, Technical Sergeant John Eva Lawrence, "denied she knew anything about the statement she was supposed to have signed." Casey alleged that after her friend's denial

Captain White took Lawrence to the judge advocate's office and "frightened her to death, that if she did not stick to her statement in the case she would be given a dishonorable discharge."[84]

Given the embattled position of the women's corps in general, Captain White's actions reinforced the overall position of WAC administrators that women whose conduct "reflected badly" on the corps should be removed. Her actions may also have signaled her understanding of the precarious situation of black women within a largely white organization, and reflected her desire to protect that position by eliminating those who posed a threat to it. Her rank as an officer gave her the power to do so.

As I demonstrated above, the relationships between black officers and black enlisted women were often not only scenes of solidarity on the basis of race, but also arenas in which conflicts rooted in differential status and rank were negotiated. In her letter to Hobby, Casey asked that Hobby not refer her case to Major Harriet West, the ranking black member of Hobby's headquarters staff, because West and Captain White were friends and "nothing will be done about it." In this light, Casey's appeal to Hobby, like Pound and Chambers' petition to their congressman, can be understood as a desire to gain sympathy and support from someone whose position placed them outside the power structures they believed responsible for their dismissal. For Pound and Chambers, who blamed the WAC and Army for their plight, an appeal to civilian authority made sense. For Casey, who considered black WAC officers culpable, an entreaty to the white WAC director was equally understandable. Although Pound and Chambers did not succeed in getting their case reopened, their congressman's queries on their behalf warranted a response from the Army. In Casey's case, her letter to Hobby resulted in the director forwarding her file and discharge records to the Secretary of War's Discharge Review Board for reevaluation. Unfortunately, there is no evidence as to whether or not her discharge status was changed as a result of this evaluation.[85]

"Undesirable" discharges stigmatized former servicewomen in the eyes of their families and larger communities, denied them all veteran's benefits, and made it difficult for them to get jobs.[86] Most employers required that job applicants who had served in the military bring in their discharge papers as a condition of employment. Undesirable discharges, printed on blue paper, labeled women like Pound, Chambers, and Casey as social misfits, and most employers were unwilling to hire individuals whom the military had deemed unacceptable. As Casey wrote, "I can't get work with this blue paper—to whom do you think I would present it?"[87] This situation most likely affected women who did not have a college education more severely than those who did. Even if they wanted to hide their military service and their blue discharges, they still needed references from previous employers. More importantly, they could not directly refer to job skills they learned in the military that might have made them more employable.

While Captain White was depicted by Casey as typical of black WAC officers in her behavior toward enlisted women, evidence suggests that other black officers were more tolerant of incidences of homosexuality. Captain Charity Adams, CO of the only black WAC unit in the ETO recalled her reaction to Army directives that she and other unit commanders "be alert to homosexual activity." She understood that such relationships probably existed in her unit but also judged as unnecessary suggestions from Army Hq that she make "surprise inspections during the hours when troops were in bed." She believed that as long as her unit performed well, there was no need for her to unduly examine enlisted women's behavior. Her philosophy is captured in her statement: "I cannot swear to the kind of social activity that took place with all the members of the 6888th, but I will swear that the efficient performance of the unit was not impaired."[88]

The power that officers wielded over enlisted women was formidable when allegations of homosexuality were made. Lesbians' reactions to the pressures of Army and WAC investigations were sometimes dictated by their rank, and the greater authority and status they held in relation to their enlisted counterparts. While some lesbian officers were themselves the subject of investigations, others protected themselves by using their authority to indict enlisted women. During the court-martial of Technical Sergeant Julie Farrell, letters she had written to her officer lover were used as evidence against her. The tender and explicit discussions of their relationship contained within these letters were crucial to the decision of WAC officers to bring charges against Farrell. In one letter Farrell referred to Lieutenant Pines by her well-known, masculine moniker, "Little George," and asserted her love for Pines. Farrell went on to recall several sexual encounters between them and closed by saying she wanted to "hold you in my arms and kiss your eyelashes."[89]

During Farrell's trial it became clear that WAC officers had attempted to insure the incrimination of Farrell while clearing their friend and colleague Lieutenant Pines of all "blame." For example, two female lieutenants called a meeting of all enlisted women in the month prior to the trial that specifically excluded Farrell. During the meeting Lieuetenants Gould and Creighton explicitly connected Farrell with the rumors of homosexuality on the post. Lieutenant Pines avoided prosecution by claiming that the reason she was so often in the company of Farrell was that she was "observing" her behavior to determine if charges should be brought against her. She also contended that the interactions described in Farrell's letters occurred only in the sergeant's imagination. Pines covered herself by asserting that she had kept the letters because of her own suspicions of Farrell. When asked by the board how she planned to prefer charges against Farrell "in view of the contents of the letter concerning you," without incriminating herself, Pines replied, "My word, I hope, is good as an officer."[90] Thus, Pines invoked her status as an officer to save herself, and in doing so sealed the fate of her lover.

The most extensive formal military investigation of homosexuality in the WAC began in June 1944, at the 3d WAC Training Center, Fort Oglethorpe, Georgia. The investigation was initiated when the mother of a Wac private stationed at Fort Oglethorpe read love letters sent to her daughter by a female sergeant also at Fort Oglethorpe. The mother, Mrs. Adams, sent a letter to the judge advocate's office at the War Department claiming the training center was "full of homosexuals and sex maniacs." She contended that there were "others practicing this terrible vice" and submitted their names as well. She also threatened to make her allegations public unless the military took immediate action. In response Army and WAC officials instituted an investigation of the general conditions at Fort Oglethorpe and the specific women mentioned by Mrs. Adams in her letter.[91]

Lesbians' responses to the Army's investigation ranged from denial to self-indictment to blaming others. Some, like Lieutenant Forrest, claimed that their relationships were not sexual but were simply those of good friends. Forrest said she was guilty of associating with enlisted women but nothing else. Others, like Mrs. Adams' daughter and her lover, Sergeant Baker, blamed one another. Baker said that Private Adams came on to her and "followed her around like a sick puppy," but denied having engaged in homosexual practices with Adams. Baker also contended that in writing explicitly sexual letters to Adams she was simply following her father's advice that "if a girl ever tried that kind of stuff just to give her her way and play her game and she would let you alone."[92]

Private Adams in turn laid the responsibility for their relationship on Baker. In doing so she tried to place herself within the Army's psychiatric discourse that assigned greater blame to women who were the "aggressors" in homosexual relationships and viewed more leniently those whose age or rank made them likely in Army officials' eyes to have been the "victim" of a more experienced and powerful woman. She did this by claiming she was afraid of the sergeant and wrote her letters to "calm her down." Adams also maintained that she hadn't a "chance" with Sergeant Baker because the sergeant was so much older than she was and had a great deal more "experience." Her attempt to portray herself as both sexually passive and an innocent victim, unknowledgeable about sexual issues, especially homosexuality, becomes clear in the following excerpt from her interrogation:

Q: You stated that one night, while Sergeant Baker was with you . . . she accomplished her desire. What do you mean by that?

A: Well, you probably know as much about Lesbians as I do.

Q: You mean you waked up and she was embracing you?

A: Yes.

Q: I believe you said that you were asleep at the time.

A: I was asleep before—I mean while this was happening, and, of course, the minute that anything like that happened, naturally I was awakened. The girl was clever, sly as a panther.[93]

In contrast, some lesbians who appeared before Army and Wac investigators acknowledged their relationships and attempted to protect their lovers from persecution. Under questioning Corporal Cooper "admitted" that her involvement with Lieutenant Douglas was "abnormal" but testified that they "love each other and enjoy each other's company more than that of men." Douglas tried to take all the responsibility for her association with Corporal Cooper. Although Douglas had been transferred to another post, when Corporal Cooper called to ask her what she should do when asked to testify, Douglas returned to Fort Oglethorpe to voluntarily address the inquiry board. Douglas told the board she simply "wanted to take all the blame for and clear the kid." She also testified that she "could not deny" her behavior and that "not even doctors" could explain it. Moreover, the WAC technician involved with Lieutenant Forrest told officials that she was "truly in love" with Forrest and would "hate to give her up."[94]

It is not surprising that lesbians' reactions to Army inquiries varied so widely. Brutal Army interrogations were designed to erode a woman's dignity and pit lesbians against one another in the interest of the military, and investigative methods were intended to coerce women into incriminating themselves or others in their unit. Under these circumstances lesbians' denial of their sexuality cannot be accepted at face value but must be understood as potentially delaying tactics used by Wacs to avoid incriminating themselves or others. Lieutenant Douglas' use of contemporary psychiatric theories to explain her behavior, for instance, could be evidence of her internalization of these ideas. Yet her use of this discourse also allowed her to resign her commission and save her lover. These interrogations, however, when combined with threats of familial censure, loss of career, reputation, and benefits forced some lesbians to make heartbreaking choices between defending themselves, their friends, or their partners.[95]

Army and WAC officials' decisions as to the disposition of individual cases at Fort Oglethorpe were influenced by the recommendations of the WAC psychiatrist, Captain Ross, who examined those women called to testify. Ross based her suggestions to the Board of Inquiry on her evaluation as to whether or not these women could be "rehabilitated" through psychiatric treatment. In making these judgments she followed War Department policy and the Army's psychiatric discharge regulations. These regulations demanded that the psychiatrist make an assessment determining if the individual was a "confirmed homosexual" or simply had been involved in "accidental" homosexual relationships.[96]

Within this framework a variety of criteria were used in calculating the category of homosexuality in which individuals belonged. Butch women were defined as "true homosexuals or addicts" while femmes were characterized as the "victims" of their "seduction." In addition, "first offenders" who "acted as a result of immaturity especially if influence was exercised by a person of greater years or superior grade" were more likely to be depicted as "victims."[97] The woman's class background and educational status were also figured into the equation. In a discussion of Sergeant Baker's behavior, board members characterized her as the "ringleader" of homosexual activities at Fort Oglethorpe, noting for the record that she had not graduated high school. In contrast, Captain Ross spoke quite highly of Private Adams, portraying her as a victim and noting that she was from a good background and had "high moral ideals."[98] Finally, the type of sexual activity in which women engaged was a factor. Despite evidence that the six women discussed here had made love to one another, because they described their sexual activities in terms of kissing, fondling, and embracing, they were not defined as "true perverts" as they did not engage in "oral practices."[99]

The decision of the Board of Inquiry was that Lieutenant Douglas should be asked to resign her commission "for the good of the service" as she "admitted all allegations" and intimated that she was "afflicted with an abnormal condition." The other five women were ordered to the First WAC Training Center at Fort Des Moines, Iowa, to be "hospitalized . . . for psychiatric treatment . . . with a view to being either restored to duty or separated from the Service, depending upon the results of such treatment."[100] Although ordering this course of action, board officials also qualified their recommendations by commenting on the possibility for reclamation of these women. Members suggested that Sergeant Baker should be "carefully examined" to determine whether she should be put through Section VIII proceedings (psychiatric discharge-undesirable), while also observing that Private Adams' "exemplary conduct" since her "experience" was a good indicator that she could still be useful to the corps. In addition, the board indicated that because both Corporal Cooper and Technical Sergeant Edwards "evinced no desire to discontinue their relationships," their potential for rehabilitation depended on their willingness to do so.[101]

The board's decision to order psychiatric treatment as opposed to undesirable discharge allowed the women's corps to avoid the potentially crippling publicity that most likely would have accompanied an extensive purge of lesbians at the training center. Colonel Hobby's follow-up actions after the Fort Oglethorpe investigation were undertaken with similar discretion. Women who under coercion "named names" presented Colonel Hobby and the WAC with another dilemma with much greater ramifications. In response, the Fort Oglethorpe Board of Inquiry recommended that "discreet inquiries" be made by "responsible commanding officers and psychiatrists" as to the status and conduct of women who had been incriminated but were stationed elsewhere. Board members felt that "nationwide" investigations launched by the inspector general's office would "adversely affect WAC morale" and result in unwanted publicity.[102] Hobby followed this advice and issued memoranda for the WAC staff directors in each service command, providing them with lists of servicewomen and officers serving in their area who had been named in the Fort Oglethorpe testimony. Hobby informed these WAC administrators:

> These names are furnished you in order that you may quietly inquire into their present conduct on any inspection trips made by officers of your office. If there is any indication that their present conduct warrants further investigation, copies of the testimony pertaining to the individual concerned, will be furnished you.[103]

This technique, in effect, enabled Hobby to engage in a hidden national witchhunt of alleged homosexuals in the WAC.

The atmosphere of terror created by military investigations, whether overt and extensive, like the one at Fort Oglethorpe, or covert, like Hobby's personal campaign, cannot be overemphasized. As Allan Berube has argued, although only a small percentage of gays and lesbians were actually victimized by these inquiries, they "nonetheless had a tremendous impact on lesbian and Gay GIs." In fact, the procedures developed by the WAC adminstration for eliminating "suspected" lesbians during the war were widely used in purges of lesbians from the military in the immediate postwar years. Certainly, many lesbians, some who had served years in the WAC, must have been outraged when their status changed from necessary to expendable as the Army demobilized.[104]

Some lesbians were eliminated quietly by simply being declared "excess" from a command and discharged. In one such situation Major Helen Hart, the WAC supervisor for the 6th Army, headquartered in San Francisco, announced her intention to use this method to "dispose of" three "maladjusted females" from the WAC Band at Camp Stoneman. She sent WAC Headquarters a list of their names and suggested that they be immediately discharged. She believed this would be an easy procedure since most re-enlistees had signed up "for the duration plus or for the convenience of the government" and remarked "This is certainly the time when the convenience of the government is at stake."[105] Other lesbians were removed by much larger, systematic witchhunts launched at posts in the United States and overseas. In these efforts the Army and WAC utilized the techniques they had honed at Daytona Beach and Fort Oglethorpe. Methods based on coercion and intimidation left lesbians battered and with few opportunities to protect themselves. Pat Bond described one purge at an Army post in Japan:

> After the war, when we were no longer needed, they decided to get rid of the dykes. So they had court martials. Every day you came up for a court martial against one of your friends. They turned us against each other. When I was living it, I didn't have any idea why they were doing this to us. I only knew they were throwing us out of the army with dishonorable discharges.[106]

Some escaped by accusing others of lesbianism. Others got married or pregnant in order to leave the Army and protect themselves and their lovers; Pat Bond married a gay GI to avoid prosecution. Although she regretted leaving her lover behind she felt the "only way I could figure out to save my lover was to get out. If I had been there, they could have gotten us both because other women would have testified against us."[107]

The postwar crackdown on homosexuality in the WAC signaled the expansion of explicit policies aimed at screening for and eliminating lesbians from the women's corps. The new WAC director, Colonel Westray Boyce, picked up where Hobby left off, insisting on stringent criteria for admission to the corps. Faced with a congressional battle to make the WAC a permanent part of the Army, Boyce felt it was imperative to exclude all those of "undesirable traits of character," including "homosexuals and promiscuous women." To accomplish this objective she enlarged existing WAC psychiatric screening programs and added new ones. Moreover, she provided for the addition of a WAC psychiatrist to all induction stations. The function of such an officer was in part to circulate among the WAC candidates and "observe the groups in order to attempt to spot any action that perhaps one could keep under cover during the short period they could be on guard in front of a psychiatrist."[108] This type of observation, like methods used during the war, hinged on defining mannerisms, behavior, language, and appearance as indicators of social or sexual deviance.

Lesbians' experiences in the WAC during World War II must be understood within the complex and often contradictory policies and practices framing their existence and actions. Some of these policies, generated by a need to avoid negative publicity and to create a space within the male military for women in general, provided the conditions within which lesbians could be tolerated. The limits of this toleration were expanded by lesbian soldiers and officers who developed strategies for recognizing one another, socializing together, and building communities. Yet, the process of creating and sustaining a lesbian identity or relationship within the WAC was also fraught with danger and uncertainty. Lesbians, moreover, unlike their gay male counterparts, also battled suspicions and restrictions based on their precarious position as women within a male military. In particular, butch lesbian soldiers epitomized the "threat" of female military service, combining the overlapping possibilities of female power and sexual agency as expressed through their own "masculinity." Thus, because of their centrality to larger debates over gender and sexual deviance, lesbians' attempts to create identities and communities for themselves within the military were critical to both lesbian visibility and to the creation of a category of "female soldier" during and after the war.

Epilogue

In this book I have outlined the process by which women were formally incorporated into the Army and analyzed the ways in which the category of "female soldier" was created and continually constructed during World War II. I have demonstrated that understanding the process by which women were accepted into this "masculine" institution, and a new category of "female soldier" was constructed, helps us to better evaluate the competing meanings of gender, race, and sexuality in twentieth-century American culture. Because the formation of the WAC became the focus of public fears that the mobilization for war would undermine established racial, gender, and sexual systems, Army and WAC leaders attempted to create a place for women within the military without disrupting contemporary definitions of "masculinity" and "femininity" or contemporary military and community policies of segregation.

The construction of the World War II Wac, however, was not a binary process. In other words, it is too simple to view this process as only a tale of institutional Army sexism; there were a number of different actors who offered competing visions of what the "female soldier" could, should, and might be or represent. Significantly, white feminists, for the most part, did not directly influence or shape the discourse on women's military service during the war; most white women's organizations did not argue for women's *right* to participate in the military as women. Rather, they defended women's military service as a temporary aberration that would end with the war when women would be discharged and return to their respective homes and families. In contrast, throughout the war African-American women's groups, especially the National Council of Negro Women, depicted black women's military experience as important both for African-American people and as crucial to the advancement of all women in postwar American society.

The negative publicity plaguing the WAC throughout the war, especially the slander campaign, shaped both the lives of female soldiers and the tenor of WAC leaders' vision of military women. The images of the scatterbrained, ineffectual woman playing at soldier and the female soldier as sexual victim, for instance, both emphasized certain definitions of "femininity" and "womanhood." Key aspects of these definitions were women's inability to function well in arenas defined as male and their inherent sexual vulnerability when stepping beyond the circle of protection found within the home. The former was a disparagement of women's capabilities and the latter a warning of the consequences for moving outside one's prescribed gender sphere. Simultaneously portraits of Wacs as potential sexual victims were balanced by the equally threatening specter of military women as sexual agents and actors. Negative public depictions of Wacs were rooted in particular gendered constructions of "women" and "soldiers." These archetypes were set in direct opposition to one another and resulted in the creation of two separate but overlapping ideological paradigms circumscribing female soldiers' experiences. Both placed Army women in an absolute double bind. In the first, if women maintained their femininity they would be viewed as incompetent soldiers and if they succeeded as soldiers they must have lost or rejected their femininity and become mannish. In the second, women who maintained their femininity were relegated to the role of sexual victim, used and discarded by a male military which violated their trust and their virtue. In this scenario the dangers of losing or rejecting one's femininity were inscribed in the images of sexually independent women: dykes or whores.

Anticipating controversy, female and male military leaders, as well as civilian proponents of the women's corps, agreed that female soldiers must not seem to threaten either male power in the military or the notion that masculinity was integrally tied to the definition of "soldier." Consequently, the parameters created by WAC and Army leaders in carving out a space for women in the military greatly circumscribed the ability of women to be soldiers or to be perceived as soldiers. Given that during World War II, gender, racial, and sexual hierarchies were in enormous flux, this defensive posture meant that military systems of regulation and the Army's employment of women were often more reflective of prewar conditions and standards. Thus, while both civilian and military women engaged in extramarital sex during the war, WAC leaders imposed a regulatory system that penalized or eliminated women for engaging in heterosexual activity. To Colonel Hobby, sexually active women threatened all women's place within the military and the larger WAC organization itself.

Despite, and in some ways because of, the position staked out by WAC leaders women's military service during the war was a significant factor in the emergence of a modern lesbian identity and the continuing development of lesbian cultures, both within and outside the military itself. The struggles by lesbians to carve out a space for themselves in the WAC despite the risks, for instance, underlay some lesbians' resistance to the purges of homosexuals in the immediate postwar period. The intensified repression of lesbians by the military in the immediate postwar period then created a situation in which some lesbians began to define themselves as deserving of civil rights and laid the basis for the later struggles of gay men and lesbians for equal rights and justice.

Similarly, the World War II military experiences of black women were crucial to succeeding struggles for racial justice and personal dignity. During the war black women's efforts to overcome individual and institutional bias made visible the Army and WAC's poor treatment of them and were crucial to public debates over racial discrimination and equal rights for black people after the war. Moreover, the ways in which they opposed discrimination, including letter-writing, sit-ins, and sit-down strikes, presaged the tactics used by civil rights activists in succeeding decades. As a result, black women's military service must be understood as important not only to the status of black people and all women in the military, but also to black men and all women within the larger civilian culture.

One of the most important measures of the World War II experience for women was the sense of empowerment many ex-Wacs took with them from their military service. This empowerment was articulated by some as a "greater sense of themselves." As white WAC veteran Martha Ward remembered, "I liked the new experience, new friends, new places, and *Pride* in something . . . and mostly I liked myself . . . I was the one who made myself."[1] This empowerment was also articulated in ex-Wacs' sense of entitlement to the benefits and programs previously available only to returning male GIs and officers. While most historians have characterized the postwar period as one which encouraged women to return to the home, many returning servicewomen and female officers took advantage of the GI Bill and other veteran's benefits to maintain their economic independence and further their education.

The GI Bill and its provisions of higher education, on-the-job training, and business and home loans has been identified as a significant factor in some men's economic choices and opportunities in the postwar period. Few, however, have addressed the similar actions of female soldiers and the significance of women's eligibility for these benefits. Fully one-half of both male and female Army veterans, for example, took advantage of readjustment allowances providing them with $20/week for the year following their military service. Equally important, one-third of all ex-Wacs began college or made definite plans to enter school shortly after their discharge. In addition, 50 percent of all former Wacs returned to the work force immediately following their discharge. Of those who went to work in the civilian labor force, 40 percent did not return to their previous civilian employment but moved into new jobs for which they were trained and had developed skills during their military service. While few servicewomen took advantage of the low-interest business loans provided by the GI Bill, those who did opened cafes, hat shops, beauty parlors, and bookstores in the postwar period.[2] "I believe I have gotten so much as a direct result of my service," observed white Wac Loretta Howard, "my degree which gave me a better job and consequently better pay, which of course, resulted in a better standard of living. I have always been so thankful I did enter the WAC."[3]

Although most ex-servicewomen characterized their service as the best time of their lives and as crucial in making them feel good about themselves and their capabilities, many came out of the war to face a culture that had not changed as much as they had and which in many ways tried to restrict women's opportunities. Juanita Waters recalled that after the war she returned to her husband and his family, but "because I had served in the WAC I was accused of everything imaginable . . . ultimately the marriage ended in divorce."[4] Although most WAC veterans were happy to see the war come to an end, and glad to return to their husbands or families, many also expressed regret at the end of their military service. White Wac Laura Frank captures the difficulties some ex-servicewomen had reconciling the end of their "great adventure" with the more mundane routine of daily life. She characterized her military service as "wonderful" and as offering her the opportunity to "find myself, be independent. I like it because it was *my* choice." To Laura Frank, life in the WAC was "as close as I could get to the feel of college. At that age it was the way I could make something better of myself." Returning home after the war she was caught up in the cultural desire for normalcy and made the choice to marry shortly after her discharge. Of her postwar experience she noted, "I became a housewife and mother of four, and worked part time at the railroad. Didn't seem to change much. Right?" [5] As white Wac Doris Samford remarked:

Now, the ending was really here. The war was over. I was out of the army. There were no wartime buddies, no strict regulations, no practical jokes, no uniform of the day, no long working hours . . . I hung my uniform on a hook on the back of the bathroom door . . . I was, and felt, stripped and exposed. I stepped into the tub and sat down in an abundance of hot water. I held the washcloth in trembling hands and pressed it to my face. I would have to figure out later why I was crying, when I knew that I must be so very happy.[6]

The ambivalence expressed by Doris Samford at the ending of her "great adventure," the disappointing conclusion to Juanita Waters' military service, the confusion of Wacs in the midst of the slander campaign, the courage of the sit-down strikers at Fort Devens, and the bitterness of lesbians "purged" during and after the war all encompass both the possibilities and problems involved in female military participation.

While conditions today have changed dramatically since the 1940s, current debates about women in combat and lesbian and gay soldiers in many ways reflect similar tensions. Arguments against the employment of female soldiers in combat jobs, for instance, remain overwhelmingly ideological. As Cynthia Enloe has contended, military forces, historically and today, rely on "ideological beliefs concerning the different stratified roles of women and men" to justify their policies and practices.[7]

Today, for instance, the resiliency of sexual images of servicewomen as camp followers and the legacy of these sexual systems is epitomized in the public and congressional response to bills intended to more fully integrate women into combat roles. After the passage of a House bill in July 1991 that would allow women limited access to combat roles, for instance, there was a "fierce whispering campaign" on Capitol Hill. This new slander campaign included "wild tales of women's misdeeds in the Gulf—everything from rumors of women soldiers turning tricks to stories about the high number of pregnancies (36) aboard a single Navy ship."[8] These rumors placed the responsibility and blame for sexual activity on women and made no mention of their male sexual partners. As Representative Pat Schroeder remarked, "Unless there was a star shining over that ship, I'd say it takes two . . . what kind of military discipline do we have that we blame only women?"[9] Both female victimization and agency, today as in World War II, are used as arguments against the full employment of women within the modern military.

Further, accusations of lesbianism, aimed at women who join the military, or who in other ways make claims to traditionally male power and status, continue to work to marginalize women's performance in "masculine" arenas. Currently "dyke-baiting" of female soldiers has attained a level of cultural sanction that makes military women's lives increasingly difficult. Recently, military women testifying before the Defense Advisory Committee on Women in the Armed Services (DACOWITS) reported that enlisted women and female officers were routinely harassed through the mechanism of "gay-baiting." One female Navy Petty Officer displayed a sign with the word "DYKES" in a circle with a slash through it and stated that enlisted male personnel commonly displayed such signs were aboard ships to intimidate women. She and other servicewomen asked that DACOWITS handle the matter of dyke-baiting as an issue of sexual harassment.[10]

Feminist participation in debates about women's military service is often impeded by the assumption that the military is not an appropriate venue for fighting for equal rights and justice. It may be beyond us all to imagine an equal place for women in the military or a military that reflects "feminine" as well as "masculine" values. To continue to ignore the military, however, is to continue to ignore a critical state institution through which a stratified citizenry, based on race, gender, and sexual orientation, is constructed. To remove ourselves from the debate over heterosexual women's, gay men's, and lesbians' rights to participate fully within the military because of a strong and justified critique of the military and its function in American society and worldwide is to cede authority to challenge current limitations on women's access to state power generally. Military women's experience must be continually historicized and understood, not only to shape the discourse about servicewomen, but also to shape the discourse about women's position and status within the larger culture.

Meyer Oral History Questionnaire

This questionnaire is an important part of my research for a history of the WAAC/ WAC during World War II. If you need more space for your answer to a particular question, please use the back of the page and indicate the number of the question. I appreciate very much your cooperation in completing this form.

1. Name   Rank
2. Units served in. Indicate the years of service in each unit.
3. On which posts did you serve? Which did you like the best? and worst? Why?
4. Birthplace and date
5. Where did you spend your childhood? If on a farm, say so and give name of nearest town.
6. What was your father's occupation?
7. What was your mother's occupation?
8. How much education did you have before you entered the WAAC/WAC?
9. Did you initially enroll in the Women's Army Auxiliary Corps (WAAC) or did you enlist in the Women's Army Corps?
10. If you were originally enrolled in the WAAC, how did you feel when the WAAC became an official part of the Army in 1943?
11. Did you have a job before you enlisted? If so, what was it and how did your pay compare to the pay received as a WAAC or WAC?
12. What did you know about the Army before you enlisted/enrolled? Had you seen much of soldiers?
13. Why did you enlist/enroll in the WAAC or WAC?
14. When and where did you enlist/enroll?
15. What did your family and friends think about your enlisting/enrolling? What was your marital status when you enlisted?
16. How did your WAAC/WAC pay and the types of jobs you were doing compare to that of your female friends in civilian life?
17. How did your WAAC/WAC pay compare to that of male soldiers of comparable rank?

18. Where did you receive your recruit training?
19. Briefly describe this training. Did it adequately prepare you for your job?
20. Evaluate generally the equipment, clothing, and food rations as well as the living quarters on the base.
21. Briefly describe a typical day's routine on the base where you were assigned/stationed. What was your job?
22. As you saw it, what was the purpose of the WAAC/WAC?
23. Were male soldiers and WAAC/WACs assigned similar jobs or did they have different occupations? Briefly explain.
24. Evaluate the discipline and morale of the women in your unit.
25. Were promotion policies fair?
26. Were there any problems in your unit? If so, briefly describe.
27. How would you describe the relationship between the women of the WAAC/WAC and male soldiers and officers?
28. Were there any specific fraternization policies addressed to WAAC/WACs interaction with male soldiers?
29. Was homosexuality an issue?
30. Was pregnancy an issue?
31. What is your opinion of military justice? For example, when there was a breach of discipline, were the punishments proper for the crime?
32. Did you attend any Army schools for special training? If so, which ones? How long were the courses? Evaluate the instruction?
33. Evaluate medical facilities, doctors, and health care.
34. Was there much interest in religion? Evaluate the religious facilities and the chaplains.
35. How much free time did you have in a typical week? How did you spend this time?
36. How often did you get into town?
37. How did you get along with civilian personnel either on base on in town? Was there much contact with civilians?
38. What was the reputation of the WAAC/WAC while you were serving?
39. Was there much interest in politics? Did you vote prior to 1941?
40. How did you spend your pay? Were you able to save much?
41. How did you spend your leave time?
42. Did you have any desire to be stationed overseas? If so, why? If not, why not?
43. Describe and evaluate other women in your unit. Did they generally have the same civilian background? If so, what? Were many foreign born? Did a majority of the women in your unit come from a particular region of the country? If so, which region? Roughly, how many in your unit were married?
44. Describe and evaluate your officers. Were they good/bad? fair/unfair? strict/lax? Did they know their jobs? Were they good leaders?
45. Did your life in the WAAC/WAC change much as the war progressed?
46. How long did you stay in the WAAC/WAC?
47. If you re-enlisted or re-enrolled in the WAAC/WAC, why did you do so?
48. What did you like the most about being in the WAAC/WAC?
49. What did you like the least about it?
50. What did you do after you left the WAAC/WAC?

Discussion of Sources

Because the Army is a powerful state institution, there are numerous federal records available at the National Archives, which detail the difficult process involved in the creation of the WAC, as well as its constant battle to achieve legitimacy within a male military establishment during World War II. Most significant in illuminating this struggle are the WAC administrative records and the records of the WAC director (RG 165, RG 319). While these record groups provide a wealth of material on the organization and structure of the women's corps, they also include vital information on the formulation of WAC policies concerning the regulation of "female soldiers" throughout the war. Discussions between female and male Army leaders available in memos, transcripts of "secret" telephone conversations, and correspondence, shed light on the articulated reasons behind WAC regulations addressing servicewomen's social and sexual lives, and highlight the conflict between male and female Army leaders over whether Wacs should be treated and controlled as "soldiers" or "women." The corps' methods of regulating service women's social and sexual lives, and the philosophy behind such methods, are also articulated in classified court-martial transcripts and discharge reports found within these record groups. In addition, confidential reports of Army investigations into the negative publicity that plagued the corps throughout the war provide useful information concerning the content, breadth, and source of these rumors, particularly during the "slander campaign" against the WAC from mid-1943 through early 1944.

Further, these record groups contain hundreds of letters from civilians and Wacs themselves to the War Department, President Roosevelt, and WAC Headquarters. While some civilians supported the women's corps others condemned the idea of female soldiers, and examining their respective arguments helps clarify why the creation of the WAC was so controversial. Moreover, letters from servicewomen, articulating both praise and criticism for the corps and their positions within it, serves to give at least a partial voice to the women who served within the WAC during the war.

In an effort to understand more fully the arguments of both proponents and opponents of the women's corps, I scrutinized the *Congressional Record* for the 77th and 78th Congresses and the transcripts of the hearings of the House and Senate

Committees on Military Affairs. The issues raised on the House and Senate floors in debates over the initial WAAC bill and the later WAC legislation were relevant not only to the eventual passage of the bills but also portended public debates over the creation of a corps of "female soldiers." To understand these broader public discussions I used public opinion data collected by Corps' advertising agencies through Gallup Polls during the war. I also surveyed contemporary mainstream periodicals, including *Time, Newsweek, Saturday Evening Post, Ladies Home Journal, Woman's Home Companion, Christian Science Monitor,* and *Life.* In addition, I examined editorials in the mainstream press and nationally syndicated cartoon series' to clarify the competing discourses about women's military service.

Most of my discussion of newspaper sources results from my perusal of articles about the women's corps included in both the WAC records at the National Archives as well as in the archives of the WAC Museum at Fort McClellan, Anniston, Alabama. The latter collection is more reflective of regional diversity, as the newspaper files of the WAC Museum contain literally hundreds of columns clipped from papers throughout the United States. including materials that portrayed the corps in positive and negative terms.

Moreover, I analyzed the black press' coverage of the WAC to determine the similarities and differences between black newspapers and their white counterparts in reporting on female military service. In doing so I focused on the Philadelphia *Afro-American,* one of the top five "Negro newspapers" in terms of circulation during World War II. I also scanned articles on the WAC in the *Pittsburgh Courier,* the *Chicago Defender,* and in the black periodicals *Opportunity* and *The Crisis.*

In examining WAC policies concerning the sexual regulation of female soldiers and analyzing the Army framework for the sexual control of all military personnel, the records of the American Red Cross (RG 200, NA) and the Office of Community War Services, Social Protection Division (RG 215, NA) were invaluable. The American Red Cross was one of the major organizations providing support and services to Army personnel (including Wacs) during the war. These records illustrate the key role played by the ARC in developing maternity programs for pregnant servicewomen and ARC officials' roles overseas as mediators between pregnant local civilian women and the GI fathers of their children. As such, these records were crucial to my understanding of Army attitudes and policies toward the non-U.S., civilian women with whom male soldiers associated, and illustrate the Army's emphasis on the "protection" of male soldiers from civilian women's claims, not the shared responsibility of these GIs for civilian women's predicaments. This Army paradigm of "protection" not "responsibility," was bolstered by civilian and military social protection programs aimed at decreasing the spread of venereal disease among male soldiers by controlling civilian women's sexuality and is clearly illuminated in the records of the Office of Community War Services.

Colonel Oveta Culp Hobby, who served as the director of the WAC throughout World War II, was the key figure in formulating both formal and informal WAC policies and practices. As a result, her papers, located at the Library of Congress, including correspondence with male and female military leaders, prominent civilian women, and Wacs, as well as her responses to both criticisms and suggestions from civilian and military sources, illustrate her own perspective on the struggles of the women's corps and individual service women during the war.

I explored the holdings of the Bethune Museum and Archives to better understand the situations and perspectives of African-American women on women's participation in the Women's Army Corps. The museum's archives include the records of the National Council of Negro Women (NCNW), which detail the tensions between Colonel Hobby and NCNW President Mary McLeod Bethune over the WAC's segregation policies, and the ways in which Bethune's organization acted as both support and advocate for black service women during the war. Further, the Dovey Johnson Roundtree Papers, also at the Bethune Museum, provided information on one black WAC officer's role within the corps and her attitudes toward the position of African-American women in the WAC during the war.

The greatest drawback of institutional and public sources is the difficulty they present in attempting to draw out the attitudes and opinions of individual Wacs on their military service. To provide some balance I used oral histories and memoirs, and explored records focusing on enlisted women who made up the majority of women serving during World War II. The personnel records located at the Air Force Historical Research Center, Maxwell Air Force Base, Montgomery, Alabama, provided me with much needed data on enlisted women, as well as general information on Wacs attached to the Army Air Forces (AAF) during the war and a large amount of material on Wacs stationed in Europe during the war.

I also developed a twelve-page questionnaire and distributed it to WAC veterans of World War II. I sent out a total of 350 questionnaires and received 95 responses. My contact list in this project represents a snowball sample, in that I sent out questionnaires to several individual ex-Wacs and to the WAC Veterans Association, who then forwarded the questionnaires to others who served during the war or provided me with additional contact names. As a result, the potential for generalizing from this sample is limited. However, the responses increased my ability to present a more complex picture of WAC life than that gained solely through institutional records. I supplemented these questionnaires with five oral history interviews.

In addition, the WAC Museum collection included oral history tapes of World War II WAC leaders and unpublished memoirs of enlisted Wacs. I also examined several published memoirs including Charity Adams Earley's One Woman's Army: A Black Officer Remembers the WAC (College Station: Texas A & M Press, 1989) and Doris Samford, Ruffles and Drums (Boulder, Colo.: Pruett Press, 1966). I also took advantage of the recent publication of several collections of letters from military women during the war, Anne Bosanko Green, One Woman's War: Letters Home from the Women's Army Corps, 1944–1946 (St. Paul: Minnesota Historical Society Press, 1989) and Judy Barrett Litoff and David C. Smith, We're In This War, Too: World War II Letters from American Women in Uniform (New York: Oxford University Press, 1994).

Except for marginal treatment in larger works exploring women's work in the civilian labor force, secondary historical literature for this project is in short supply. Ex-Wac Mattie Treadwell's official history of the Women's Army Corps, The United States Army in World War II, Special Studies, The Women's Army Corps, is the only historical work focusing solely on women's service in the WAC during the war. Published in 1954 by the Office of the Chief of Military History, Treadwell's work is important in offering a detailed description of the auxiliary and the WAC, and the respective struggles of each for legitimacy and respect.

Notes

Prologue

1. Anthony Rotundo, *American Manhood: Transformations in Masculinity from the Revolution to the Modern Era* (New York: Basic Books, 1993), 284–293.

2. As quoted in "Our Women in the Desert," *Newsweek*, September 10, 1990, p. 23.

3. For a discussion of this point see Cynthia Enloe, *Does Khaki Become You?: The Militarization of Women's Lives* (London: Pandora Press, 1983, 1988), pp. xvii–xviii.

4. The growth of women's military history as a field is evident in the creation of a scholarly journal devoted solely to issues of women's past military experience, *Minerva*, and the increasing number of works analyzing women's military particpation. For example see: Jeanne Holm, *Women in the Military: An Unfinished Revolution* (Novato, Calif.: Presidio Press, 1982, 1993); Judtih Hicks Stiehm, *Arms and the Enlisted Woman* (Philadelphia: Temple University Press, 1989). That said, there has been little work done on military women within the historiography of World War II. Both D'Ann Campbell, *Women at War with America: Private Lives in a Patriotic Era* (Cambridge: Harvard Publishers, 1982), and Susan Hartmann, *The Homefront and Beyond: American Women in the 1940s* (New York: Twayne, 1982), address women's military service during World War II within their work on women's participation in that war more generally. Mattie Treadwell's study of the WAC during the war remains the most comprehensive document to date on women's service within the United States Army. Although an incredible resource it remains trapped within its author's intent: to both defend women's military service and to create a blueprint for further use of women within the Army. Like other works, such as Holm's, it serves as a report of progress and setbacks without a full discussion or analysis of the gender, race, class, and sexual ideologies framing women's military service. The best works to date analyzing women's military experience and the military as a state institution are: Ruth Roach Pierson, *"They're Still Women After All": The Second World War and Canadian Womanhood* (Toronto, Ont.: McClelland and Stewart, 1986); Stiehm, *Arms and the Enlisted Woman*; and Enloe, *Does Khaki Become You?*

5. John D'Emilio and Estelle Freedman, *Intimate Matters: A History of Sexuality in America* (New York: Harper and Row, 1988), pp. 260, 288–89.

6. Lillian Faderman, *Odd Girls and Twilight Lovers: A History of Lesbian Life in Twentieth-Century America* (New York: Columbia University Press, 1991), pp. 123–25.

7. My understanding of the ways in which "repression" also functions to increase both discussions of lesbianism and the possibilities for women in same-sex relationships to identify themselves as lesbians has been greatly enhanced by the work of Michel Foucault. See Michel Foucault, *The History of Sexuality*, vol. 1: *An Introduction* (New York: Random House, 1980), pp. 15–50.

1. Creating a Women's Army

1. *Congressional Record*, 77th Congress, 1st sess. (March 17, 1942), 88, pt. 55:2682. File: Congressional Record (hereafter referred to as *Congressional Record*), Box 217, Series 55, RG 165, National Archives and Record Administration (hereafter referred to as NA).

2. *Congressional Record*, Appendix, Women's Army Auxiliary Corps, 77th Congress, 1st sess. (March 17, 1942). vol. 88, part 56: 2658–59. Rogers argued, "So far back as the first World War, when I was in England and France, I saw the need for such an adjunct to our military forces."

3. Ibid.

4. Ibid.

5. Constructions of "citizens" as those who are willing to take up arms in defense of country and die in such service date back to the American Revolution. For a discussion of the relationship between military service and citizenship during the early national period, see Linda Kerber, "May All Our Citizens Be Soldiers, and All Our Soldiers Citizens: The Ambiguities of Female Citizenship in the New Nation," in Joan R. Challinor and Robert L. Beisner, eds., *Arms At Rest: Peacemaking and Peacekeeping in American History* (Westport, Conn.: Greenwood Press, 1988), pp. 1–21; Charles Royster, *A Revolutionary People at War: The Continental Army and the American Character, 1776–1783* (Chapel Hill: University of North Carolina Press, 1979). See also Kathleen Jones, "Dividing the Ranks: Women and the Draft," in Jean Bethke Elshtain and Sheila Tobias, eds, *Women, Militarism, and War: Essays in History, Politics, and Social Theory* (Savage, Md.: Rowman and Littlefield, 1990), pp. 125–36.

6. For a discussion of the Women's Overseas Service League, see Leisa D. Meyer, "Miss Olgivy Finds Herself," pp. 77–85.

7. Lee Finkle, *Forum For Protest: The Black Press During World War II* (Cranbury, N.J.: Associated University Presses, 1975), pp. 61–66, 82, 84, 88–89. See also Bernard Nalty, *Strength for the Fight: A History of Black Americans in the Military* (New York: Free Press, 1986), pp. 29–46, 107–24, 141. As Bernard Nalty has argued, "Instead of assuming good will on the part of white authority, they sought to trade military service for measurable progress toward full citizenship." Black men's participation in the U.S. military was perceived by both themselves and the larger African-American community as crucial to black people's claims to full citizenship. The equation of military service with full citizenship, for example, was made by African-American men during the Civil War who believed that their service in the Union Army was an assertion of their

status as free citizens of the United States. Similarly, during World War I the service of black men in the military was deemed by the African-American community an irrefutable statement of the claim of black Americans to the rights and privileges due American citizens. After World War I many of these "claims" were negated when some uniformed African-American men were subjected to ridicule and physical violence, including lynchings. These incidents made clear that military service in and of itself was not sufficient to overturn entrenched racial hierarchies and grant African-Americans the rights and status of citizenship allocated to white servicemen. The violent reaction of some white people to black men in uniform, however, also demonstrated the perceptions of some that African-American military service might indeed threaten these hierarchies.

8. Susan Hartmann, *The Homefront and Beyond: American Women in the 1940s* (New York: Twayne, 1982): and Nalty, *Strength for the Fight*, pp. 29–46, 107–24, 141.

9. *Congressional Record*, p. 2682; cited in note 1.

10. For a discussion of Britain's women's auxiliaries, see Jenny Gould, "Women's Military Services in First World War Britain," in eds. Margaret Randolph Higonnet et al., *Behind the Lines: Gender and the Two World Wars* (New Haven: Yale University Press, 1987), pp. 114–25; and Diana Condell and Jean Liddiard, *Working for Victory? Images of Women in the First World War, 1914–1918* (London: Routledge and Kegan Paul, 1987), pp. 124–25.

For a discussion of American women's service with the American Expeditionary Forces in France, see Dorothy and Carl J. Schneider, *Into the Breach: American Women Overseas in World War I* (New York: Penguin Books, 1991), pp. 177–87; Mattie Treadwell, *The United States Army in World War II, Special Studies, The Women's Army Corps* (Washington, D.C.: Office of the Chief of Military History, 1954), pp. 6–7.

11. In fact Baker argued that "The enlistment of women in the military forces of the United States has never been seriously contemplated and such enlistment is considered unwise and highly undesirable." As quoted in Treadwell, p. 8. See also Schneider aand Schneider, *Into the Breach*, pp. 177–78.

12. For a discussion of the woman suffrage movement in the twentieth century, see Nancy Cott, *The Grounding of Modern Feminism*, (New Haven: Yale University Press, 1987).

13. Treadwell, *U.S. Army in World War II*, pp. 6–10, 13; Wesley Frank Craven and James Lea Cate, eds., *The Army Air Forces in World War II: Services Around the World*, vol. 7 (Chicago: University of Chicago Press, 1958), p. 504.

14. As quoted in Treadwell, pp. 10–11. For a discussion of female pacifism during World War I, see Barbara Jean Steinson, "Female Activism in World War I: The American Women's Peace, Suffrage, Preparedness, and Relief Movements," Ph.D. dissertation, University of Michigan, 1977.

15. The Army's new director of Women's Relations was supposed to secure the support of American women and in particular "powerful women's groups," for the War Department and convince women that the Army was "a progressive, socially minded human institution" that women voters should not "fanatically demand the dissolution of [as] a ruthless military machine." As quoted in Treadwell, pp. 10–11.

16. Ibid., pp. 10–12.

17. In 1928 the Army also appointed a chief Army planner for a women's corps. The models developed by Maj. Everett Hughes, like those of Anita Phipps, suggested that women be formally accepted into the Army, and not granted only auxiliary status. However, his final designs, like those of Anita Phipps, were shelved until such time as a need for a women's corps was more pressing. As Treadwell notes, both Phipps' and Hughes' plans were "buried so deep in the files that they were recovered only after the WAAC was six months old and War Department planners had already made most of the mistakes he had predicted." Treadwell, pp. 13–15.

18. Treadwell, *U.S. Army in World War II*, pp. 15–16.

19. Ibid., pp. 16–17.

20. Ibid., p. 17.

21. Ibid., p. 18.

22. Rogers later remarked, "In the beginning, I wanted very much to have these women taken in as part of the Army. . . . I wanted them to have the same rate of pension and disability allowance. I realized that I could not secure that. The War Department was very unwilling to have these women as a part of the Army." As quoted in Treadwell, p. 18. The full text of her remarks can be found in the *Congressional Record*, p. 2657; cited in note 1.

23. In a letter to the House majority leader, Marshall noted: "I would like to say that I regard the passage of this bill at an early date as of considerable importance. In general, we have secured most of the legislation required for the complete mobilization of the Army so that we can go ahead with its development and definitely plan for the future. However, we lack Congressional authority for the establishment of a Women's Army Auxiliary Corps, and as a result we can make no definite plans." Gen. George C. Marshall, chief of staff, U.S. Army, to Congressman John W. McCormack (D, Mass.), House majority leader, February 6, 1942, in *The Papers of George Catlett Marshall: "The Right Man for the Job" December 7, 1941–May 31, 1943*, vol. 3, eds. Larry I. Bland and Sharon Ritenour Stevens (Baltimore: Johns Hopkins University Press, 1991), p. 99.

24. Treadwell, *U.S. Army in World War II*, pp. 20–21.

25. Susan Ware, *Beyond Suffrage: Women in the New Deal* (Cambridge: Harvard University Press, 1981), pp. 126–28.

26. Ware, pp. 130–31; see also Treadwell, pp. 267–68; "Oveta Culp Hobby," File: Biographies, Box 209, Series 55, RG 165, NA.

27. Oveta Culp Hobby served as the parliamentarian of the Texas House of Representatives, 1925–31, and again 1939–43. "Oveta Culp Hobby," cited in note 26. See also James A. Clark with Weldon Hart, *The Tactful Texan: A Biography of Governor Will Hobby* (New York: Random House, 1958), pp. 176–203.

28. In the early 1950s, Oveta Hobby became increasingly active in national politics and helped organize the "Democrats for Eisenhower" during his presidential campaign in 1952. As a result of her support and his service with her during World War II, President Eisenhower made Oveta Hobby the first woman cabinet member of any Republican administration when he appointed her as secretary of the Department of Health, Education and Welfare in 1953. As a member of Eisenhower's cabinet, moreover, Hobby pressured a number of feminists appointed by Roosevelt to resign their positions. Hobby, for example, forced Jane Hoey out of her position with the Bureau

of Public Assistance, saying that Hoey held a "policy-making" position that should be filled by an appointee of the Republican administration. Ware, *Beyond Suffrage*, pp. 128, 147, 193n2; Phyllis J. Read and Bernard L. Witlieb, eds. *The Book of Women's Firsts* (New York: Random House, 1992), pp. 208–10. See also Clark, *The Tactful Texan*, pp. 176–203.

29. "Oveta Culp Hobby," cited in note 26.

30. Ibid. Among the groups included in the Advisory Council were the League of Women Voters, the American Association of University Women, the National Business and Professional Women's Clubs, and the National Council of Negro Women.

31. Treadwell, *U.S. Army in World War II*, pp. 28–29.

32. Memo to Secretary of War Stimson from Gen. George C. Marshall, Subject: Chief of WAAC, March 18, 1942, in *The Papers of George Catlett Marshall*, eds. Bland and Stevens, pp. 135–36.

33. Ibid., pp. 25–26.

34. One example of this is the way the House Rules Committee held up the WAAC bill for several weeks, prompting a frustrated aide of Gen. Marshall to remark that he "had never seen anything like it" in all his years of service. The committee eventually succumbed to Army and War Department pressure and sent it along for discussion in the full House, noting that they "dared not oppose their opinions to the Chief of Staff's on the matter of measures required for national defense." As quoted in Treadwell, p. 25.

35. Robert Westbrook, " 'I Want a Girl Just Like the Girl That Married Harry James': American Women and the Problem of Political Obligation in World War II," *American Quarterly* 42, no. 4 (December 1990): 603–6.

36. Ibid. See also Judith Stiehm, "Women, Men, and Military Service: Is Protection Necessarily a Racket?" in *Women, Power, and Policy*, ed. Ellen Boneparth (Oxford: Pergamon Press, 1982), pp. 287–291; see also Judith Hicks Stiehm, *Arms and the Enlisted Woman* (Philadelphia: Temple University Press, 1989), pp. 224–30. I am indebted to Judith Stiehm's work and Robert Westbrook's article for clarifying my thinking on the concept of reciprocity as a means of analyzing the gendered obligations of citizenship during World War II.

37. For example see the discussion in the *Congressional Record*, p. 2682; cited in note 1.

38. Ibid., p. 2668.

39. As Kathleen Jones has argued in her essay on female citizenship: "Women cannot become active in their own defense without either calling into question their identity as women or threatening the sexual iconography upon which the discourse [of citizenship] is based." Kathleen Jones, "Citizenship in a Woman-Friendly Polity," *Signs* 15, no. 4 (Summer 1990): 786.

40. For a discussion of the American fascination with British women's military service, see John Costello, *Love, Sex, and War: Changing Values, 1939–45* (London: William Collins, 1985), p. 61. For examples of the coverage of British women's military service by the American media, see "Women Man the Guns," *The American Magazine*, October 1941, pp. 14–15, 72–73; and "British Women" *Life*, August 4, 1941, pp. 70–80.

41. *Congressional Record*, p. 2660; cited in note 1. See also letter from Hobby to Rep. Edith Nourse Rogers, May 26, 1943, File: 000.7, Box 2, Series 54, RG 165, NA.

The chair of the House Committee on Military Affairs also clarified this position when he stated: "The reason the women of America are so strong for this bill is that it is one of their ways of protecting their home, which they know is their citadel." *Congressional Record*, 77th Congress, vol. 88, part 56, Extension of Remarks, March 17, 1942, p. 2670.

42. *Congressional Record*, Extension of Remarks, p. 2670; cited in note 41. A similar point was made by Congressman Robison (D, Ky.), who pointed out that women's service in the WAAC would be voluntary, not compulsory, and argued that there were "tens of thousands of women . . . who have *no dependents* [emphasis mine] . . . who will welcome this opportunity to be of service to the Nation." *Congressional Record*, ibid., p. A1166.

43. Treadwell, *U.S. Army in World War II*, pp. 15–21.

44. In discussing the work that women would perform, Rogers remarked that several "high-ranking officers of the Army" had informed her that the "one task enlisted men disliked the most was that of telephone operator. It is definitely a woman's work and men admittedly do not make good operators as a rule." *Congressional Record*, p. 2660; cited in note 1.

45. Ibid., p. 2670.

46. Congressman Hare (D, S.C.) began his statement against the bill, "I can appreciate the patriotism and ambition . . . of those favoring this proposition," and another adversary, Congressman Randolph (D, Va.) remarked, "Before I leave this House I want it clearly understood that I appreciate the fact that the women of America have stood side by side with the men of the country through its history." Ibid., pp. 2660–61, 2683.

47. See, for example, Congressman Robison's (D, Ky.) comments: "In the defense of our country and to insure victory there is some task that each one of us may perform, and the services of none can be more effective than those who love our country and are impelled by patriotic desire to volunteer his or her services to protect and defend it." *Congressional Record*, Extension of Remarks, p. A1166; cited in note 41. See also *Congressional Record*, pp. 2659–60, 2670; cited in note 1. The most difficult question for those against the bill to answer was that articulated by Senator Austin (R, Vt.) who remarked, "Are we to deny the patriotic, courageous, women of America the opportunity of participating in this war? It is as much their war as ours." *Congressional Record*, 77th Congress, vol. 88, part 90, Senate Bill No. 425 (May 1942), p. 4228.

48. *Congressional Record*, p. 2670; cited in note 1.

49. Ibid., p. 2681. See also Congresswoman Norton (D, N.J.), who contended that the "patriotic" women of the nation were wholeheartedly behind the bill and in response to a male member's opposition queried, "Does not the gentleman believe that the women of the country know about as much regarding this question as the men of the country do?" Ibid., pp. 2667, 2683.

50. Congressman Hoffman (R, Mich.) even claimed that he had heard several members of the House say that they would vote for the bill though they didn't actually believe it would help the war effort. Ibid., p. 2668–70; also *Congressional Record*, Senate Bill No. 425, p. 4226; cited in note 47.

51. *Congressional Record*, pp. 2668–70, cited in note 1; *Congressional Record*, Senate Bill No. 425, p. 4226, cited in note 47.

52. *Congressional Record*, pp. 2659, 2672–73, cited in note 1.

53. Ibid., p. 2666.

54. Ibid., p. 2672.

55. *Congressional Record*, Senate Bill No. 425, p. 4223.

56. Ibid., p. 4223. The amendment to grant Waacs the same benefits as male sol-diers was rejected by a two to one majority. For a full reading of this debate, see *Congressional Record*, pp. 2673–80, cited in note 1.

57. For a discussion of the ways in which the Army denigrated African-American servicemen's participation during World War I and World War II, see Nalty, *Strength for the Fight*, pp. 107–24, 168–77.

58. Senator Johnson's (D, Colo.) proposed amendment would have explicitly pro-hibited any discrimination on the grounds of "race or color" within the WAAC. *Congressional Record*, Senate Bill No. 425, p. 4223.

59. Ibid., p. 4222.

60. In her testimony before the Senate Committee on Military Affairs, Mrs. Manikin, president of the Women's Overseas Service League, stated that when sta-tioned in areas with large "colored" and white populations, "white women should serve in the white section and the colored women in the colored section." Her opin-ion was seconded by Brig. General Hilldring who, speaking on behalf of the War Department, stated that "the War Department intends, and has so stated in both hear-ings, to recognize colored units for service at appropriate stations." Ibid., p. 4223.

61. The proposed amendment to the WAAC bill was withdrawn when Senator Austin (R, Vt.) claimed that passing the amendment would require sending the bill back to the House for agreement and would most likely result in a lengthy post-ponement of the measure's passage. Despite his acquiescence Johnson voted against the version of the WAAC bill. One possible explanation for his no vote is that he did not consider a verbal guarantee that the Army would not practice racial discrimina-tion sufficient to insure black women's equal treatment within the WAAC. Another possible scenario, however, is that he offered the initial amendment, and demanded verbal assurance concerning racial equity, to either delay passage of the bill or kill it entirely by raising the specter of racial mixing within the women's corps. Ibid., pp. 4223–24, 4229.

62. *Congressional Record*, p. 2684, cited in note 1; *Congressional Record*, Senate Bill No. 425, p. 4229; cited in note 47. Treadwell, pp. 44–45. The final vote in the House was 249 yeas, 86 nays, and 96 abstentions. In the Senate the final vote was 38 yeas, 27 nays, and 31 abstentions. In both the House and the Senate Democrats and Republicans were fairly evenly divided among the yeas and nays. In other words there was no significant difference by party in how members of Congress voted on this bill.

63. "Catholics v. Waac's," *Time*, June 15, 1942, p. 39.

64. Laura McEnaney, "Women and the America First Movement During WWII," M.A. thesis, University of Wisconsin/Madison, 1990.

65. "No Babies for the WAACs?" Another interesting cartoon showed a service-woman in uniform standing underneath a waterfall, her hand upraised as if to stop the water's flow; on the surface of the waterfall was inscribed in capital letters "BIRTHRATE." All in File: Newspaper Clippings, WAAC 1942, Box 3, Oveta Culp Hobby Papers, Library of Congress. Hereafter referred to as Hobby Papers, LC.

66. See, for example, "Army's Most Unusual Rookies Are 'Processed' Into WAACS," *Newsweek*, July 17, 1942, pp. 29–30; " 'Major' Hobby's WAACS," *Time*, May 25, 1942, p. 72, and "Waacs First Muster," *Time*, June 8, 1942, pp. 71–72. For an additional perspective on the relationship between the WAAC and the media, see Ann Allen, "The News Media and the WAAC: Protagonists for a Cause," *Military Affairs* 50, no. 2 (April 1986): 77–83.

67. "Army's Most Unusual Rookies Are 'Processed' Into WAACS," pp. 29–30.

68. File: Cartoons/Humor, WAC Reference Files, WAC Museum, Fort McClellan, Anniston, Ala.

69. "War Women," July 21, 1942, *Racine (Wisc.) Journal-Times*, and Rowene Byers, "WAAC Training to Keep 'Em Fit but Feminine," June 28, 1942, *Washington, D.C. Times-Herald*, File: Newspaper Clippings, Box 8, Hobby Papers, LC. See also File: Miscellaneous, Box 1, Hobby Papers, LC. See also Ethel Mocklen's exclusive to the *Brooklyn Eagle*. Mocklen was a representative of the USO in New York City and was one of a group of thirty women officials and executives of national organizations who visited Fort Des Moines, Iowa, and Camp Crowder, Missouri. She wrote, "they are doing their work with military precision, but managing to remain wholly feminine, too." File: USO, Box 15, Series 54, RG 165, NA.

70. File: Clippings, Box 3, Hobby Papers, LC.

71. In another series, a "rough looking" WAC officer sat at her desk with a scared male private in her lap taking dictation. Dave Breger, *Private Breger Abroad* and Phillips, "Glory Hallelujah," both in File: Cartoons/Humor, WAC Reference Files, WAC Museum, Fort McClellan, Anniston, Ala.

72. File: Cartoons/Humor, cited in note 71.

73. Walter White, secretary of NAACP to Mary McLeod Bethune, National Council of Negro Women (NCNW), June 19, 1942; Jesse Daniel Ames to Walter White, June 15, 1942; Walter White to Jesse Daniel Ames, June 19, 1942; File: 513 Correspondence W, Box 36, Series 5, NCNW Papers, Bethune Museum and Archives, Washington, D.C. See also Treadwell, *U.S. Army in World War II*, pp. 58–59.

74. Mary McLeod Bethune to Mrs. Harriet B. Hall concerning segregation at Fort Des Moines, November 10, 1942. Bethune writes, "There is only one thing I can say regarding segregation there—that I never have and never will give my consent to segregation at Des Moines or any where else. . . . Nobody is more grieved than I at the growing tendency toward any segregated set-up at Des Moines." See also Jeanetta Welch Brown, executive secretary, NCNW, to Charles P. Howard, general manager, Howard News Syndicate, September 29, 1943; she writes, "We feel that any move which will make permanent the policy of segregation is not in keeping with our present day idea of full integration." File: 237 Correspondence H, Box 14, Series 5, NCNW Papers, Bethune Museum and Archives. See also Mary McLeod Bethune for NCNW to Hobby circa November 1943; File 291.2, Box 49, Series 54, RG 165, NA.

75. Finkle, *Forum for Protest*, pp. 61–66, 82, 84, 88–89.

76. For a discussion of this point, see Paula Giddings, *When and Where I Enter . . . The Impact of Black Women on Race and Sex in America* (New York: William Morrow, 1984), pp. 231–60. See also Alice Kessler-Harris, *Out to Work: A History of Wage-Earning Women in the United States* (New York: Oxford University Press, 1982), pp.

273–99, and Gerda Lerner, *The Majority Finds Its Past: Placing Women in History* (New York: Oxford University Press, 1979), pp. 63–82.

77. For an example of this column see Charles P. Howard, "At Home and Abroad with the WAACs," *Philadelphia Afro-American*, January 2, 1943, p. 16. This feature ran in a majority of the issues of the *Afro-American* during the war and generally headlined the section of the paper called "The Feminine Front." For examples of the African-American press criticizing the WAAC/WAC's Jim Crow policies, see *Philadelphia Afro-American*, March–December 1943; *The Crisis*, February 1943; *The Opportunity*, 1943–1945; File: Scrapbook, *Headlines and Pictures: A Monthly Negro News Review*, Box 2, Series 54, RG 165, NA; "Turn Down Negro Wacs for Overseas Service," *Chicago Defender* (December 1943) and excerpts from the *Ohio News* (December 1943), Dovey Johnson Roundtree Papers, Bethune Museum and Archives.

78. Mrs. Bethune Endorses WAACs, File: 535, Box 38. See also Bethune to Mrs. Harriet B. Hall, Boston, concerning her opinion on segregation at Fort Des Moines, November 10, 1942, File: 237, Box 14; Jeanetta Welch Brown, executive secretary, NCNW, to Charles P. Howard, general manager, Howard News Syndicate, concerning segregation at Fort Des Moines, September 29, 1943, File: 230, Box 14; Major General J. A. Ulio, adjutant general to Mary McLeod Bethune, concerning the Army's general practice of segregation, September 21, 1944, File: 67, Box 4—all in Series 5, NCNW Papers, Bethune Museum and Archives.

See also National Non-Partisan Council of Public Affairs of AKA Sorority to Secretary of War Henry Stimson concerning planned segregation of the WAAC organization, May 17, 1942, File: Box 10, Series 54, RG 165, NA.

79. Treadwell, pp. 19–20. For a discussion of the different grades and ranks provided for women vis-à-vis men, see *Congressional Record*, p. 2659, cited in note 1. For example, alternate designation were used when referring to women occupying positions similar to those held by men: a female first officer was equivalent to a male captain, a female second officer to a male first lieutenant. In the enlisted grades there were three types of WAAC noncommissioned officers: first leader, leader, and junior leader, as opposed to the five grades available within the Army's regular structure. In addition, auxiliaries, who were roughly equivalent to Army privates, had the opportunity to qualify for specialist ratings that would improve their pay and status. For example, specialist: first, second, and third class.

80. As quoted in Treadwell, p. 120.

2. The Slander Campaign Against the WAC

1. John O'Donnell, *New York Daily News*, June 8, 1943. O'Donnell's column also appeared in the *Washington Times-Herald* and the *Chicago Tribune*. His columns on this topic were published on three successive days, June 8, 9, and 10, with his last word on the subject taking the form of an ambivalent retraction forced by War Department pressure. See also subsequent articles discussing the O'Donnell columns in other newspapers and periodicals, for example: "Waac Whispers," *Newsweek*, June 14, 1943, pp. 34–35; "Waac Rumors," *Newsweek*, June 21, 1943, p. 46.

2. John D'Emilio and Estelle Freedman, *Intimate Matters: A History of Sexuality in America* (New York: Harper and Row, 1988), pp. 260, 288–89. See also John

Costello, *Love, Sex, and War: Changing Values, 1939–45* (London: Williams Collins, 1985); Allan Berube, *Coming Out Under Fire: The History of Gay Men and Women in WWII* (New York: Free Press, 1990), p. 6; Elaine Tyler May, *Homeward Bound: American Families in the Cold War* (New York: Basic Books, 1988), p. 69.

3. Richard A. Koch, M.D., Chief, Division of VD, Department of Public Health, City and County of San Francisco, Calif. and Ray Lyman Wilbur, M.D., Chancellor, Stanford University, President American Social Hygiene Association (ASHA), "Promiscuity As A Factor in the Spread of VD," reprinted from the *Journal of Social Hygiene* 30 (December 1944); File: Films, Scripts, etc., Box 9, Series 37, RG 215, OCWS, NA.

4. Elaine Tyler May, *Homeward Bound*, pp. 69–71.

5. May, pp. 68–69. In fact, women's presence within the preeminently masculine environment of the Army gave rise to presumptions that they would embrace the same type of sexual freedoms and the same kind of active sexuality popularly associated with their male counterparts.

6. Christina Simmons, "Modern Sexuality and the Myth of Victorian Repression," in Kathy Peiss and Christina Simmons, eds., *Passion and Power: Sexuality in History* (Philadelphia: Temple University Press, 1989), pp. 157–59.

7. For a discussion of shifts in the contemporary discourse on birth control, see Linda Gordon, *Women's Body, Women's Right: Birth Control in America* (New York: Penguin Books, 1974, 1976), pp. 186–245.

8. For a discussion of this shift, see George Chauncey, "From Sexual Inversion to Homosexuality: The Changing Medical Conceptualization of Female Deviance," in Peiss and Simmons, eds., *Passion and Power*, pp. 105–7; Estelle Freedman, "The New Woman: Changing Views of Women in the 1920s," *Journal of American History* 61 (1974): 372–93; Carroll Smith Rosenberg, *Disorderly Conduct: Visions of Gender in Victorian America* (New York: Oxford University Press, 1985), pp. 245–96.

9. Simmons, "Modern Sexuality," pp. 167–71.

10. For an excellent discussion of how the ideal of passionlessness functioned as a sexual ideology promoted by feminists of the nineteenth century and its basis in the constructed categories of "good" versus "bad" women, see Ellen Carol Dubois and Linda Gordon, "Seeking Ecstasy on the Battlefield: Danger and Pleasure in Nineteenth-Century Feminist Sexual Thought," in *Pleasure and Danger: Exploring Female Sexuality*, ed. Carole S. Vance (London: Routledge and Kegan Paul, 1984), pp. 31–49.

11. Patricia Hill Collins, *Black Feminist Thought: Knowledge, Consciousness, and the Politics of Empowerment* (New York: Unwin Hyman, 1990), p. 177; Kathy Peiss, *Cheap Amusements: Working Women and Leisure in New York City, 1880–1920* (Philadelphia: Temple University Press, 1986)

12. See Oral History of Colonel Mary A. Halleran, May 1979, Tape # VT 79.02 #8, WAC Oral History Program (WAC Foundation), WAC Museum, Fort McClellan, Anniston, Ala. See also Report, June 25, 1943, Advisory Council Meeting Washington, D.C., p. 6, File: 522, Box 37, Series 5, Records of the National Council of Negro Women, 1935–1976, Bethune Museum and Archives; and Charity Adams Earley, *One Woman's Army: A Black Officer Remembers the WAC* (College Station: Texas A & M University Press, 1989), p. 70.

13. D'Emilio and Freedman, *Intimate Matters*, pp. 262–63. For a discussion of the new sexual discourses as social control mechanisms see Simmons, "Modern Sexuality," pp. 157–77.

14. This book does not take on the subject of female military nurses serving with and in the Army. However, women as caretakers have often had a place on or near the battlefield as nurses, but because this was an eminently "female" pursuit highly differentiated from the masculine "warrior" culture, military nurses did not threaten constructions of "soldier" as male or military service as the obligation of male, not female citizens. Women served as nurses or matrons with the U.S. Army throughout the eighteenth and nineteenth centuries and in 1901 received official recognition when the Army Nurse Corps was established. The enrollment of women as nurses within the Army in 1901 was met with some initial resistance, but it soon faded for several reasons. First, nursing was acceptable as a "woman's" occupation. Second, though the Medical Corps was part of the Army, its members were not considered soldiers. Third, nurses were granted only "relative rank," meaning that they had authority only in relation to one another and no power over men, thus having no real place within the military hierarchy. Although this book does not deal directly with the Army Nurse Corps, military nurses' battle to be granted full membership within the Army Medical Corps is another aspect of women's attempts to gain acceptance within the U.S. military. Although not stigmatized in the same manner as women who gained admittance into the military itself, nurses struggled both for official recognition of their work as citizens, and for benefits and rights comparable to those granted military men.

For a discussion of female nurses during the late nineteenth and early twentieth centuries, see Leisa Meyer, "Miss Olgivy Finds Herself: American Women's Service Overseas During WWI," Master's thesis, University of Wisconsin-Madison, 1986, pp. 28–55. On female nurses during World War I, see Carl and Dorothy Schneider, *Into the Breach: American Women's Service Overseas in World War I* (New York: Penguin Books, 1991). For a brief summary of the service of nurses during World War II and their struggle for rank, see Phillip A. Kalisch and Margaret Scobey, "Female Nurses in American Wars: Helplessness Suspended for the Duration," *Armed Forces and Society* 9, no. 2 (1983): 215–44; Phillip A. Kalisch, "How Army Nurses Became Officers," *Nursing Research* 25, no. 1 (May–June 1976): 64–77. See also Julia Flikke, *Nurses in Action: The Story of the Army Nurse Corps* (New York: Lippincott, 1943).

The most useful coverage of women's work with the American military historically is Maj. General Jeanne Holm, USAF (Ret.), *Women in the Military: An Unfinished Revolution* (Novato, Calif.: Presidio Press, 1993; rev. ed. 1982).

15. Cynthia Enloe, *Does Khaki Become You? The Militarization of Women's Lives* (London: Pandora Press, 1983, 1988), pp. 1–6. For a discussion of one woman's role with the military during the Civil War, see Susie King Taylor, *A Black Woman's Civil War Memoirs: Reminiscences of My Life in Camp with the 33rd U.S. Colored Troops, Late 1st South Carolina Volunteers* (New York: Marcus Wiener, 1988). See also Lynda Grant De Pauw, "Women in Combat: The Revolutionary War Experience," *Armed Forces and Society* 7, no. 2 (Winter 1981): 210.

16. As feminist scholar Cynthia Enloe has observed, the very fact that "she was a woman who allegedly *chose* to make her life among 'rough' men was presumed proof enough of her loose character." Enloe also argues that the blanket labeling of all women

attached to revolutionary armies as camp followers meant that a military commander who "wanted to rid himself of women in his trains could claim that camp followers were fundamentally nothing more than whores. Furthermore, they could be replaced by other women when the need again arose." Enloe, pp. 2–4. For information on the nineteenth-century military and the "camp-follower" designation, see Patricia Y. Stallard, *Glittering Misery: The Dependents of the Indian Fighting Army, 1850–1890* (San Rafael, Calif.: Presidio Press, 1978); and Edward M. Coffman, *The Old Army: A Portrait of the American Army in Peacetime, 1784–1898* (New York: Oxford University Press, 1986). Also for information on the relationship between the military and prostitutes during this period, see Anne M. Butler, *Daughters of Joy, Sisters of Misery: Prostitutes in the American West* (Champaign: University of Illinois Press, 1987), pp. 126, 135, 145–46.

17. Deborah Samson passed as Robert Shirtliffe during the Revolutionary War, fighting for the 4th Massachusetts Regiment, while Lucy Brewer, the "first woman marine," served on the USS *Constitution* during the War of 1812 as George Brewer. Perhaps the most colorful cross-dressing soldier was Loreta Velasques, who during the Civil War pasted on a moustache in order to pass as Lt. Harry T. Buford and commanded a Confederate Cavalry unit. Holm, *Women in the Military*, pp. 18–21. See also Julie Wheelwright, *Amazons and Military Maids: Women Who Dressed as Men in Pursuit of Life, Liberty, and Happiness* (London: Pandora Press, 1989).

18. Wheelwright, pp. 75, 132–35.

19. Ibid., p. 155.

20. I am indebted to Cynthia Enloe's work, which enabled me to make these connections between the military's dependence on women and its marginalization of them as soldiers. See Enloe, *Does Khaki Become You?* pp. 1–17.

21. Mattie Treadwell, *The United States Army in World War II, Special Studies, The Women's Army Corps* (Washington, D.C.: Office of the Chief of Military History, 1954), pp. 113–15.

22. Testifying before the Senate Committee on Military Affairs, Marshall noted, "I am now certain that the women's organization will be of great value to the military service." Speaking in favor of the conversion bill he went on to cite the needs to simplify WAAC operations in order to improve efficiency and remedy potential injustices and inequalities within the WAAC as the chief reasons why Congress should pass the bill. Treadwell, pp. 117–19.

23. Letter to Mrs. Gold (mother of a Waac), June 9, 1943. File: Rumors, Box 192, Series 55, RG 165, NA.

24. Letter from Cpl. Badgett to Cpl. Helen Stroude, August 11, 1943; see also Letter from 1st Lt. Roland to Sgt. Ray Coley caught by Base Censor, December 2, 1943. File: Rumors, Box 192, Series 55, RG 165, NA.

25. Memo for director, War Department, BPR, re: Problems and Deterrents in Connection with WAC Recruiting, February 18, 1944, "Early Problems, July 1942–April 1943," Box 64, Series 54, RG 165, NA. See also Report filed by 1st Officer Treila M. Welch, Inspection of 4th and 8th Service Commands (June 1943) and Report of 1st Officer D. Myer on 802d WAAC, Columbus Army Air Base, Columbus, Miss., and Col. Nostrande, Report of Rumors, Fort Ethan Allan, Vt., Box 190/2, Series 55, RG 165, NA. See also Report on Rumors, Headquarters Recruiting and Induction, Harrisburg, Pa., July 3, 1943, File: Rumors, Box 192, Series 55, RG 165, NA. In this

report the officer notes: "Attempts to trace these rumors have failed, but it is believed that they are not without foundation and are the result of some question on the part of officers as to the advisability of utilizing women to do the work of soldiers, and opposition on the part of some enlisted men who preferred their present assignments rather than combat duty." See also File: Study of the WAC in the ETO, vol. 1, sec. 5 and 7, Box 502.101–3, 502.101–11 (1943–45) ETO, Air Force Historical Research Center, Maxwell Air Force Base, Montgomery, Ala.

26. Earley, *One Woman's Army*, p. 187.

27. Memo to director, WAAC, from 1st Officer Martha E. Eskridge, Hq. branch officer, Special Services Division, Los Angeles, File: WAAC Film SWPA 062.2, January 22, 1943; Box 9, Series 54, RG 165, NA; File: What the Soldier Thinks of the WAC, Report no. B-80, Copy no. 2, December 10, 1943, Research Branch Morale Services Division, Army Service Forces, Box 8, Series 54, RG 165, NA; Report no. B-50, Attitudes of 348 Enrolled Women in WAAC, Special Services Division, Research Branch, Army Service Forces, July 7, 1943, Box 991, RG 330, NA.

28. File: Young and Rubicam, "A National Study of Public Opinion Toward the WAC," Gallup Poll, Prepared for the U.S. Army by the Research Department, Young and Rubicam, Inc., Spring 1944. Box 188, Series 55, RG 165, NA.

29. Report of Rumors from Seventh Service Command, Army Service Forces, Col. Jacob J. Gerhardt, director, Personnel Division, 1st Officer Mary S. Bell, WAAC staff director, reporting, July 9, 1943, File: Rumors, Box 192, Series 55, RG 165, NA.

30. Letter from Mr. John Warren to Commander Neil B. Wolcott, June 11, 1943; File: Rumors, Box 192, Series 55, RG 165, NA.

31. For example, at Fort Riley, Kansas, soldiers were under the impression that Waacs were assigned to posts only to pleasure soldiers and were "glorified prostitutes and issued rubbers." Report of Rumors from 7th Service Command, cited note 29.

32. Letter from AFC Annie L. Dishough, Fort Des Moines, Iowa, to WAAC Recruiting and Induction Station, Houston, Texas, reply to letter of June 19, 1943. File: Rumors, Box 192, Series 55, RG 165, NA.

33. Report of Rumors from 7th Service Command, cited note 29.

34. Cpl. Vic Herman, *Winnie the WAC*, Foreword by Carole Landis (Philadelphia: David McKay), WAC Museum, Fort McClellan, Anniston, Ala.

35. WAAC Recruiting Station, Baltimore, Md., Reports of Rumors and Occurrences, July 6, 1943, Box 92, Series 54, RG 165, NA.

36. List of Rumors Submitted, 3d Officer Alta R. Joffee, Recruiting and Enrollment Station, Roanoke, Va., June 23, 1943, Box 92, Series 54, RG 165, NA.

37. It is important to note that while the rumor campaign stretching from June 1943 to early 1944 marked the height of the negative publicity surrounding the WAAC/WAC negative portrayals of service women did not cease in 1944, but continued throughout World War II and into the postwar period. For example, see Mrs. Ray Thurman to Hobby concerning Wac drunkenness and heterosexual immorality. March 16, 1945, Box 21, Series 54, RG 165, NA. See also Maj. Chance (WAC) and Mr. Marples (phone transcript) concerning *Time* editorial for that month (October 1945) in which Mr. Bradley, head of the Office of Surplus Property in the Department of Commerce, claimed that the office had 10 million pounds of contraceptive jelly and then implied that this was issued to Wacs. Box 21, Series 54, RG 165, NA.

38. Hon. Ed. C. Johnson (Senate) to Hobby, April 30, 1943; and Mrs. R. L. Loucks to Hobby, June 16, 1943, both concerning rumors they had heard of the public behavior of Waacs stationed in Hattiesburg, Miss.; Box 14, Series 54, RG 165, NA.

39. Ruth Schreiber of the Women's Overseas Service League to Hobby, December 6, 1943. Box 14, Series 54, RG 165, NA.

40. Reports of Rumors: Hq. Recruiting District Kansas, Kansas City; Hq. Minneapolis Recruiting District, Minneapolis, 2d Officer WAAC, Temporary Recruiting Duty in Minnesota; Harrisburg Armed Forces Recruiting and Induction District, 1st Officer Lovella M. Jones, assistant WAAC recruiting officer, July 3, 1943; File: Rumors, Box 192, Series 55, RG 165. See also Syracuse Rumor Clinic to Hobby, March 10, 1943; Getrude Breslau Fuller, state chair National Defense Activities Pennsylvania Federation of Democratic Women, to Hobby, May 26, 1943. Box 13, Series 54, RG 165, NA.

41. Jack Kofoed, *Miami Florida News*, May 20, 1942, in Center for Military History Manuscript Files, Mattie Treadwell's Background Files, Box 9, RG 319, NA.

42. Mrs. Walter Ferguson on the appointment of Oveta Culp Hobby as director, WAAC, July 13, 1942, File: Newspaper Clippings, WAAC 21–40, Box 8, Hobby Papers, LC.

43. See, for example, Reports on Rumors: Hq. Minneapolis, Harrisburg, cited note 40. See also Reports on Rumors, 5th Service Command, Fort Hayes, Columbus, Ohio, 1st Officer Helen Y. Hedekin to Hobby, July 10, 1943; Box 92, Series 54, RG 165, NA.

44. Esther Newton, "The Mythic Mannish Lesbian: Radclyffe Hall and the New Woman," in *Signs: The Lesbian Issue*, eds. Estelle B. Freedman, Barbara C. Gelpi, Susan L. Johnson, Kathleen M. Weston (Chicago: University of Chicago Press: 1982, 1983, 1984, 1985), p. 16.

45. Joan Younger, Interview with Colonel Oveta Culp Hobby, *Ladies Home Journal*, June 2, 1952, File: *Ladies Home Journal*, Article on WAC, 1952, Box 9, Hobby Papers, LC.

46. Mattie Treadwell, *The U.S. Army in World War II*, p. 625.

47. *Congressional Record*, 78th Congress, vol. 89, part 97, May 27, 1943, p. 4995.

48. Ibid., p. 4998.

49. Ibid., pp. 5001–2.

50. Ibid., pp. 4996, 4999.

51. Ibid., p. 4999.

52. Ibid., pp. 4996–5000.

53. Ibid., p. 5002.

54. One member opposed Vincent's amendment on the grounds that "We are giving women the responsibility, as an integral part of the Army, to perform military services and no valid reason has been given that should cause us to deny them any benefits or any privileges that we give the armed forces of the U.S." Ibid., pp. 4996, 5001–2.

55. This change in the Army's bill was recommended by the House Military Affairs Committee. Chair of the Committee, Andrew May (D, Ky.), reported, "We do not provide in this measure that the members of the WAC may have the benefits of the service men's dependency allowances, but we do provide that they shall be entitled to all other benefits and privileges of other members of the Army of the U.S." Ibid., p. 4995.

56. Ibid., pp. 4996, 5001–3.

57. The amendment, though passing the House, was later removed from the bill in conference when Army and War department officials argued that it was necessary to include women under all military regulations with no exceptions. Nevertheless, Army administrators demonstrated their own understanding of the threat presented by women's eligibility for soldiers' dependency allotments. After the WAC bill was passed on May 27, 1943, Army officials took great pains to announce publicly the parameters of female soldiers' access to this benefit; under no circumstances would husbands of Wacs be eligible to receive any dependency benefits. *Congressional Record*, Conference Report, 78th Congress, part 595 (June 24, 1943). See also Treadwell, pp. 220–21, for a discussion of this and other amendments she terms "narrowly averted."

For a statement of Army policy on dependency allotments for Wacs, see Press Release, "Allowance for WAC Dependents Can Be Paid in Certain Cases," October 13, 1943, File: Press Releases, Box 216, Series 55, RG 165, NA. Despite the heated opposition to the measure the WAC bill passed the House by a wide margin, 260 yeas, 39 nays, and 132 abstentions. While some Southern Democrats did support the measure, the vocal opposition of other Southern Democrats and their resistance to the idea of women as soldiers is reflected in the fact that of the 39 nays on the WAC bill, 29 were cast by Democrats from southern areas, including Mississippi, Georgia, Texas, South Carolina, Alabama, North Carolina, and Kentucky. See *Congressional Record*, 78th Congress, vol. 89, part 97 (May 27, 1943), p. 5004.

58. "Waac Whispers," June 14, 1943, pp. 34–35 and "Waac Rumors," June 21, 1943), p. 46. See also Treadwell, pp. 200–206 for a list and description of the rumors surrounding the Corps at this time. The *Newsweek* quote comes from House members discussion of the WAC bill which granted women full status in the regular Army. See *Congressional Record*, 78th Congress, vol. 78, part 97 (May 27, 1943), pp. 4998–5000.

59. These types of statements were widespread. One example is: "WACs in the European Division, ATC, June 1944–August 1945, Historical Record Report," January 31, 1945, File: WACs in the European Division, Box 308.04-1-308.072, Air Force Historical Research Center, Maxwell Air Force Base, Montgomery, Ala. This report discusses in depth the function of WAC units in terms of morale, especially overseas. One male officer remarked: "Although the Wacs resented most emphatically either the statement or the insinuation that they were primarily a morale factor overseas, the longer they remained overseas the more willing they were to agree that . . . simply because they were American women (they were) something more than mere manpower," p. 108.

See also Box 502.101-3-502.101-11 (1943–1945), File: Study of the WAC in the ETO, vol. 1, section 5: Military Discipline, Courtesy, Justice, p. 38; Air Force Historical Research Center, Maxwell Air Force Base, Montgomery, Ala.

60. Memo to Gen. Somervell from Brig. General W. B. Smith, August 3, 1942, File: 320.0 75th and 76th Post Headquarters Companies (August 18, 1942) (1) Sec. 1, Box 79, Series 54, RG 165, NA; Colored Requisitions, June 30, 1943, Box 43; Memo to Col. Catron re: Negro WAAC companies for duty with 92d Division, January 5, 1943, File: Activation of post hq. companies and photographic lab companies, Aerial 320.2 1-1-43 (1) Sec. 2, Box 74; all in Series 54, RG 165, NA. See also Report of AAFTC, Sioux Falls, S.D., on status of requisitions for colored Waacs, July 1943, File: Assignment and Classification, Box 190, Series 55, RG 165, NA.

61. Treadwell, *The U.S. Army in World War II*, pp. 597–98.

62. James McDonald, "Sending of Women to Germany Urged," *New York Times*. December 5, 1944; "WACS, ATS Plenty Angry at New 'Role,' " December 8, 1944; Letter to Hobby from Miss Gertrude M. Puelicher, National Federation of Press Women, Inc., December 16, 1944; Letter to Miss Puelicher from Lt. Colonel Jessie Rice, executive, WAC, December 26, 1944; Box 14, Series 54, RG 165, NA.

63. Dr. K. F. Scott to Hobby, re: WTIC Radio Program, Hartford, Conn., January 14, 1945, and Memo for Capt. Chance, Office of Director from Col. E. M. Kirby, chief, Radio Branch, re: radio program, January 19, 1945. In this memo Col. Kirby noted that the station manager apologized and was willing to retract but also stated in his defense that the press carried a similar article which supported the broadcaster opinions. File: 330.14, Box 91, Series 54, RG 165, NA.

64. Censorship Division, 1st Lt. Roland to Sgt. Ray Coley, December 2, 1943, File: Rumors, Box 192, Series 55, RG 165, NA.

65. Confidential cable, no. 2384, Chief of Staff Gen. George Marshall to Gen. MacArthur, December 30, 1943; Confidential cable, no. C-1760, February 16, 1944; Restricted cable, No. 4292, Gen. Ulio, TAG to CINC SWPA, Brisbane, Australia, February 17, 1944; Secret cable, Brisbane from Military Attaché Melbourne to MILID M90, February 24, 1944. In sum these cables are requests for commissioning three Australian women directly into the WAC and the permission to do so from Chief of Staff George Marshall. All in Box 26, Series 54, RG 165, NA.

66. Undated Letter from J. C. Calhoun to WAC Director Hobby, Box 26, Series 54, RG 165, NA.

67. For a discussion of the Army investigation into the relationship between Lt. Gen. Kenny and Mrs. (Capt.) Elaine Bessemer Clark, see Transcript of telephone conversations, June 6, 9, 12, 1945, between Gen. Weckerling and Col. Hammond, WDC, in which Col. Hammond makes clear that the investigation showed a definite "mistress connection" between Lt. General Kenny and Capt. Clark. Also Transcript of telephone conversation, July 1, 1945, between Col. Hammond and Lt. Colonel Earman, G-2 Secretariat. All in Box 26, Series 54, RG 165, NA.

68. SWPA 320.2 Memo for assistant chief of staff, G-1, from Hobby, re: Commissioning of WAC officers from civil life, February 25, 1944, File: 314.7, History of Organization of WAC in U.S. After January 1, 1944, Box 56, Series 54, RG 165, NA.

69. Treadwell, pp. 413–14, 477.

70. Letter from Mrs. Ceil Howard (Waac mother) to Hobby, July 19, 1943, Box 90, Series 54, RG 165, NA. See also File: NCAC Forum, Box 191, Series 55, RG 165, NA.

3. *The WAC Strikes Back: Constructing the "Respectable" Female Soldier*

1 Mattie Treadwell, *The U.S. Army in World War II, Special Studies, the Women's Army Corps* (Washington, D.C.: Office of the Chief of Military History, 1954), pp. 47–49. See also "Speech to Poor Richard Club," Philadelphia, January 16, 1943. Box 13, Series 54, RG 165, NA.

2. Joyce Melva Baker, *Images of Women in Film: The War Years, 1941–45* (Ann Arbor: University of Michigan Research Press, 1981). In particular she argues that

Rosie the Riveter was not the most heroic image during World War II, rather it was the housewife who sacrificed all to keep the "home fires burning."

3. For examples of this type of argument, see Susan Hartmann, *The Home Front and Beyond: American Women in the 1940s* (New York: Twayne, 1982); Maureen Honey, *Creating Rosie the Riveter: Class, Gender, and Propaganda During World War II* (Amherst: University of Massachusetts Press, 1984); and D'Ann Campbell, *Women at War with America: Private Lives in a Patriotic Era* (Cambridge: Harvard University Press, 1984). Hartmann's *Home Front and Beyond* and Campbell's *Women at War* are two of the few historical works to substantially discuss military women within their larger analysis of women's role during World War II.

4. Reinterpretations of the "feminine mystique" which have emerged in recent years question the emphasis on domesticity emerging from the war. Though once again focusing on civilian women, the work of Joanne Meyerowitz, Nancy Gabin, and Leila Rupp and Verta Taylor suggests a more complex view of the postwar years as a period of contradictory messages about gender and women's position in American culture. Joanne Meyerowitz, "Beyond 'The Feminine Mystique': The Discourse on American Women, 1945–1950," paper presented at the Berkshire Conference on the History of Women, June 1990. See also Nancy Gabin, "Wins and Losses: The UAW Women's Bureau After World War II," in Carol Groneman and Mary Beth Norton, eds. *"To Toil the Livelong Day": America's Women at Work, 1780–1980* (Ithaca: Cornell University Press, 1987); Leila Rupp and Verta Taylor, *Survival in the Doldrums: The American Women's Rights Movement, 1945 to the 1960s* (New York: Oxford University Press, 1987). It should be noted that Susan Hartmann also concludes "Although the popular ideology that women's primary role was in the home survived the war both in the public discourse and in the beliefs of most women, the military crisis did create an ideological climate supportive of women's movement into the public realm." Susan Hartmann, *The Homefront and Beyond*, p. 20.

5. Brief statement on "The Role of the Negro Woman in the Postwar World," Executive Secretary Jeannetta Welch Brown, NCNW, File: 239, Box 14, Series 5, NCNW Papers, Bethune Museum and Archives.

6. This "public relations consciousness" meant that the WAC administration carefully scrutinized all "future plans" for the corps "in the light of their possible effect upon public sentiment." As quoted in Treadwell, p. 33. See also Ruth Roach Pierson, *"They're Still Women After All": The Second World War and Canadian Womanhood* (Toronto, Ont.: McClelland and Stewart, 1986).

7. "Our Girls in Uniform," *Ladies Home Journal* 60 (January 1943): 63.

8. For a discussion of this issue, see Barbara Epstein, *The Politics of Domesticity: Women, Evangelism, and Temperance in 19th-Century America* (Middletown, Conn.: Wesleyan University Pres, 1981), and Paula Baker, "The Domestication of Politics: Women and American Political Society, 1780–1920," *American Historical Review*, vol. 89, June 1984.

9. Alma Lutz, "It's Time to Draft Mary," *Christian Science Monitor* (April 8, 1944), p. 6.

10. Blake Clark, "Ladies of the Army," *Readers Digest* 42, no. 253 (May 1943): 85–88, condensed from *This Week Magazine, New York Herald Tribune* (April 14, 1943). See also D'Ann Campbell, "Servicewomen of World War II," *Armed Forces*

and Society 16, no.2 (Winter 1990): 254. Campbell argues that "patriotic" state-ments concerning women joining the WAC because of male family members and friends danger and a desire to hasten the end of the war were much used by Army and WAC publicists.

11. "A WAC Talks Back," Feburary 11, 1944, Tech/Sgt. 5th Grade Bernice Brown of the New York Port of Embarkation. Box 1, Series 54, RG 165; "Idea Sheet for WAC Allocation," February 20, 1944," File: 330.13, Box 90, Series 54, RG 165, NA. See also S/Sgt. Blanche A. Bordeaux, "What the Wac Has Meant to Me," *Christian Science Monitor* (May 11, 1946): 10. See also Joyce Melva Baker, *Images of Women in Film*. Baker argues that films depicting women in uniform focused predominantly on nurses and that their public acceptance was conditional on them giving first priority to the men they loved.

12. In speeches to women's groups and in WAC newletters Colonel Hobby described these actions as evidence that while Wacs "shar[e] the rigors of the military war effort" they "los[e] nothing as women," retaining their "feminine attitude and charm, and the respect of their men and their nation." "Speech by Hobby to Women's Clubs of Montreal," January 29, 1943, Box 12, Series 54, RG 165, NA. See also "My First Day at Fort Devens," partially reprinted in *Petticoat Soldiers* 1, no. 2 (June 14, 1943): 2, Fort Devens, WAC Newsletter, File: History of 4th WAC Training Command, Fort Devens, Mass. (March 15, 1943–August 1943), Box 219, Series 55, RG 165, NA.

13. "Off the Waac's Record," *Waac News* 1, no. 31 (May 15–22, 1943): 6, Box 212, Series 55, RG 165. See also "Wac's Wiles Are Womanly," *Recreation* 39, no. 2 (June 1945): 108. One female journalist even went so far as to describe normal Army rou-tines, such as inspections, as servicewomen's opportunities to show off their skills at keeping their kitchens and rooms "clean and sparkling . . . just like any Army wife." Mrs. Ruth Massey, "From an Army Wife," *Dallas News*, March 15, 1945, File: Clippings, WAAC 1942, Box 3, Hobby Papers, LC. See also Transcript of Larry Lesueur interviewing Hobby in London, File: Col. Hobby Overseas, Box 188, Series 55, RG 165, NA.

14. "Restless Wacs Demand Hand in War," n.d., File: 330.14, Box 92, Series 54, RG 165, NA. See also Ernest O. Houser, "Those Wonderful G.I. Janes," *Saturday Evening Post* 217 (September 9, 1944): 26–28, 60, 63. He noted that "soldiering has-n't transformed these Wacs into Amazons—far from it. They have retained their fem-ininity, and if you ask them what they want to do after the war, the majority will reply, 'Have a home and babies.' "

15. Mrs. A. Guttentag to Mr. Stimson (secretary of war), June 17, 1943, Box 90, Series 54, RG 165; see also WAC *Newsletter* 1, no. 14 (September 1944), Box 218, Series 55, RG 165. See also File: SPWA 080 USO, Box 15, Series 54, RG 165, NA. See also "Statements by Members of the Advisory Council," at the conclusion of their trip to Fort Des Moines and Camp Crowder, April 16–18, 1943. File: 536 WAC 1945–47, Box 38, Series 5, Bethune Museum and Archives.

16. Honey, *Creating Rosie the Riveter*, pp. 113–17. See also *The WAC in the ETO*, part 5: Public Relations and Health, ch. 1: Public Relations. This chapter included guidelines for public relations officers dealing with the WAC. These advisory rules sug-gested avoiding any negative stories about servicewomen, stressing only the positives of

Wac experience. It also recommended that Wacs be portrayed both as soldiers as well as feminine women and that the work they did within the Army be described as important and necessary. File: The WAC in the ETO, WWII, vol. 1, Box 502.101-3-11 (43-45), ETO, Air Force Historical Research Center, Maxwell Air Force Base, Montgomery, Ala. See also Treadwell, *The U.S. Army in World War II*, pp. 701-2.

17. *The WAC in the ETO,* cited in note 16. See also Treadwell, pp. 701-2.

18. As quoted in Nona Brown, "The Army Finds Woman Has Place," *New York Times Magazine*, December 26, 1948, p. 14. See also *The WAC in the ETO*, cited in note 16.

19. Blake Clark, "Ladies of the Army," *Readers Digest*, May 1943, pp. 85-88, reprinted from *New York Herald Tribune*, May 18, 1943. See also Octavius Roy Cohen, "The Lady's a Soldier," *Colliers*, October 10, 1942, pp. 32-54.

20. File: Young and Rubicam, "A National Study of Public Opinion Toward the WAC," Gallop Poll, Prepared for the U.S. Army by the Research Department, Young and Rubicam, Inc. Spring 1944, File: Box 188, Series 55, RG 165, NA.

21. Draft of Army/WAAC response to WMC limitations on recruiting, June 4, 1943, File: 000.7, Box 4; Telephone conversation between Col. Barron and Mr. J. A. Smith, War Manpower Board re: Recruiting in Massachusetts, Box 94, Series 54, RG 165, NA. On August 12, 1943, the director of War Mobilization, Justice James Byrnes, sought to end the conflict, by issuing a decree that forbade the WMC from interfering in national WAC recruiting campaigns even in labor-short areas. Treadwell, pp. 233-43.

22. Editorial in Hartford *Courant*, October 2, 1942, and Rice to Hobby, October 2, 1943. re: Problems with WMC in Connecticut, Box 94, Series 54; WMC directive forbidding the Army from recruiting "women employed in essential industry," January 26, 1943, File: Recruiting-WMC, Box 197, Series 55; all in RG 165, NA. See also Treadwell, pp. 171-72, 233-35.

23. For example, see John A. Wood, secretary Teachers' Pension and Annuity Fund, State of New Jersey, to the adjutant general, U.S. Army, July 11, 1942; also Charles A. Allen, councilman 8th district City Council of Los Angeles to the judge advocate general, re: Military bonuses and leave for those entering service and leaving state civil service positions, October 5, 1942; Judge Advocate General Ulio reply to John A. Wood, a boilerplate response repeated verbatim to all requests for such information, July 29, 1942, Box 47, Series 54, RG 165, NA. Army officials reinforced this differential treatment of male soldiers and Wacs. When asked by state officials and employers to clarify women's military status, Army officials invoked the logic used by members of Congress to deny Waacs benefits and responded that Waacs were not actually *soldiers* entitled to the privileges and benefits afforded by federal law, and that individual states and employers must make their own decisions as to what Waacs were entitled.

24. Memo from Colonel Hobby to Administrative Services, re: Enlistment of school teachers in the WAAC, April 2, 1943; Major B. P. Cody, Cavalry, adjutant to director of personnel division, Hq. 9th Service Command, Fort Douglas, Utah, re: Policies being established that interfere with WAAC recruiting, April 19, 1943; 3d Officer Milian Parrick, Salem, Ore., to Col. J. J. Fulmer, re: Meeting of school board, April 15, 1943; letter from Marjorie L. Christenson to Margaret N. Horn, Oregon Recruiting hq., Salem, Ore., April 14, 1943; Hobby to commanding general, 9th

Service Command Fort Douglas, Utah, re: Response from National Education Association, April 27, 1943. All in Box 47, Series 54, RG 165, NA.

25. In fact, even after conversion when the WAC became a part of the regular Army the only women eligible for benefits such as jobs as returning veterans, military leave, and bonuses, were those women who left a civilian job to enter the WAC. Women who were originally members of the WAAC and reenlisted in the WAC or who were discharged after conversion were never eligible for any benefits under the Selective Service Act or the Soldiers and Sailors Relief Act, 1940. For example, see Col. Charles W. West, JAGD, chief of Military Affairs Division to Col. Hobby, re: Eligibility for reemployment benefits upon release from active service of members of the WAAC and WAC, August 19, 1943, Box 47, Series 54, RG 165, NA.

26. Treadwell, pp. 204–7. See also Letter from Hobby to Miriam J. Cohen on behalf of Mrs. Roosevelt, July 10, 1943, based on Army press release dated July 1, 1943, File: Rumors, Box 192, Series 55, RG 165.

27. Hobby consistently emphasized that the jobs women were doing in the WAC were not "heroic" but "necessary" and that women joined the service simply because they understood that they were needed. Transcript of Larry Lasueur Laseuer interviewing Colonel Hobby in London concerning WAC service overseas in Britain, January 16, 1944, File: Colonel Hobby Overseas, Box 188, Series 55, RG 165, NA. Hobby stressed the importance of women feeling appreciated and remarked, "They know now, how much they are needed, and that's especially important to women. It means a lot to them to know that they are appreciated." See also LaVerne Bradley, "Our Girls in Uniform," National Geographic 84, June 12, 1943, pp. 445–48. She writes "Their desire to serve can never be more than partially fulfilled, but they are willing to stand by, just in case. In the meantime, theirs is the biggest job of all: learning to do the unheroic, to serve where needed." See also "Stepsister Corps," Time, May 10, 1943, pp. 55–56 and "Waacs 1st Muster," Time, June 8, 1942,pp. 71–72.

28. Treadwell, p. 204–5. In particular see ch. 11: "The Slander Campaign," which goes into great detail about this episode in WAAC/WAC history. See also Oral History, Col. Mary A. Hallaren, WAC Oral History Program (WAC Foundation) May 1979, Tape #VT 79.02 #8, March 1947–January 1953, WAC Director. WAC Museum, Fort McClellan, Anniston, Ala.

29. "Lament," WAC Songbook, p. 39, File: WAC Songbooks, WAC Files, WAC Museum, Anniston, Ala.

30. "Life in the WAAC," recruiting pamphlet prepared by Young and Rubicam, File: 062.001, 1942–43, Box 9, Series 54; Letter Laura Hobson, War Writers Board to Clifton Fadiman, re: Young and Rubicam Meeting on WAAC Recruiting, April 23, 1943, File: War Writers Board, Box 15, Series 54, RG 165; "WAC Recruiting Guide as Recommended by Young and Rubicam," File: 000.7 (April 15, 1943) Box 3, Series 54, RG 165; File: ASF, 7th Service Command, War Recruiting Conference, Omaha, Neb., March 3, 1944, pp. 1–9, 42, Box 206, Series 55, RG 165, NA. "This same decision concerning 'glamorization,' " notes WAC historian Mattie Treadwell, "was also deemed essential at different times, by both British and WAVES recruiters, in both cases over the objections of the women leaders." Treadwell, pp. 187, 232–33.

31. "A Plan for Increasing Enrollment in the WAAC," manual designed to give information to WAAC recruiters, Box 199, Series 55, RG 165.

32. Ibid. See also WAC Recruiting Posters, File: Advertising, Box 221, Series 55, RG 165, NA.

33. Letter, Manuel Y. Ings, Madison, Wisc. to Hobby, re: Problems of WAC advertising, Box 21, Series 54, RG 165, NA. See also Alma Lutz, "It's Time to Draft Mary," p. 6.

34. Recruiting, July 21, 1945, File: 320.2, December 1943, Box 64, Series 54, RG 165, NA.

35. Press release, June 11, 1943, "Statement from nine church leaders," and Memo SWPA OOO.3 (5–8–43)W from Director Hobby to commandant, 1st WAAC TC, Fort Des Moines, re: Religious activities. All in Box 21, Series 54, RG 165, NA.

36. Address by Chaplain (1st Lt.) George W. Casey on the Catholic Hour (NBC), July 4, 1943, File: Press Releases, Box 216, Series 55; Field Memo #31 (August 5, 1944) Lt. Colonel Johns to All Service Commands, re: Indorsement of WAC by religious leaders and publication of their statements; Inclosure no. 1, Bishop Boyle of Pittsburgh diocese for the Catholic Church, File: Field Memos, Box 219, Series 55; Speech by Monsignor Michael J. Ready, general secretary, National Catholic Welfare Conference, June 3, 1943, Box 1, Series 54; all in RG 165, NA. See also "Bishop Toolen Salutes the Wacs," *Mobile Press Register*, January 20, 1944, File: Notecards of Treadwell, Box 9, RG 319, G-1, NA. It is interesting to note here that the WAC as an all-female organization with female leadership but within a male military institution was very similar to the convent structure, which was an integral part of the Catholic Church. This might be another of the reasons why the Catholic Church moved from antagonism to approval of the women's corps.

37. "A Plan for Increasing Enrollment in the WAAC," cited in note 31; "Statement by Mrs. Emily Newell Blair," first address as chief of the War Department Women's Interest Section to the Women's Advisory Council, June 15, 1942; and "Report on Work of Women's Interest Section in Connection with the Advisory Council," no. 4 "Cooperation in Recruiting Program of WAAC," pp. 5–6, June 25, 1942, File: 22, Box 37, Series 5, NCNW Papers, Bethune Museum and Archives, Washington, D.C.

38. Hobby speech to Advisory Council of Women's Interest Section, June 25, 1943. Box 14, Series 54, RG 165, NA.

39. Treadwell, p. 171.

40. Memo to commanding generals AAC Command, Army Ground Forces Replacement Depot #1, re: Replacement and school command, from Lt. Colonel Herbert L. Nelson, AGD, May 10, 1944, Hq., Army Ground Forces, Army War College, Subject: WAC recruiting, Tab 16, Box 189, Series 55, RG 165; Field memo no. 20, Attn.: Army Service Forces SPIPR 431 (General) May 9, 1944, to commanding general, Fort Bragg, N.C., Attn.: Post chaplains, Subject: WAC procurement talk by chaplains at reception center, File: Field Memos, Box 219, Series 55, RG 165. See also "Idea Sheet for WAC Allocation," February 20, 1944, File: 330.13, Box 90, Series 54, RG 165, NA.

41. As feminist theorist Patricia Hill Collins has argued, African-American women "inhabit a sex/gender hierarchy in which inequalities of race and social class have been sexualized." Therefore, descriptions of black women as well as working-class and poor women as "sexually aggressive and immoral" all encompass African-American women and define them as "sexually available." Patricia Hill Collins, *Black Feminist Thought:*

Knowledge, Consciousness, and the Politics of Empowerment (Boston: Unwin Hyman, 1990), p. 165. See also Paula Giddings, When and Where I Enter: The Impact of Black Women on Race and Sex in America (New York: Bantam Books, 1984), pp. 31–35.

42. File: 535-WAC 1942–45, Box 38, Series 5, NCNW Papers, Bethune Museum and Archives. News File: 000.7, Three Native Americans sworn into the WAAC, June 11, 1943, Box 2, Series 54, RG 165; File: 291.2, Enrollment of Japanese-American women, Box 49, Series 54, RG 165; Kathleen Iseri to Major Kathleen McClure, WAC Recruiting Hq., January 26, 1944, Box 21, Series 54, RG 165; Lt. Colonel M. D. Seil, Air Corps, PRO to Hobby, and Capt. H. E. Jewett, Air Corps, assistant AG for commanding general to Hobby, re: Swearing in of Benito Juarez Squadron at Randolph Field, Texas, March 14, 1944, File: 095, Box 17, Series 54, RG 165, NA.

43. Joan Younger, interview with Oveta Culp Hobby, February 25, 1952, File: Ladies Home Journal, Article, Box 9, Hobby Papers, LC.

44. Kathy Peiss and Christina Simmons with Robert A. Padgug, eds., Passion and Power: Sexuality in History (Philadelphia: Temple University Press, 1989), pp. 4–6.

45. Treadwell, pp. 55–56. See also "Waac News," WAAC Newsletter 1 no. 33 (June 5–12, 1943): 3, Fort Des Moines, Iowa, Box 212, Series 55, RG 165, NA.

46. Memo to recruiting officer, Military District of Washington, Lt. Helen K. Cooper, re: Recruiting program for women's colleges, March 24, 1944, File: Field Memos, Box 219, Series 55, RG 165; WAC Recruiting Poster, LX-102-RPB-1/15/43–100M, An Appeal "To College Women in Their Senior Year," File: Advertisements, Box 221, Series 55, RG 165, NA. See also D'Ann Campbell, "Servicewomen of World War II," pp. 251–70. She reports that while WAC officers had to have at least two years college education, enlisted women were also better educated than civilian women: 32 percent had some high school, 41 percent were high-school graduates, 15 percent had some college, and 7 percent were college graduates. Only 6 percent had never attended high school, compared with 42 percent of civilians that age (p. 252).

47. Pamphlet: Life in the WAC, the Women's Army Corps, "A Word to Parents," Box 12, Hobby Papers, LC. For an example of how this message gets articulated in the media, see Lula Jones Garrett, "Forrest Wac's Not Ward Boys/ Hold Varied Jobs in Mixed Post Hospital/ Colonel Says Morals High, Morale Fair," Philadelphia Afro-American, February 26, 1944. p. 3. Occasionally, this focus on the connections between class and race status and respectability was used to mediate rigid applications of the Code of Conduct in favor of servicewomen whose civilian class status was "above reproach." White officer candidate Mildred Hindman, for example, was caught with a companion coming back to Officer Candidate School (OCS) drunk. She was dismissed from OCS but the overall recommendation of the investigating board was that "because of her excellent background" she be returned to service and "encouraged to reapply to OCS" at a later date, Subject: Report of investigation regarding elimination from OCS of Mildred W. Hindman, October 29, 1943, To: Director, Field Survey, Branch, WAC HQ, Washington, D.C., File: H, Box 27, Series 54, RG 165, NA.

48. Memo for director, WD BPR, Subject: Problems and deterrents in connection to WAC recruiting, February 18, 1944, Box 64, Series 54, RG 165, NA. See also Treadwell, p. 169.

49. WAC historian Mattie Treadwell has documented the problems created by an Army Recruiting Service that never really had to engage in intensive campaigning because of the depression and the draft, suddenly expected to "bring in greater num-

bers of women than it ever had men, in a nation endorsing the idea of women in the home." She further remarked on the difficulties generated by the Army BPR which lacked information and made a number of errors early on because of the absence of any coordination and screening of publicity on servicewomen. Treadwell, *The U.S. Army in World War II*, pp. 168, 699–700.

50. Ibid., pp. 169–183, 699–702.

51. Ibid., pp. 182–83.

52. Ibid., pp. 183–184.

53. See, for example, letter to Hobby from Mrs. Ruth Clellan, February 3, 1944, File: Rumors, Box 192, Series 54, RG 165, NA.

54. File: Young and Rubicam, "A National Study of Public Opinion Toward the WAC," cited in note 20.

55. Vera Clay, "Bounding WAVES," *Newsweek*, November 1, 1943, pp. 46, 48, 53. See also "Women" in "US At War," *Time*, March 12, 1945, pp. 20–23.

56. Col. Hobby to Mary McLeod Bethune, June 19, 1942; Major Grant, recruiting officer, to Sgt. Stephenson, recruiter, May 27, 1942; Mary Elnora White to War Department, July 1, 1943, Box 50, Series 54, RG 165, NA.

57. Horace R. Claying, director of housing for recruits, to the Armed Forces, Induction Station, 1639th Service Unit, Chicago, Ill., July 8, 1944, File: 535-WAC 1942–1945, Box 38, Series 5, NCNW Papers, Bethune Museum and Archives.

58. Harry F. Tarving, regional reports officer, Associated Press, to Mr. Dillen S. Myer, director, War Relocation Authority, December 13, 1943, File: 291.2, Enrollment of Japanese-American Women, Box 49, Series 54, RG 165, NA.

59. Telegram from Walter White to Col. Hobby, July 12, 1943, File: NAACP, SPWA 291.2; Memo for assistant secretary of war from John J. McCloy, Executive Committee of the Negro Newspaper Publishers Association, July 16, 1943; L. Virgil Williams, Dallas Negro Chamber of Commerce, to Col. Hobby, July 2, 1943, File: 291.2, Box 49, Series 54, RG 165; ARL 543, WD HG WAAC 6th Service Command, Chicago, Ill., re: Lt. Ruth L. Freeman's removal as WAC recruiting officer (Negro) in Chicago, June 10, 1943, File: Assignment, WAAC Officers to All Training Centers, June 1, 1943, Box 37, Series 54, RG 165, NA.

60. Col. Hobby to Walter White, July 12, 1943, File: NAACP, SPWA 291.2; 1st Officer Elizabeth C. Strayhorn, WAAC to Mr. L. Virgil Williams, executive secretary, Dallas Negro Chamber of Commerce, July 17, 1943, File: 291.2, Box 49, Series 54, RG 165; ARL 543 WD HG WAAC 6th Service Command, Chicago, Ill., June 20, 1943, File: Assignment, WAAC officers to all training centers, June 1, 1943, Box 37, Series 54, RG 165, NA.

61. WAAC memo to Col. Catron from Major Harold Edlund, Subject: Negro recruiting, File: Untitled, Box 39, Series 54, RG 165; Internal memo Edlund to Hobby, July 14, 1943, File: 291.2, Box 49, Series 54, RG 165, NA.

62. Rep. George Mahon of Texas to Col. Howard Clark, chief, Operational Services, April 22, 1943; Col. Hobby to Rep. George Mahon, May 5, 1943; Rev. Palfrey Perkins, president, and Seaton W. Manning, executive secretary, Boston Urban League, to Col. Hobby, November 17, 1942, and Hobby's response, December 2, 1942; Box 50, Series 54, RG 165, NA.

63. Hobby speech to United Daughters of the Confederacy, Columbus, Ohio, National Convention, November 19, 1943. In this speech Hobby lauds the "heroes of

the great Confederacy" who fought in a "noble losing cause, but who had so much honor," and characterizes the WAC as made up of their women descendants. Obviously, she is not including African-American women in her list of "descendants." Box 15, Series 54, RG 165, NA.

64. 1st Officer Bernice L. Keplinger, district director, Military District of Washington, to: Director WAAC, re: Discipline, January 25, 1943, Box 48, Series 54, RG 165, NA.

65. Joan Younger, interview with Oveta Culp Hobby, cited in note 43. See also Capt. Todd Report: Medical Deficiencies in the WAC, Box 191, and Notes from Director's Daily Journal, January 23, 1943, File: Office of the Director, Daily Journal, vol. 1, Box 200, Series 55, RG 165, NA.

66. Treadwell, pp. 616–19.

67. Board proceedings, Auxiliary Agnes R. Skipper, Hq. 8th Service Command, SOS, JA Branch, acting chief of WAAC Branch, July 13, 1943. A ranking male officer's opinion of court-martial proceedings concerning WAC personnel, given that the WAC was recently made a formal part of the regular Army was as follows: "The women who make up the WAC are, therefore, to be treated as enlisted and commissioned personnel of the Army rather than as inmates of some well-chaperoned young ladies seminary. As long as they conduct themselves decently and without bringing discredit or disgrace upon the uniform or the military service, their private life is and ought to be recognized as a matter for their own direction." File: 250.1, Box 49, Series 54, RG 165, NA. See also Joan Younger interview with Hobby, p. 3; cited in note 43.

68. Treadwell contends in her history of the women's corps that the director believed: "Whatever the merits of a theoretical single standard, the practical fact was that at the current moment in society, and in recruiting, the habits and traits that rendered a woman undesirable as an associate of enlisted women were somewhat different from those that made a man an undesirable associate of enlisted men." As a result, Hobby believed, on the basis of her legal training and study of reports from the field, that the clue to a solution lay in the Army's "well-recognized duty" to protect the rights of all individuals. For example, while Hobby pointed out that the female moral offender, in strict justice, could not be punished more severely than a male soldier for identical offenses, she also argued that the 149 other members of a WAC unit also were entitled to "protection from damage to physical or mental health or well-being, and the Corps, as a volunteer group, had the right to choose its members and give honorable discharges to the unfit." Treadwell, pp. 498–99. See also Margaret D. Craighill, M.D., "A Psychological Approach to Social Hygiene for Women," *Journal of Social Hygiene* (April 1946): 200.

69. Joan Younger, interview with Hobby, p. 3, citedd in note 43. See also Treadwell, pp. 498–99.

4. "Women's Work" and Resistance in the WAC

1. Susan Hartmann, *The Homefront and Beyond: American Women in the 1940's* (New York: Twayne, 1982), p. 47, passim. The military's need for trained personnel was not completely new; General Pershing's American Expeditionary forces had used 5,000 civilian women in France during World War I to run their switchboards. The Army, however, expanded enormously during World War II and its need for compe-

tent office staffs had increased as well. As I noted above, Army leaders, especially Chief of Staff General George C. Marshall, did not believe that civilian women were an appropriate solution to the clerical shortage because the Army needed more control over these workers than it could have over civilians. Thus, creating a women's corps for work with the Army seemed the best answer.

2. William Chafe, *The American Woman: Her Changing Social, Economic and Political Roles, 1920–1970* (New York: Oxford University Press, 1972), p. 181.

3. Karen Anderson, *Wartime Women: Sex Roles, Family Relations, and the Status of Women During World War II* (Westport, Conn.: Greenwood Press, 1981), pp. 173–75; Hartmann, *The Homefront and Beyond.*

4. For example, see Anderson and Hartmann, and D'Ann Campbell, *Women at War with America: Private Lives in a Patriotic Era* (Cambridge: Harvard University Press, 1984). The only historian to have focused completely on women's service with the Army during World War II is Mattie Treadwell, *The United States Army in World War II, Special Studies, The Women's Army Corps* (Washington, D.C.: Office of the Chief of Military History, 1954). Her tome on the Women's Army Corps is an invaluable resource, largely because it was designed to document in minute detail the inner workings of the organization throughout the war, including all the difficulties encountered with the aim of creating a blueprint for future uses of women in the military.

5. Campbell, ch. 1. Campbell argues that public antagonism was the most critical factor in the Army's lack of success in meeting its quotas.

6. Treadwell, p. 767, appendix A, table 3: "WAAC Personnel Statistics"; Samuel Stouffer, "The American Soldier in World War II," Survey S-194, Question 5, as cited in Campbell, p. 23; Anderson, pp. 4–5. It should be noted that the age limits for the WAAC were initially 21–40, these were extended to 20–50 after conversion when the WAAC became part of the regular Army.

7. Treadwell, p. 767, Samuel Stouffer, as cited in Campbell, p. 23, Anderson, pp. 4–5, as cited in note 6. In addition, a 1944 study of 18,000 Wacs stationed at the First WAC Training Center at Fort Des Moines, Iowa, demonstrated that while 50.3 percent came from urban communities, 49.7 percent hailed from rural communities and small towns. See Major Albert Preston, Jr., *History of Psychiatry in the Woman's Army Corps* (Spring 1946): 5, File: 700, Box 143, Series 54, RG 165, NA.

8. Campbell, *Women at War with America*, p. 23; D'Ann Campbell, "Servicewomen of World War II," *Armed Forces and Society* (Winter 1990): 252–53. Campbell also argues that white women from the South were underrepresented because the Southern military tradition was heavily male and while being a military wife was a "high prestige role" for a Southern woman, being in the military proper was not.

9. Campbell, "Servicewomen of WWII," p. 252. A comparison of black and white women in May 1943 demonstrates that of approximately 3,000 African-American Waacs 33.3 percent were high-school graduates compared to 42 percent for white women, while 9 percent of black Waacs were college graduates relative to 8 percent among white Waacs. Treadwell, p. 767, as cited in note 6. See also Statistical History of the WAAC, May 1943, File: HQ—Historical Branch, Box 209, Series 55, RG 165, NA.

10. Meyer Oral History Questionnaires, Phyllis Allen, no. 3, Questions 13 and 48.

11. As quoted in Charity Adams Earley, *One Woman's Army: A Black Officer Remembers the WAC* (College Station: Texas A & M University Press, 1989), p. 23.

12. Excerpts from interviews of black women applying for the WAAC, File: Director's Evaluation Board, Box 189, Series 55, RG 165, NA.

13. Meyer Oral History Questionnaires, Martha Ward, no. 4, Juanita Waters, no. 5, Question 13. See also Campbell, "Servicewomen of World War II," p. 243, Table 6: "Labor Force Movement of Wives by Status of Husband, 1941–44." It is clear that civilian women whose husbands were absent also had a much higher participation rate in the labor force than those whose husbands were present throughout the war. See also Earley, p. 23.

14. File: Young and Rubicam, "A National Study of Public Opinion Toward the WAC," Spring 1944, Gallup Poll, Box 188, Series 54, RG 165, NA.

15. For example, see Meyer Oral History Questionnaires, Beatrice Brown, no. 6, Question 14. "Women Honored at WAC Rally," *Toledo Blade*, March 27, 1944. This article carried the text of Lt. Lillian Duncan's recruiting speech given at the Frederick Douglass Community Center, the last event in Negro WAC Day in Toledo, honoring Negro women from that city. Duncan reported, "Negro women serving in the WAC are winning a respect and admiration throughout the nation that will reflect in greater race equality after the war." Dovey Johnson Roundtree Papers, Bethune Museum and Archives, Washinton, D.C..

16. Excerpt from Radio Broadcast by Harriet M. West, April 23, 1943, WINX 6:30–7:00 P.M., File: Negro, Box 211, Series 55, RG 165, NA.

17. Mary Nyasaka to Col. Hobby, March 1, 1943; Col. Scobey memo for Col. Catron, re: Capt. Norman Thompson's attached report from Gila River Relocation Center, March 17, 1943; 2d Officer Manic M. Hill, WAAC to commanding general, 8th Service Command, Dallas, Texas, re: Investigation of attitude of women in Rohwer Relocation Center toward the WAAC, McGehee, Ark., March 4, 1943; 2d Officer Henriette Horak to Hq, 9th Service Command, WAAC Branch, re: Tule Lake Relocation Center Report, March 7, 1943; File: Enrollment of Japanese-American Women in the WAAC (January 13, 1943), Box 49, Series 55, RG 165, NA.

18. Information Guide on Wacs, p. 4, File: News Media/PR IV-F-24, Box 61, Series 55, RG 165, NA.

19. A Study of the WAC in the ETO, chapter II: Performance in the ETO, section 3: Manner of Performance, pp. 97–98, File: A Study of the WAC in the ETO, WWII, G-1; no. 11; V.1, Box 502.101-3;-11, 1943–45, Air Force Historical Research Center, Maxwell Air Force Base, Montgomery, Ala. Also, File: 4th Air Force Historical Study, No. V-4; vol. 1, 1942–45, section 5: The WAAC May 1943, pp. 246–51, File: Box 450.01-13, 1941–45, V.2, Air Force Historical Research Center, Maxwell Air Force Base, Montgomery, Ala.

20. Col. Hobby speech to graduation of Women's Reserve of Coast Guard (SPARS), November 3, 1943, p. 3, Box 13, Series 54, RG 165. See also Background Information for Public Relations Films on WAC Work Overseas, File: WDWAC 062.3 Photography January–December 1945, Box 9, Series 54, RG 165, NA.

21. Col. Hobby to House Committee on Military Affairs, re: WAC Budget, File: Budget Material for 1944, WAC Director, Box 22; Memo to Col. T. B. Catron, executive officer, WAAC, re: Study of all military occupations in Army with view to determining jobs appropriate for WAAC Auxiliaries, File: Reports of Military Occupations Suitable for WAAC Auxiliaries, Box 32, Series 54; Statement by Oveta Culp Hobby,

director, WAAC to Congress, May 27, 1943, File: Congressional Committee Notes, May 27, 1943, Box 185; Memo to the Director, re: Utilization of WAAC from Adjutant General J. A. Ulio, File: Utilization of WAAC 13; May 1943, Box 189, Series 55, RG 165, NA.

22. Treadwell, *The U.S. Army in World War II*, pp. 767 and 559, as cited in note 6. Stouffer, "Jobs Before and After Enlisting in the WAC," fig. 2, as cited in Campbell, *Women at War*, p. 24. It should be noted that although both Treadwell and Campbell agree that office and administrative work was the job category to which most enlisted women were assigned their numbers and percentages differ, with Treadwell's figures reflecting a decrease from 53 to 45 percent of Wacs employed in administrative and office jobs from 1943 to September 1944, while Campbell's figures show an increase to 75 percent of women holding "clerical" type jobs in the WAC by 1945. Hartmann, *Homefront and Beyond*, p. 40.

23. A Study of the WAC in the ETO, chapter 2, section 2: Types of Jobs Performed by Enlisted Women, p. 96, File: as cited in note 19.

24. Clerical and sales jobs were dominated by white women and African-American women entering the military were less likely to have these skills and more likely to have been employed in the service sector or agriculture and thus were more likely to be utilized in service work in the Army. Treadwell, p. 767 and pp. 559, 596, as cited in note 6; Stouffer, as cited in Campbell, *Women at War*, p. 24; Paula Giddings, *When and Where I Enter: The Impact of Black Women on Race and Sex in America* (New York: William Morrow, 1984), p. 232.

25. The following shows Army promotion of enlisted women and enlisted men:

Grade	Percent	
	EW	EM
Master and 1st Sgt.	0.6	1.5
Technical Sgt.	0.6	2.9
Staff Sgt and Tec/3	3.5	8.1
Sgt. or Tec/4	11.8	14.1
Corporal or Tec/5	19.6	21.0
Private 1st Class	25.4	28.1
Private	38.5	24.3

Source: Treadwell, p. 562.

See also Meyer Oral History Questionnaires, Anne Clark, no. 7, Question 17, she noted that when men and women worked side by side "men were given the supervisory jobs," and said in terms of promotions that the "longer women were present in command the fairer promotions became, but men still had that supervisory advantage."

26. Letter, June 11, 1943, George A. Martin, Jr. to Hobby, Box 11, Series 54; Memo, November 4, 1943, for Commanding General ASF from Maj. General White, assistant chief of staff, re: Officers for Negro Troops, WAC, Box 199, Series 55, RG 165, NA.

27. Bernard Nalty, *Strength for the Fight: A History of Black Americans in the Military* (New York: Free Press, 1986), pp. 29–46, 107–24, 141.

28. File: General Information and Documentation on the WAAC, Box 188, Series 55, RG 165, NA. See also Treadwell, pp. 54–55.

29. File: Officer Candidate Testing Procedure, Box 207; "Questions Asked OCS Candidates by OCS Board at Fort Des Moines," File: General Information and Documentation on the WAAC, Box 188, Series 55, RG 165, NA.

30. Transcript of telephone conversation between Capt. Strayhorn (WAAC) and Capt. Rice (WAAC), re: Ratings for OCS, July 19, 1943, File: Negro, Box 211, RG 165, NA.

31. Memo for director, Control Division, report by Harriet West, 1st officer, WAAC Training Command, May 29, 1943, File: Negro, Box 211, Series 55. See also Treadwell, pp. 174–76, 589–600; Hartmann, p. 40.

32. Col. Hobby to the director of Military Personnel Division, SOS, May 5, 1943, "Negro Personnel," Box 76, Series 54, RG 165, NA.

33. Conference between Mrs. Bethune (NCNW) and Col, Hobby, Col. Catron, Capt. Strayhorn (WAC hq), August 16, 1943, File: Office of Director, Daily Journal, V.1, Box 200, Series 55, RG 165; File: Approval and Disapproval of Requests for WAAC Personnel, Box 69, Series 54; Report on Field Trip to 6th and 7th Service Commands made by 1st Officer Harriet West, May 17, 1943, File: Negro, Box 211, Series 55, RG 165, NA.

34. For an example of this, see Col. Catron, executive officer to commanding general 2d Army Memphis, re: Negro WAAC companies for duty with the 92d Division, Fort McClellan, January 5, 1943; Capt. James A. Gibbs, Hq Fort McClellan to commanding general 4th Service Command, Atlanta, re: Negro WAAC companies for duty with 92d Division, February 2, 1943; Col. L. B. Clapham, director Personnel Division to Hq 4th Service Command, Atlanta, Attn: Chief of Administrative Services, February 5, 1943. He says that the request that "Negro Waacs be used to replace enlisted men at Fort McClellan shows a basic misunderstanding of the utilization of black soldiers. . . . No colored soldiers are performing the duties it is suggested Waacs could replace them in, they are employed in labor and service type detachments only. . . . No Negro WAAC companies are qualified to relieve colored general service men." File: 320.2 March 43, Box 73, Series 54, RG 165, NA.

35. Report of Inspection and Investigation, 4th WAAC Training Command, Fort Devens, Mass., June 20–23, 1943, June 28, 1943, File: Negro, Box 211, Series 55; SPWA 291.21 (5/24/43-C), Memo for the director, re: Enrollment and assignment of Negro personnel, from Maj. George F. Margin, director, Control Division, May 24, 1943, File: Negro, Box 211, Series 55, RG 165, NA.

36. File: Approval and Disapproval of Requests for WAAC Personnel, Box 69, Series 54; Col. McCoskrie, commandant, to director, WAAC, re: Designation and use of colored unit, May 13, 1943, File: Misc Section 320.2 (1/1/43-1), Sec. 10, Box 75, Series 54, RG 165, NA.

37. Report by 2d Officer Dorothy L. Myer, Fort McClellan, Ala., July 28, 1943, Box 190, Series 55, RG 165. See also SPWA 291.21 (5/24/43)C, Memo for the director, re: Enrollment and assignment of Negro personnel, from Maj. George F. Martin, director, Control Division, May 24, 1943, File: Negro, Box 211, Series 55, RG 165, NA. See also Nalty, *Strength for the Fight*, p. 179, for a discussion of the assignment of black women at Fort Breckinridge, Ky., where their jobs consisted predominantly of "sweeping the floor of a warehouse, ladling out food at a service club, or surviving the heat and humidity of a quartermaster laundry."

38. Study of the WAC in the ETO, part 6: Special Problems, chapter 1: Utilization of Colored WAAC/WAC Personnel, File: as cited in note 19.

39. Letter, anonymous Wac to Mr. Eugene Meyer, May 10, 1944, File: F, Box 26; Letter, Edith Nourse Rogers to Hobby, May 25, 1943, Box 11, Series 54, RG 165, NA. File: 4th AF Historical Study, No. V-4; vol. 1, 1942–45, pp. 246–51, Box 450.01–13, 1941–45, vol. 2 and Box 432.01, December 7, 1941–December 31, 1942 (vol. 13) and 1943 (vol. 3) History of the 2d Air Force, chs. 1 and 2, Air Force Historical Reserach Center, Maxwell Air Force Base, Montgomery, Ala.

40. "The WAC Program in the AAF," by Lt. Colonel Betty Bandel, File: 141.33, November 1945, Box 141.287–1(1945) - 142.01 (1918), Air Force Historical Research Center, Maxwell Air Force Base, Montgomery, Ala.

41. Ibid. See also 3d Officer Hazel K. Miller to director WAAC for commanding general 5th Service Command, re: Utilization of WAAC personnel, November 6, 1942, Box 76, Series 55, RG 165, NA.

42. File: Negro, Reports of Utilization of Negro Female Personnel, Box 211, Series 55, RG 165, NA.

43. Col. Hallaren Discussing WAC Problems with Treadwell, May 16, 1947, File: Notecards of Treadwell, Box 9, RG 319, NA. See also Treadwell, *The U.S. Army in World War II*, pp. 319–20, 326–28.

44. Memo for the commanding general, AGF, from Joseph T. McNarney, deputy chief of staff, sent to all commanding generals, August 11, 1944, File: 210.31, Box 36, Series 54, RG 165, NA. Also Treadwell, pp. 565–66.

45. Treadwell, pp. 546–47.

46. At several posts personnel officers assigned women to KP duties not only for their own unit but for the male detachments as well, believing that these tasks were more suitable employment for women than men. On the homefront the small size of most WAC units vis-à-vis men's created difficulties because there were so few enlisted women eligible for KP that these women were sometimes assigned KP two to three times a week as compared to their male counterparts, who usually received the assignment no more than once a month. This resulted in a disruption of office routines as women assigned to KP would be gone from their normal assignments for anywhere from one-half to a full day two or three times a week. Some male officers were upset with the adverse impact this situation had on office efficiency and proposed as a solution giving selected women "permanent KP" duties, thus allowing other women to continue uninterrupted at their "real" jobs. See Box 247.91 (n.d. V. 5A)–248.1011 (April 1930), Air Force Historical Research Center, Maxwell Air Force Base, Montgomery, Ala.; Treadwell, pp. 546–47. Overseas, this was less of a problem as local civilian women were hired by the Army and employed as servants and maids for all Army personnel in the various theaters. See 1st Officer Boyce, WAAC service command director to director, WAAC, re: Report of visit to 148th WAAC Communications Company, Miami Beach, Fla., April 12–13, 1943, April 29, 1943, File 320.2 148th Communications Company, Box 77, Series 54, RG 165, NA; also Treadwell, pp. 369–70, 548.

47. 1st Lt. Martha Settle, 9951 TSU SGO WAC Detach, Fort Custer, Mich., to Office of Director, File: S, Box 29, Series 54; WD Circular #86, February 26, 1944, File: Staff Reports, Box 190, Series 55, RG 165, NA. Also Treadwell, pp. 547–48.

48. Memo for the director from the War Department, re: KP, File 220.6 Kitchen Police, August 14, 1943, Box 45, Series 54; Transcript of telephone conversation, Capt. Elizabeth Strayhorn and Capt. Jessie Rice, July 19, 1943, File: Negro, Box 211, Series 55, RG 165, NA.

49. Report of Elizabeth W. Stearns, 1st officer, WAAC Fort Dix, N.J., July 19, 1943, File: Negro, Box 211, Series 55; 1st Lt. Harriette Gould, classification officer, WAC Camp Forrest, Tenn., to commanding general, 4th Service Command, WAC Camp Forrest, Tenn., re: Survey of classification and assignment of WAC, October 19, 1943, Box 30, Series 54, RG 165, NA.

50. Treadwell, pp. 767 and 559; Stouffer, as cited in Campbell, *Women at War*, p. 24.

51. Project 13, "O'Rourke Self-Instructional Training Program," Folder 1, "Planning Projects May–September 1943," Box 188 Director's Desk File, 1942–45, Series 55, RG 165, NA.

52. A Study of the WAC in the ETO, chapter 2: Performance in the ETO, section 3: Manner of Performance, p. 98, File: cited in note 19. Treadwell, pp. 289–90. See also Allan Berube, *Coming Out Under Fire: The History of Gay Men and Women in World War Two* (New York: Free Press, 1990), pp. 34–66. Berube makes an intriguing argument in his work, contending that jobs within the military that were cross-gendered were often given to gay men and lesbians, i.e., that women engaged in "men's jobs" were likely to be lesbians and men engaged in "women's jobs" were likely to be gay.

53. Study of the WAC in the ETO, ch. 2, sec. 3, p. 98; and Major Mary Hallaren, WAC staff director, ETO, to Hobby, August 23, 1944, Appendices 95 and 96, File: see note 19.

54. Study of the WAC in the ETO, ch. 2, sec. 3, p. 98, File: see note 19.

55. "The WAC Program in the AAF," cited in note 40; "History AAF, Eastern Flying Training Command (EFTC)," File: V.1 January–June 1944, Box 222.01 (January–December 1943)–(January–June 1944), Air Force Historical Research Center, Maxwell Air Force Base, Montgomery, Ala.

56. Meyer Oral History Questionnaires, Ruth Thomas, no. 1, Supplement, p. 42. Ruth Thomas, who was stationed at Goodfellow Field, Texas, wrote that when the male cadet pilots had radio trouble they almost always blamed it on the female radio technicians, when it was usually a consequence of their failure to plug in their headsets.

57. Meyer Oral History Questionnaires, Ruth Thomas, no. 1, Supplement. See also "The WAC Program in the AAF," cited in note 40; and Treadwell, *The U.S. Army in World War II*, pp. 288–293.

58. Treadwell, pp. 562–63.

59. Hearing Before the Committee on Military Affairs, U.S. Senate, 77th Congress, 2d Session, on S. 2240, "A Bill to Establish a WAAC for Service with the Army of the U.S." February 6, 1942. Brig. General J. H. Hilldring, assistant chief of staff, speaking for General Marshall, p. 27. File: Legislation on "WAAC," Series 55, RG 165, NA.

60. For a discussion of the ways that the Army denigrated African-American servicemen's participation during World War I and II, see Nalty, *Strength for the Fight*, pp. 107–24, 168–77.

61. Judith Stiehm, "Women, Men, and Military Service: Is Protection Necessarily a Racket?" in Ellen Boneparth, ed. *Women, Power and Policy* (Oxford: Pergamon Press, 1982), pp. 287–91.

62. Memo W635 1943, "Prohibition of the Use of Weapons or Arms by Members of the WAAC/WAC," September 1, 1943, File: WAAC Circulars, Bulletins, Regulations, Box 215, Series 55, RG 165, NA.

63. Although the judge advocate general declared the project illegal, the Army persisted. When the judge advocate general was approached about the legality of the project he ruled that Waacs could not be utilized in this type of combat duty without an amendment to the original legislation creating the corps. In accordance with this ruling, Army administrators drafted an amendment providing for women, with their consent, to be used in "combatant service within the U.S. and its territories and territorial possessions." Though the amendment was never passed, the formation of the unit proceeded as planned. See Conference held on suggestion to use Waacs in fixed AAC installations, November 18, 1942; 150th and 151st WAAC AAAC Companies constituted, January 1, 1943; Draft of Amendment to WAAC Act of May 14, 1942; File: WAAC, SPWA 320.2, Series 55, RG 165, NA; also Treadwell, pp. 302–3.

64. Study reported by Col. Hobby to chief of staff, re: Use of British women in fixed AAC gun installations in British Isles, November 16, 1942; Conference held on suggestion to use Waacs in fixed AAC installations, November 18, 1942; 150th and 151st WAAC AAAC Companies constituted, January 1, 1943; Draft of Amendment to WAAC Act of May 14, 1942; File: WAAC, SPWA 320.2, Series 55, RG 165, NA; also Treadwell, pp. 302–3.

65. Operations Division, liaison secretary, Theater Group, May 30, 1943, WDOPD, Box 66, Series 54, RG 165, NA.

66. Study of the WAC in the ETO, chapter 2, section 3, File: see note 19.

67. Meyer Oral History Questionnaires, Olive Crandall, no. 9, Supplement, p. 3. Wacs served in every overseas theater during World War II, with the largest numbers serving in the European Theater (8,316), the Southwest Pacific Area (5,500), and the Mediterranean and North African theaters (over 2,000). Treadwell, pp. 380, 410, and appendix A, table 7, "Strength of Women's Army Corps in Overseas Theaters: 1943–46," pp. 772–73.

68. On several occasions after they returned, they found considerable damage to their billets and the surrounding building. After one such raid a WAC described the situation they found as they emerged from the shelter: "We saw before us the crumpled ruins of a large corner of the billet which had housed many of our girls as well as our company officers . . . for many days it was necessary for those who had been bombed out to share cots with the more fortunate ones or set up their beds in the mess hall or day room." "Housing," p. 7, File: European Division ATC Historical Record Report, WACs in the European Division ATC, June 1944–August 1945, Box 308.04-1 (January 31, 1945)–308.072 (June 1944–August 1945), Air Force Historical Research Center, Maxwell Air Force Base, Montgomery, Ala. See also Edith Davis, WAAC and ETO Experiences, Oral History #1, May 16, 1986, 5th WAC Reunion, Fort McClellan; WAC Museum Oral Histories, Fort McClellan, Ala.

69. Study of the WAC in the ETO, chapter 2, section 4: Headquarters to Which Assigned, Continental Assignments, p. 99, File: see note 19. See also Treadwell, pp. 366–68.

70. Treadwell, p. 410.

71. File: WDWAC 314.7 Military Histories, Historical Data and Notes on SWPA Wacs, Box 55, Series 54, RG 165, NA. See also Treadwell, *The U.S. in World War II*, pp. 418–50.

72. Ibid.

73. John J. McManus, president of Rolls-Royce, to Hobby, February 8, 1945, Box 19, Series 54, RG 165, NA. See also "History AAF, Eastern Flying Training Command (EFTC), p. 59, "Training," File: cited in note 55.

74. David E. Kahn to Hobby, re: Letter from Auxiliary Ruth Freudenthal, Includes sworn statement from Ruth Freudenthal to Brig. General Don C. Faith, September 15, 1943, File: 330.14, Box 92, Series 54, RG 165, NA.

75. Charles P. Howard, Howard News Syndicate, to Mrs. Mary McLeod Bethune, re: Handling of Negro officer candidates, August 26, 1942, File: 291.21, Series 54, RG 165, NA.

76. Earley, *One Woman's Army*, pp. 19–20.

77. Lt. Col. J. Noel Macy, assistant director, WAAC, Fort Des Moines, to Mr. Harry McAlpin, Chicago *Defender*, a response to McAlpin's inquiries about the problems experienced by Negro Waacs at Fort Des Moines, September 8, 1942; Howard to Bethune, re: Handling of Negro officer candidates, August 26, 1942, see note 75. For examples of articles in the black press, see "WAC Follows Army Pattern; Sets up Jim Crow Unit in Des Moines," and "Protest Fails to Halt J-C Battalion at Fort Des Moines," in *Philadelphia Afro-American*, September 4, 1943, p. 13, and Pvt. Joan Willis, "Diary of a WAC Private," *Philadelphia Afro-American*, October 2, 1943, p. 5.

78. For an example of this, see Howard to Bethune, re: Handling of Negro officer candidates, August 26, 1942; Howard to Bethune, August 27, 1942; and Mary McLeod Bethune to Judge William H. Hastie, civilian aide to the secretary of war, September 2, 1942, File 291.21, Box 50, Series 54, RG 165, NA. In this correspondence Bethune requested that Howard, as a representative of the black press visit Fort Des Moines and investigate the conditions there for African-American women. Howard sent a report on the results of his investigations to Bethune and held off using them in the media until she gave him the okay. In the meantime, Bethune sent his report on to Hastie, who was in charge of "Negro Affairs" for the War Department.

79. Bethune to Mrs. Harriet B. Hall, re: Fort Des Moines, November 10, 1942, File: 237, Box 14 Correspondence H, Series 5, Records of the NCNW 1935–1976, Bethune Museum and Archives, Washington, D.C.; Conference with Mrs. Bethune and NCNW, Col. Hobby, Col. Catron, Capt. Strayhorn (WAC HQ), August 16, 1943, File: Office of Director, Daily Journal, V. I, Box 200, Series 55, RG 165, NA.

80. Ibid., and Report on Field Trip to 6th and 7th Service Commands, 1st Officer Harriet West, May 17, 1943, File: Negro, Box 211, Series 55, RG 165, NA.

81. "Beginning a Who's Who of WAC Officers," *The Aframerican Women's Journal* 3, no. 2 (Summer 1943): 32. Transcript of Telephone Conversation Between Colonel Hobby and Mr. Jonathan Daniels, November 29, 1944, File: 291.2, Box 49, Series 54, RG 165, NA.

82. Report on Field Trip to 6th and 7th Service Commands, cited in note 80.

83. Letter from enlisted Wacs at Laurinburg-Maxton AAB, Maxton, N.C., to Mrs. Roosevelt, October 1944; Request for investigation and report on Negro WAC detach-

ment, Maxton, N.C., from Lt. Colonel Jessie Pearl Rice, executive, Women's Army Corps, October 31, 1944; Request for investigation to air inspector from Maj. General J. M. Bevans, assistant chief of air staff, Personnel, November 2, 1944; Col. Max F. Schneider, deputy air inspector to commanding general, I Troop Carrier Command, Alleged Conditions in WAC Section 810th AAF Base Unit, November 3, 1944, Stout Field, Indianapolis, Ind.; Report of investigation of conditions in colored WAC squadron, Laurinburg-Maxton AAB, November 28, 1944; Maj. General Bevans, assistant chief of air staff, Personnel, to Col. Hobby, December 4, 1944; Col. Hobby to Mrs. Roosevelt, January 16, 1945, File: WDWAC 330.14, Box 91, Series 54, RG 165, NA.

84. Lula Jones Garrett,"Officials at Fort McClellan Would Double WAC Quota," and photo spread, "WAC's at Fort McClellan Find Plenty Facilities for Play as Well as Jobs that Hold their Interest," in "The Feminine Front," *Philadelphia Afro-American*, March 4, 1944, p. 12. See also Lula Jones Garrett, "Jim Crow Irks WAC Recruiter," *Philadelphia Afro-American*, February 5, 1944, pp. 1, 16.

85. Joe Shepard, "Two Camp Sibert Wac's Beaten by Alabama Policeman; Girls Refused to Give Up Seats to Whites on Bus; 2 Agreements Follow Investigation," *Philadelphia Afro-American*, January 13, 1945), p. 1. See also "Philly Wac Beaten in N.C.; Police Chief Wields Blow; Brutal Attack Follows Ejection from Train; MPs Witnesses —NAACP Intervenes After Victim Jailed," *Philadelphia Afro-American*, August 18, 1945, p. 1; Lula Jones Garrett, "Benning WAC's in Varied Jobs; Praised by Colonel and Soldiers," *Philadelphia Afro-American*, February 12, 1944, pp. 1, 14.

Col. Frederick D. Sharp, deputy director of Intelligence, ASF, Office of the Commanding General, Report on domestic racial estimate, July 10, 1945, and Racial situation in the United States, June 16–30, 1945, July 14, 1945, File: 291.2, Box 49, Series 54, RG 165, NA. See also File: History of the 2d Air Force, chs. 1 and 2, pp. 279–86, on similar situations arising for African-American male soldiers and being evaluated by the Army, Box 432.01, December 7, 1941–December 31, 1942 (V. 13) and 1943 (V.3), Air Force Historical Research Center, Maxwell Air Force Base, Montgomery, Ala. Evidence also suggests that racial violence directed toward black military personnel increased as the war drew to a close.

86. Sharp, Report on domestic racial estimate, and Racial situation in the United States, June 16–30, 1945, cited in note 85.

87. "2 Wacs Slugged by Kentucky Cop," *Philadelphia Afro-American*, July 28, 1945, p. 1; ASF, Hq. of the 5th Service Command, Report of Investigation of Incident at Elizabethtown, July 27, 1945, File: 291.2, Box 49, Series 54, RG 165, NA. See also "WAC Slapped for Drinking at Columbia Fountain," *Philadelphia Afro-American*, December 22, 1945, p. 22. This article discusses the plight of a Wac from Pennsylvania who, along with another Wac, accompanied two white male MPs who were transporting an injured third Wac into town. While awaiting orders to return to the fort one of the women went to get a drink of water at an unmarked fountain. She was having trouble getting the water to come out and one of the MPs helped her. As she was finishing the drink a civilian officer rushed up, swearing, pushed her back from the fountain, and slapped her in the face because "n—s are not supposed to drink from this fountain." This all occurred in the presence of the other Wac and the two white male MPs, who did nothing to prevent the incident or help the woman after it was over.

88. "Army Offers No Rotation Relief for WACs 'Buried' in the South: Six Months in South Enough Says Disillusioned Officer," *Philadelphia Afro-American*, September 30, 1944, p. 12.

89. "Wacs' Crossing Fair; Find English Hospitable, Entertainment Plentiful, Exchange Confusing," *Philadelphia Afro-American*, March 10, 1945), p. 16. This article quotes from a letter written by a black Wac private to her friend in the States. See also Richard R. Dier, "British, French Reception Cited by 4 Wacs Returned to States," *Philadelphia Afro-American*, September 1, 1945, p. 9, and "200 WAC Postal Unit Members Back After 2 Years Overseas," *Philadelphia Afro-American*, March 23, 1946, p.

90. "WACs Recall Segregated Service," *Atlanta Journal*, October 5, 1984, clippings from 4th Black WAC Reunion, October 3–7, 1984, Atlanta, File: History of WAAC-WAC Black, Fort McClellan WAC Historical Museum Files, WAC Museum, Fort McClellan, Anniston, Ala.

91. Earley, *One Woman's Army*, pp. 161–66; B. M. Phillips, "ARC Jim Crows Women Officers," *Philadelphia Afro-American*, March 26, 1945; "WACs Recall Segregated Service," *Atlanta Journal*, October 5, 1984; cited in note 90.

For more information on the only African-American unit to serve overseas, the 6888th postal battalion, see "Employment of Colored WACs in the ETO," File: Study WAC in ETO, V.III, G-1, #11, Box 502.101–11;-16 1943–45, Air Force Historical Research Center, Maxwell Air Force Base, Montgomery, Ala.

92. Lt. Colonel Jessie Pearl Rice, executive WAC, to Mrs. Mary McLeod Bethune, National Council of Negro Women, Mr. Ike Smalls, chairman, Des Moines Inter-racial Commission, Mrs. Thomasina W. Johnson, legislative representative of Alpha Kappa Alpha sorority, Mrs. Jeanetta Welch Brown, executive secretary, National Council of Negro Women, in response to their protests over the dissolution of the black WAC Band, August 16, 1944; Telephone conversation between Col. Rice and Mr. Lautier (Mr. Gibson's office), July 26, 1944; Telephone conversation between Col. Rice and Mr. Holloway, July 24, 1944, File: 291.2, Box 49; Mary McLeod Bethune to Col. Hobby, August 14, 1944; Memo for Gen. White from Lt. Col. Rice, re: Negro WAC Band, August 3, 1944; Form letter from members of WAC Band #2, July 18, 1944, Box 91, Series 54, RG 165, NA. Telegram from Walter White to Secretary of War Stimson, re: Deactivation of Negro WAC Band, July 18, 1944; S. A. Hull to Bethune, re: Band, July 22, 1944; John S. Coleman, president, Des Moines Branch NAACP, to Bethune, re: Band, July 25, 1944; 2d Lt. Thelma B. Brown, former officer-in-charge WAC Band #2 to Bethune, July 25, 1944; Jeanetta Welch Brown to Col. Hobby, re: Negro Band, July 26, 1944; All in File: 535 WAC 1942–1945, Series 5, Box 38, Records of the NCNW, Bethune Museum and Archives, Washington, D.C. See also Oral History no. 4. Tr 920-1310691B, May 12, 1988, WAC Foundation Oral History, TSgt (Ret) Gurthalee Clark, member of WAC Band #2, interviewed by Col. Eunice M. Wright, WAC Museum Oral Histories, WAC Museum, Fort McClellan, Anniston, Ala.

93. "Conditions at Lovell General Hospital," memo for Capt. Chance, WAC, from Col. O. G. Haywood Jr., GSC, executive, March 23, 1945; Memo for General Berry, re: Response of Truman Gibson's office to Fort Devens situation, April 5, 1945; Maj. Kathryn Johnson, Office of the Director WAC to War Dept., April 10, 1945; Rep.

William T. Granahan to secretary of war, March 13, 1945; "Complaint of Negro Wacs at Lovell General Hospital, Fort Devens, Mass., to Office of Director WAC from Office of Director of Personnel, ASF, March 28, 1945; "Negro Wacs, Lovell General Hospital," Maj. General Sherman Miles, commanding general 1st Service Command, to commanding general, ASF, Attn: director of personnel, March 20, 1945; File: 330.14, Box 91; "Situation at Fort Devens," transcript of conversations between Maj. Herman and Capt. Chance, WAC, File 291.2, Box 49, Series 54, RG 165, NA.

94. Ibid. See also Rita Gomez DeArmond, "The Strike of Black Wacs at Fort Devens," paper given at Organization of American Historians Conference, April 1988, Washington, D.C., pp. 11, 14.

95. For example, see *Philadelphia Afro-American* "Deven WAC Strike Ends; 4 Get Hard Labor Term," March 31, 1945, p. 1. See also Lee Finkle, *Forum for Protest: The Black Press During World War II* (Cranbury, N.J.: Associated University Presses, 1975), p. 180.

96. Mary McLeod Bethune to Col. Hamilton, re: Touring black WAC Posts, January 22, 1945, File: 241; Harriet Hall, circulating manager, *Aframerican Woman's Journal*, to Bethune, NCNW, March 18, 1945; Bethune to Hall, March 20, 1945, File: 242, Box 15, Series 5, Records of the NCNW, 1935–1976, Bethune Museum and Archives, Washington, D.C. Memo for Col. Hobby, re: Request by Bethune that investigation be made into situation of African-American Wacs at Lovell Hospital, March 20, 1945; Box 191, Series 54, RG 165, NA.

97. "Devens WAC Strike Ends; 4 Get Hard Labor Term," *Philadelphia Afro-American*, March 31, 1945, p. 1.

98. Ibid.

99. Bethune to Jane E. Hunter, president, Ohio State Federation of Colored Women's Clubs, re: Campaign to reverse the conviction of the black Wacs at Lovell Hospital, April 3, 1945. She wrote, "We have made personal contacts with Mrs. Roosevelt, and Colonel Hobby . . . The Secretary of War has ordered a technical investigation and we hope to get good results from it. The NCNW is deeply concerned about the outcome of these four WACs and, in the name of womanhood, we are working diligently to get the sentence changed." Bethune to Dr. Frank S. Horne, re: Donations to help fund the investigation of the court-martial of the 4 Negro members of the WAC at Fort Devens, April 13, 1945:"We felt that the case should not be closed until we know the reasons for this action by Colonel Crandall and the exact nature of the circumstances which motivated the stand taken by the girls." File: 242, Box 15, Series 5, Records of the NCNW, 1935–1976, Bethune Museum and Archives, Washington, D.C. DeArmond, "The Strike of the Black Wacs at Fort Devens," pp. 24–28.

100. Ann Washington Craton to Hobby, March 21, 1945; Helen Mears to Hobby, March 26, 1945; Ellen A. Kennan to Hobby, March 28, 1945; Dorothy Leon to Hobby, April 1, 1945. For example of Hobby's reply to all of these types of letters, see Hobby to Helen Mears, March 31, 1945, File: 330.14, Box 91, Series 54, RG 165, NA. See also DeArmand, p. 28.

101. DeArmond, p. 34. "4 WACS Cleared," *Philadelphia Afro-American*, April 7, 1945, p. 1; "Devens Colonel's Removal Sought," *Philadelphia Afro-American*, April 21, 1945, p. 18. It should be noted that another similar incident occurred earlier at

Camp Breckinridge, Ky., when six women refused to continue performing menial jobs assigned at the post despite their training for other occupations. There was less publicity surrounding it in part because the women were allowed to resign when the WAAC converted into the WAC. See "6 WACs Resign: WAC Clerks Decline to Scrub Floors," *Philadelphia Afro-American*, July 10, 1943, p. 1.

5. Protecting Whom? Regulating Sexuality in the World War II Army and the WAC

1. Allan Berube, *Coming Out Under Fire: Gay GIs During World War Two* (New York: Free Press, 1991), p. 2. Berube's book also includes a unique and important discussion of the changes in the way the military dealt with homosexuality occurring during the war. He demonstrates how the professions of psychiatry and neuropsychiatry influenced the military to move from policies punishing a particular sexual act, sodomy, to policies addressing a personality type defined as homosexual. For a more general discussion of the relationship between the military and venereal disease, see Allan Brandt's work *No Magic Bullet: A Social History of Venereal Disease in America Since 1880* (New York: Oxford University Press, 1985). See also John D'Emilio and Estelle Freedman, *Intimate Matters: A History of Sexuality in America* (New York: Harper and Row, 1988), ch. 9. In addition, RG 215, Series 37 and 38, Records of the Office of Community War Service, Social Protection Division, NA, contains a great deal of information on the development of military policies on prevention of VD among male troops and treatment of infected soldiers. These records also address military policy on the issue of interracial liaisons formed by African-American troops.

2. For examples of this logic, see Irwin Ross, "Sex in the Army: Uncle Sam Seeks to Safeguard His Armed Men Against Prostitution," *American Mercury*, October 21, 1941, pp. 661–69; Col. Charles S. Hendricks and Capt. John D. Winebrenner, "Some Aspects of Venereal Disease Control in the Army," *The Military Surgeon* 95, no. 1 (July 1944): 121–28; Capt. Granville W. Larimore and Lt. Colonel Thomas H. Sternberg, "Does Health Education Prevent Venereal Disease? The Army's Experience With 8,000,000 Men," *American Journal of Public Health* 35 (August 1945): 799–804.

3. AR 40–210, April 25, 1945, Medical Department, "Prevention and Control of Communicable Diseases of Man," section 7: Venereal Diseases, File: Army and Navy, Box 1, Series 37, RG 215, Office of Community War Services (OCWS), Social Protection Division General Records, 1941–1946 (hereafter referred to as OCWS records) NA. See also Brandt, pp. 163, 168.

4. Linda Gordon, *Heroes of Their Own Lives: The Politics and History of Family Violence* (New York: Viking Penguin, 1988), p. 220.

5. FSA Community War Services Social Protection Division, "Outline of Activities," File: Articles, Box 1, Series 37, RG 215, OCWS, NA.

6. "The Eight Point Agreement," May 1939, File: Articles, Social Protection Division, Box 1, Series 37, RG 215, OCWS, NA.

7. The May Act, P.L. 163, July 1941, File: 849/02 1945, Box 1, Series 38, OCWS, NA.

8. For evidence on public opinion, see Gallup Poll, asking question of regulation vs. repression, November 1942, File: Polls and Public Opinion, Box 8, Series 37, RG 215. For internal conflict within the Army and local social protection campaigns over

this issue, see War Department Office of Provost Marshal, General Emergency Operations Division, PMG 250.1 (General), To: All Provost Marshalls, Commanding Officers, and Military Police Battalions, re: Moral conditions in the vicinity of Army camps and stations, January 21, 1942, File: Army and Navy; "Military Saboteur Number One is the 'World's Oldest Profession,'" File: Articles, SPD, Box 1, Series 37, RG 215, NA.

9. File: Army and Navy; File: Articles, SPD, Box 1; File: Joint Army and Navy Disciplinary Control Board, Box 5; File: Magazines, Box 7, All in Series 37, RG 215, OCWS, 1941–46, NA. See also File: 849 (June 1945) Box 1; File: 849.1 (1944), Box 4, All in Series 38, RG 215, OCWS, 1944–46, NA. See also Brandt, *No Magic Bullet*, p. 163, for his argument that the issuance of condoms to servicemen during World War II was a significant break with World War I efforts in venereal disease (VD) prevention and marked the military's recognition of its inability to control the sex drives of servicemen. In keeping with this philosophy soldiers diagnosed as having VD prior to enlistment were not rejected by the military, but were sent to an Army hospital for treatment and placed in a unit after they were cured.

10. War Department Office of Provost Marshal General, re: Moral conditions in the vicinity of Army camps, cited in note 8; SURG 726.1 Hq 9th Corps Area Office of the Commanding General Presidio of San Francisco, To: COs of All Posts, Camps and Stations within 9th Corps Area, January 13, 1941, File: Policy Statements, Box 8; All in Series 37, RG 215, OCWS, NA. See also Brandt, p. 166. For an example of a formal policy of regulation used by the British in India, see Memo from Calcutta for the War Department, Report of Edward M. Groth, consul of Calcutta, through State Department to War Department, April 15, 1940, File: 102.2, in File: 250.18, Box 48, Series 54, RG 165, NA.

11. As the war progressed, the Army's sexual hygiene program came increasingly to emphasize the need to break down the stigma of VD for male soldiers. Army doctors argued that it was more important to guarantee timely and adequate treatment of VD than to have a falsely depressed VD rate by "enforcing punitive action which in turn caused concealed, inadequately treated or maltreated infections." See, for example, 4th Air Force Historical Study, No. V-2, p. 89, Box 450.01–13, 1941–45, V.1, Air Force Historical Research Center, Maxwell Air Force Base, Montgomery, Ala.

These attitudes were also visible in changes during the war in punitive regulations affecting male soldiers with VD. For example, though legislation existed at the outset of the war which required the Army to withhold the pay of soldiers with venereal infections the Army surgeon general recommended the repeal of such laws arguing that it discouraged men from seeking treatment. The issue was finally settled when Congress repealed the "loss of pay" provision in September 1944. Additionally, as the war progressed other Army regulations changed resulting in provisions for punishment of infected GIs only if they did *not* report their exposure and infection. Thus, by war's end formal mechanisms for punishing servicemen who contracted VD had been eliminated.

See, for example, AR 40–210, Medical Department, "Prevention and Control of Communicable Diseases of Man," section 7: Venereal Diseases, p. 12, April 25, 1945, File: Army and Navy, Box 1, Series 37, RG 215, OCWS, NA. See also 4th Air Force Historical Study, No. V-2, p. 93. See also Brandt, pp. 167–68.

12. For a discussion of the effect of these racial stereotypes on white middle-class constructions of black women as "sexually aggressive and immoral," see Patricia Hill Collins, *Black Feminist Thought and the Politics of Empowerment* (New York: Unwin Hyman, 1990), pp.: 165–66.

13. Eliot Ness, director, and Howard M. Slutes, Social Protection Section, OCWS, Field Report, Casper Wyoming, June 17, 1943, p. 3, File: Curfew (Case Studies), Box 2; Eliot Ness, to Janet S. Burgoon, Social Protection supervisor, File: Negro Groups, Box 7; All in Series 37, RG 215, OCWS, NA.

14. For an interesting angle on this issue, see "World's Oldest Profession Gives South the Jitters," Philadelphia *Afro-American*, November 13, 1943, p. 3. The author argues that the explosion of military training camps in the southern United States has created a situation in which the heretofore "secret" visits to "negro" prostitutes by white men, which he characterizes as part of an "old southern tradition," are being brought into the open by the growing numbers of white servicemen who frequent the same brothels. Thus "the new soldier in town is doing openly what the Southern white man is doing under cover."

15. "Sex Delinquency Among Girls," report submitted by Bascomb Johnson, of ASHA, November 23, 1942, File: 849, Box 2, Series 38, RG 215, OCWS, NA. See also Statements of representatives of the Army, Navy, and medical profession, re: Need for the repression, not regulation, of prostitution, Dr. William Snow, chair of executive committee, ASHA, File: Army and Navy, Box 1, Series 37, RG 215, OCWS, NA.

16. *On the Local Front* for "Municipal Review," Office of Defense Health and Welfare Services, December 31, 1942, p. 5. File: Articles, SPD, Box 1, Series 37, RG 215, OCWS, NA.

17. For a discussion of the changes in discourses on sexual psychopaths and sexual deviance, see Estelle Freedman, " 'Uncontrolled Desires': The Response to the Sexual Psychopath, 1920–1960," in Kathy Peiss, Christina Simmons, with Robert Padgug, eds., *Passion and Power: Sexuality in History* (Philadelphia: Temple University Press, 1989), pp. 199–216, especially pp. 208–10.

18. For a discussion of the shifts in the discourse on female sexual delinquency after 1910, see Gordon, *Heroes of Their Own Lives*, pp. 218–22.

19. Brandt, *No Magic Bullet*, p. 168. See also Elaine May, *Homeward Bound: American Families in the Cold War Era* (New York: Basic Books, 1988), p. 69. She notes that many "victory girls" were seen by the public as "good" women whose morals "unraveled during wartime."

20. Leo Wilson, "Sex Delinquency versus Human Resources," January 1, 1945, File: Articles, SPD, Box 1, Series 37, RG 215, OCWS, NA. See also Karen Anderson, *Wartime Women: Sex Roles, Family Relations, and the Status of Women During World War II* (Westport, Conn.: Greenwood Press, 1981), pp. 104–5.

21. WAAC Director Hobby to Chief of Staff General George Marshall, August 4, 1942, File: 300, Box 51, Series 54, RG 165, NA.

22. Letter to Col. Hobby from Commander E. H. Cushing, USNR, Division of Medical Science, re: Conference group Called by Surgeon General's Office (SGO), July 17, 1942; Memo for Director WAAC from Lt. Colonel Harold Tasker, GSC, "Report of the Conference on Prevention of VD in Female Personnel of the Armed

Forces," July 27, 1942; Memo to Col. Hobby from surgeon general (SG), May 18, 1943, Box 145, Series 54, RG 165, NA.

23. Ibid. See also Memo to Col. Hobby from Emily Newell Blair, chief, Women's Interest Section, Planning and Liaison Branch, War Department, August 13, 1942, File: 300, Box 145, Series 54, RG 165, NA.

24. Discussion of VD problem in WAC in general and specifically at Fort Oglethorpe, Memo for Col. Gorman from Lt. Col. Thomas B. Turner, Medical Corps, re: Physical standards for WAC personnel, August 2, 1943, Box 143, Series 54, RG 165, NA.

25. To: Hq WAAC, From: SG, re: Policies on VD in the WAAC, May 18, 1943, Box 145; Lt. Col. David Kirk, adjutant general (AG) to commanding general, SOS (AG), re: Basic policy to be observed concerning discharge of women, January 25, 1943; Response from Lt. Colonel Howard Clark, chief, Operating Service to AG, Operations, January 29, 1943, File: R, Box 29. All in Series 54, RG 165, NA.

26. Statement of 3d Officer Edna L. Johnson, 1st WAAC Training Command, Notarized by Warrant Officer S. J. Machuta, assistant adjutant, re: Lecture on VD by Army captain (no name given) while member of WAAC detachment, Santa Ana Army Air Base, Capt. Elizabeth A. Yancey, CO; Memo sent to director, WAC, through Maj. Margaret D. Craighill, WAC Liaison Branch by Lt. Colonel Thomas B. Turner, Medical Corps, August 13, 1943, Box 145, Series 54, RG 165, NA. See also Mattie Treadwell, *The United States Army in World War II, Special Studies, The Women's Army Corps* (Washington, D.C.: Office of the Chief of Military History, 1954), p. 618.

27. Request from 1st Officer Gretchen Thorp, director, Technical Information Division, via Director's Office to all WAAC staff directors to report re: Circulating rumors in their area and their source; Reply by 1st Officer Katherine R. Goodwin, WAAC staff drector, 1st Service Command, Boston, June 23, 1943; Statement by AFC Martha Chandler, notarized by Major William B. Collett, Jr., military intelligence officer, Bangor, Maine, May 29, 1943, File: Rumors Against the WAC, Box 93, Series 54, RG 165, NA.

28. For example, see 3d Officer Sophia J. Bogdan to chief, WAAC Branch, Personnel Division, 1st Service Command, Boston, Subject: Monthly Physical Inspections, November 7, 1942, File: Physical Inspection, Box 31, Series 54, RG 165, NA.

For an example of the WAC VD rate during 1943 and 1944, see Memo for Director, WAC from A. J. Bonis, December 8, 1944, Subject: VD Rates Among WAC personnel in the Continental United States, 1943 and 1944 (rates per thousand).

Year	Total	White	Colored
1943	8.3	6.7	37.2
1944	10.0	7.9	48.3

Memo for Maj. Margaret Janeway, Women's Health Unit, from Lt. Colonel Thomas H. Sternberg, Medical Corps, Directory, Venereal Disease Control Division, Subject: Venereal Disease Rates among WAC Personnel in the Continental United States, December 7, 1944, File: 700; Brig. General Don C. Faith to Col. Hobby, re: WAC VD Rate, August 27, 1943; Survey of VD rates at 3d WAAC Training Center, Ft.

Oglethorpe, Ga., to Hobby from Brig. General Faith, August 23, 1943; All in Box 143, Series 54, RG 165, NA. See also Treadwell, pp. 372, 398.

29. Report by 1st Officer Doris E. Epperson, WAAC staff director, 8th and 9th Service Commands, July 9, 1943, File: Unmarked, Box 190, Series 55, RG 165, NA. It is interesting to note that this continued to be a problem after the war as well. For example, see Letter from Brig. General George B. Armstrong, deputy, SG to Brig. General E. A. Noyes, Surgeon European Command, re: WAC physicals, June 10, 1947, Box 202, Series 55, RG 165, NA.

30. Meyer Oral History Questionnaires, Ruth Chambers (#1), Question #33.

31. Lillian Hanslik (Cleveland) to Col. Hobby, December 23, 1944, File: 330.14, Box 91, Series 54, RG 165, NA. See also Treadwell, pp. 608–10.

32. 3d Officer Sophia J. Bogdan to chief, WAAC branch, Personnel Division, 1st Service Command, Boston, Subject: Monthly Physical Inspections, November 7, 1942; Reply War Department SOS, SPMCE 702, Boston, From: Col. John A. Rogers, Medical Corps executive for the surgeon general, December 1, 1942, File: Physical Inspection, Box 31, Series 54; Circular letter, Subject: Physical inspection of enrolled members of the WAAC, June 28, 1943, File: 700, Box 143, Series 54; Fort Des Moines, Iowa Station Hospital Office of the Surgeon, To: Surgeon General, U.S. Army, Washington, D.C., re: Physical Inspection, October 20, 1942, File: Medical, Box 211, Series 55; Memo to WAC Directory, VIII, p. 6, Monthly Physical Exams, January 31, 1944, File: Office of the Director, Daily Journal, V. II, Box 200, Series 55; All in RG 165, NA.

33. Joan Younger interview with Oveta Culp Hobby, "Abortions and Pregnancies," *Ladies Home Journal*, February 25, 1952, p. 8. File: *Ladies Home Journal* Article, 1952, Box 9, Hobby Papers, LC.

34. Ibid. See also, Captain Todd Report: Medical Deficiencies, Box 191, Series 55, RG 165, NA.

35. War Department circular letter no. 135, from Col. John A. Rogers, Medical Corps, executive officer, section 3. Special Physical Inspections of WAC Members, July 27, 1943, File: WAC Policy File, vols. 2 and 3, Box 198, Series 55, RG 165, NA.

36. Pelvic examinations were also performed by male public health officials on any civilian woman whose behavior, manner, or dress *appeared* to place her outside the bounds of conventional norms of propriety and sexual respectability. Although used ostensibly to detect the presence of venereal disease, coercive pelvics were invasive and humiliating to women. Of equal importance, these exams, along with incarceration, were crucial aspects of state efforts to control women's behavior. For a discussion of pelvic exams as invasive and humiliating procedures, see Emily Martin, *The Woman in the Body: A Cultural Analysis of Reproduction* (Boston: Beacon Press, 1987), p. 71. Martin argues that the "position required for this exam—flat on one's back, one's feet and legs in stirrups, a sheet over one's legs, the doctor at the end of the table" alienates women from their bodies by "effectively separat[ing] the woman from the body parts the doctor is examining." See also Joan P. Emerson, "Behavior in Private Places: Sustaining Definitions of Realities in Gynecological Exams," in *Recent Society No 2: Patterns of Communicative Behavior*, ed. Hans Peter Dreitzel (New York: Macmillian, 1970), pp. 74–97.

37. For example of rumors re illegitimate pregnancy in the WAC, see Report on the Work of the Women's Interest Section in Connection with the Advisory Council, June

1942–June 1943, June 25, 1943, p. 6, Col. Hobby on the WAAC, File: 522, Box 37, Series 54, RG 165, NA. See also Women's Army Corps Separations–Enlisted and Officers, October 1943–January 1944, Inclusive; Frequency and Rate Per Thousand of Discharges for the WAAC and WAC by Month, from August 1942 through February 1944, for Pregnancy, File: Budget Material for 1944, Director WAC, Box 22, Series 54, RG 165, NA. For data on the WAC pregnancy rate, see Treadwell, *U.S. Army in World War II*, p. 620.

38. John O'Donnell, "Capitol Stuff," *Washington Times-Herald*, June 9, 1943, File: Unfavorable Newspaper Publicity, Compiled by Young and Rubicam, Box 203, Series 55, RG 165, NA.

39. "Waacs First Muster," *Time* (June 8, 1942): 71–72.

40. Statement of 3d Officer Edna L. Johnson, 1st WAAC Training Command, re: Lecture on VD by Army captain (no name given); cited in note 26.

41. Treadwell, p. 617.

42. Military Affairs Committee, conference attended by General White, Persons, Smith, Director Hobby, and Capt. Davis, June 10, 1943, file: Office of the Director, Daily Journal, V.I, Box 200, Series 55, RG 165, NA.

43. Treadwell, pp. 498–500.

44. War Department WAAC Regulations (tentative) 1942, section 4: Discharge, no. 38a. Pregnancy, File: Circulars, Box 207, Series 55, RG 165, NA.

45. For a discussion of the legalities of early pregnancy regulations, see NC #385 PREG, Letter from TAG to Honorable Joseph Clark Baldwin, House of Representatives, February 3, 1945, File: AGCH-P 321 Nurse Corps (January 15, 1945), RE: Constituent Who Became Indignant at ANC Honorable Discharge for Pregnancy, Box 10, CMH MSS File, RG 319, NA.

46. Treadwell, p. 501; Tuesday conference, Col. Hobby and Col. Catron, May 11, 1943, File: Office of the Director, Daily Journal, V.I, File: WAAC Circulars, Box 199, Series 55, RG 165, NA.

47. WAAC Circular 10, Discharge prior to expiration of service, no. 3, Pregnancy, April 9, 1943, File: WAAC Circulars, Box 199, Series 55, RG 165, NA.

48. In response to complaints stemming from this loophole, Col. Hobby issued a directive that clarified the regulation and stated: "It was not the intent of this provision to discharge an unmarried member for violation of the Code of Conduct solely for the reason of pregnancy." WAAC Intra Office Memo, To: Director, Thru: Operative Division, re: Discharge of enrolled member, May 5, 1943, Box 52, Series 54, RG 165, NA.

49. For an example of the new regulation. see SPWA 210.8 (Oct. 13, 43) O-P, Subject: Discharge of WAC officers, To: Commandant, First WAC Training Command, Fort Des Moines; By Command of General Styer, Col. Hobby, Col. Howard Clark 2d, GSC, director, Operating Division, October 13, 1943,File: 210.8, Box 43, Series 54, RG 165, NA.

50. WAAC Circular 10, April 9, 1943, cited in note 47. See also Treadwell, pp. 508–9.

51. Treadwell, p. 508. The need for the speedy discharge of pregnant servicewomen was also brought out in several letters to WAC Hq from concerned family members of Wacs who had miscarried before they were discharged. In one case the family blamed the women's corps for failure to discharge their daughter immediately and held the Army responsible for her subsequent miscarriage. Mrs. M. T. Kramer to Col. Hobby,

June 2, 1944; Lt. Colonel Jessie Pearl Rice to Mrs. M. T. Kramer, June 13, 1944; Mrs. M. T. Kramer to Lt. Colonel Rice, June 20, 1944; Lt. Colonel Jessie Pearl Rice to Mrs. Frederic A. Kramer, July 5, 1944, File: 330.14, Box 91, Series 54, RG 165, NA.

52. Treadwell, p. 502.

53. Memo to director, WAC, through Executive Officer 2d Lt. Vera A. Mankinen, Subject: Discharge because of abortion, February 23, 1944, File: 220.8, Box 46, Series 54, RG 165, NA.

54. Treadwell, pp. 502–3.

55. Ibid., p. 503. See also Transcript of telephone conversation between Col. Hobby and Maj. Margaret Craighill, April 4, 1944, File: 312, Box 78; Informal memo to Col. Hobby from Maj. Margaret Craighill, Medical Corps, consultant for Women's Health and Welfare, April 6, 1944, File: 702, Box 144; All in Series 54, RG 165, NA. Craighill's letter of April 6, 1944, was a response to Col. Hobby's request in their phone conversation of April 4, 1944, for her opinion on the procedure the WAC should adopt concerning servicewomen who were suspected of abortion. Craighill wrote: "The fact of an abortion, in itself, does not necessarily mean that she has an undesirable character, or that she will be a bad influence in the Army. It is therefore recommended that she be retained in the Army unless her conduct, either in connection with this incident or for other reasons, is of such an unsatisfactory nature that she is deemed unsuitable for the performance of her responsibilities."

56. Memo to director, WAC, February 23, 1944, cited in note 53; WDGAP 220.8, Personnel Division, G-1, G-1. MET 3026, "Discharge from WAC for Termination of Pregnancy," June 8, 1944, Box 207, Series 55. All in RG 165, NA. See also February 25, 1952, Joan Younger interview with Oveta Culp Hobby, p. 7, cited in note 33.

57. WDGAP 220.8, "Discharge from WAC for Termination of Pregnancy," cited in note 56. In a memo for the assistant chief of staff G-1, it was noted: "At present no regulation exists under which a member of the WAC may be discharged for deliberately induced termination of pregnancy. . . . Since members of the WAC certified to be pregnant are discharged, it is believed that induced termination of pregnancy should also be cause for discharge, in order that termination of pregnancy may not be encouraged." Memo, October 1944, to: Commanding Generals, AGF, AAF, ASF, All Service Commands, All Ports of Embarkation, ATC, ATC Divisions, Commanders of All Theaters, defense commands, departments and bases overseas, From: Maj. General J. A. Ulio, AG, re: Procedure for disposition of pregnant military personnel in overseas commands, Box 191, Series 55; Transcript of telephone conversation between Col. Hobby and Maj. Craighill, April 4, 1944, cited in note 55.

58. Col. J. H. Hills, AG, to Col. Hobby, re: Reconsideration of paragraph 38a WAAC Circular 17 re: Discharge of pregnancy cases, April 13, 1943, File: 300.3 WAAC Regulations, Box 52, Series 54, RG 165, NA. See also Treadwell, p. 508.

59. For an example of this plan, see Col. J. H. Hills to Hobby, re: Reconsideration of Paragraph 38a; cited in note 58.

60. Transcript of telephone conversation between Col. Hobby and Rep. Edith Nourse Rogers (D, Mass.), May 6, 1944, File: 312, Box 78, Series 54, RG 165, NA.

61. Lt. Colonel Mary-Agnes Brown to commanding general, AAFEFTC, February 22, 1944, Box 50, Series 54; Maj. Kathleen McClure, GSC, and Maj. Robert L. Graham, Jr., GSC, Memo for the executive, Subject: Maternity care for military per-

sonnel, April 27, 1944, File: 702, Box 144, Series 54; Memo for Col. Henry, from Maj. Robert L. Graham, Jr., GSC, re: Maternity care for military personnel, May 25, 1944, File: 330.31, Box 94, Series 54; All in RG 165, NA. Treadwell, p. 507. See also James L. Hicks, "Baby Is 'Family Affair' So Wacs Can't Use Vet Hospitals," Philadelphia *Afro-American*, March 23, 1946, p. 16.

62. Treadwell, p. 507.

63. In fact it was not until May 1945 that Col. Hobby was finally successful in obtaining care for pregnant discharged WAC veterans in Army hospitals. See War Department Circular 141, May 12, 1945, Box 198, Series 55, RG 165, NA. See also Treadwell, pp. 508–9.

64. ARC 416-A, Services to the Armed Forces, July 1944, ch. 3, pp. 15–23, File: 140.11 Services to Armed Forces, Creation, Functions, Organization and Discontinuation, June 1941–October 1944, Box 171, RG 200, Records of the American Red Cross National, 1935–46 (Hereafter referred to as ARC Records), NA.

65. Transcript of telephone conversation between Col. Hobby and Rep. Edith Nourse Rogers, cited in note 60.

66. Ruth L. Mann, Military and Naval Welfare Service Inter-Office Letter ARC to Mr. C. E. Heaton, November 18, 1942, p. 2, Box 963–610.2 WAC and 610.13 Hospital Service Activities, RG 200, ARC Records, NA.

67. Col. Hobby to WAC staff directors, service commands and foreign theaters, Air Force commands, ports of embarkation, and training schools, re: WAC Program Aid and Counsel for Women Discharged for Pregnancy, May 12, 1945, File: 610.12, Box 963, RG 200, ARC National Records, NA.

68. Rickie Solinger, *Wake Up Little Susie: Single Pregnancy and Race Before Roe v. Wade* (New York:Routledge, 1992), pp. 14–25.

69. Ibid., p. 24.

70. Miss Charlotte Johnson, director, Home Service, ARC, to Mrs. Kathryn N. Ellis, director, Home Service, eastern area, August 2, 1945, Enclosure: Report regarding visit to Pacific Area in the Interest of Servicewomen, August 28–October 1, 1944; Mrs. Louise N. Mumm, director, Home Service, to Miss Sterling Johnson, deputy director, Home Service National Hq., re: June Monthly Report of Service to Pregnant Servicewomen, July 6, 1945; Miss Margaret Woll, director, Home Service, to Mrs. Kathryn Ellis, director, Home Service, eastern area, June 22, 1945, and A. H. Randall to Mrs. McAdoo and Miss Leahy, re: Care for unmarried pregnant women recently released from Armed Services, S.E. Pennsylvania chapter, July 3, 1945, ARC; All in File: 610.1, Box 959, RG 200, ARC Records, NA.

71. Miss Gloria Rich, field director, Letterman General Hospital, to Mrs. Dorothy Mitchell, acting regional director, Pacific Area, Military and Naval Welfare Service, Subject: Services to pregnant enlisted Wacs at Letterman General Hospital, May 23, 1945, pp. 7–8, File: 610.1, Box 959, RG 200, ARC Records, NA.

72. Capt. Lillian Shapiro, WAC commanding, WAC detachment, ASF, 4th Service Command, Stark General Hospital, Charleston, S.C., To: Director, Women's Army Corps, Subject: Misinformation disseminated to WAC overseas troops, October 10, 1944, File: 702, Box 144, Series 54, RG 165. Miss Gloria Rich to Mrs. Dorothy Mitchell, Services to pregnant enlisted wacs at Letterman General Hospital, cited in note 71.

73. Miss Gloria Rich to Mrs. Dorothy Mitchell, Services to pregnant enlisted Wacs at Letterman General Hospital, pp. 2–3, cited in note 71.

74. For example, see Capt. Vera E. Von Stein, WAC Detachment, Hq, 9th Bombardment Division, to Col. Hobby, October 10, 1944, File: 702, Box 144, Series 54, RG 165, NA. See also Miss Elizabeth Beasom, assistant field director, Camp Kilmer, N.J., to Miss Eunice V. Willner, director, Hospital Service, re: Report of service to pregnant Wacs in debarkation hospitals, July 20, 1945, File: 610.1, Box 959, ARC Records, NA.

75. Mrs. Louise W. Forder to Miss Janet Neel, Subject: February Monthly Report on Services to Women Separated from Service Because of Pregnancy, p. 4, March 1, 1946, File: 610.1; Conference, Pentagon Building, February 8, 1945, Present: Col. Lloyd Harris, AER; Col. Hobby; Lt. Colonel Jessie Rice; Lt. Colonel Boyce, Personnel Policy Branch of the WAC; Miss Sterling Johnson, Home Service, ARC; Miss Helen Walmsley, asistant national director, Military and Naval Welfare Service, ARC, p. 2, File: 900.16, Box 1417; Report of Eastern Area, Services to Women Separated from the Service Because of Pregnancy, p. 8, File: 610.1; All in Box 959, RG 200, ARC Records, NA.

76. Solinger, pp. 14–15, 17.

77. Miss Gloria Rich to Mrs. Dorothy Mitchell, Services to pregnant enlisted Wacs at Letterman General Hospital, p. 3, cited in note 71.

78. Miss Charlotte Johnson to Mrs. Kathryn N. Ellis, Report, August 2, 1945, Enclosure: Report regarding visit to Pacific Area in the interest of servicewomen, August 28–October 1, 1945, p. 3; cited in note 70. It should be noted that additional ARC reports indicate that pressures on servicewomen to give up their babies for adoption were exacerbated by the "adoptability" of Wac children. The ARC reports noted that this adoptability was due largely to the high enlistment requirements of the WAC, which insured that prospective parents would be getting a healthy child whose mother hailed from a good background. Home Service field representatives to Mrs. Ellis, re: State resources on services to pregnant military personnel, October 3, 1945, p. 3, File: 610.1, Box 959, RG 200, ARC Records, NA.

79. Helen Walmsley to Mr. Wm. S. Hepner and Mr. J. H. Whiting, re: Care after discharge as a result of pregnancy, November 27, 1944, p. 2, File: 610.1, Box 959, RG 200, ARC Records, NA.

80. Eugene O. Fosdick to Mr. F. A. Manis, Pacific Area, ARC, re: Visit of Lt. Colonel Katherine R. Goodwin, staff director, WAC, ASF, April 4, 1945, p. 2; Samuel Kaminsky to Miss Mildred Jenkins, Subject: Report of cases handled from May 1 through May 31, 1945, in accordance with SAF&V 19.8 (Service to women separated from service because of pregnancy), June 8, 1945; Report of service to pregnant WAC in debarkation hospitals, Station Hospital, Mitchell Field, N.Y., July 20, 1945; Service to pregnant Wacs in debarkation hospitals, Halloran General Hospital, Willowbrook Reservation, Staten Island, N.Y.; Samuel Kaminsky to Mrs. Louise N. Mumm, June Monthly Report of Service to Pregnant Servicewomen, July 2, 1945; Miss Gloria Rich to Mrs. Dorothy Mitchell, Services to pregnant enlisted Wacs at Letterman General Hospital; cited in note 71. All in File: 610.1, Box 959, RG 200, ARC Records, NA.

81. Intraoffice memo to executive from Col. Clark, re: Conference in office of director of military personnel on September 13, 1943, on matter of overseas marriages,

September 14, 1943, File: 320.2 Overseas Units ETO (August 18, 1942) Section 6, Box 81, Series 54, RG 165, NA.

82. Ibid. Memo for Colonel Hobby, Subject: Marriage policy, May 3, 1945, File: WDWAC 291.1, Box 49, Series 54, RG 165, NA. Army regulations against interracial marriages affected African-American GIs seeking to marry white women, white GIs seeking to marry Asian women, as well as all GIs seeking to marry native Australian women (described as "aborigines") with "less than 50% African" blood.

83. To: General Lee, From: W. B. Smith, LG, USA, re: Applications of nurses to marry enlisted men, Appendix 39: Supreme Hq AEF, Office of the Chief of Staff, March 29, 1944, File: Study of the WAC in the ETO; G-1 Section, #11, V.2. Appendices 1–66 to V.I, Box 502.101–11, -16; 1943–45, Air Force Historical Research Center, Maxwell Air Force Base, Montgomery, Ala.

84. Treadwell, *U.S. Army in World War II*, pp. 402–4.

85. SGO, ND 319 Special, Ceylon, History of the CBI, October 25, 1944–June 23, 1945, File: CBI Section, WD, Box 10, CMH MSS File, RG 319, NA. See also Treadwell, p. 469.

86. Miss Elizabeth Beason to Miss Eunice V. Willner, Service to Pregnant Wacs in Debarkation Hospitals, p. 1; cited in note 74.

87. Intraoffice memo to executive from Col. Clark, re: Conference on overseas marriages, cited in note 81. See also Philip E. Ryan, director, Civilian Relief Insular and Foreign Operations, to Dr. Fred W. Routley, national commissioner, Canadian Red Cross Society, September 2, 1943, File: 900.16, All Theaters Red Cross Assistance in Cases of Paternity and Illegitimacy Involving Servicemen, Box 1418, RG 200, ARC National Records, NA.

88. Miss Sandra Gelband to Hobby, December 3, 1944, Box 19, Series 54, RG 165, NA.

89. Maj. Kathryn Johnson, GSC, executive, Office of the Director, to Miss Sandra Gelband, February 23, 1945, Box 19, Series 54, RG 165, NA.

90. To: Field officers in Australia, From: Frances Z. Nizell, director, Home Services, Sydney, re: Unmarried mothers claiming members of U.S. Armed Forces as fathers of their children, April 1, 1946, File: 900.611, Box 1415, RG 200, ARC Records, NA.

91. As one Army officer remarked "The man who won't fuck won't fight." As quoted in Elizabeth Fee, "Venereal Disease: The Wages of Sin?" in Peiss et al., eds., *Passion and Power*, p. 189.

6. "I Want a Man!" Pleasure and Danger in the Women's Corps

1. Much of my thinking concerning the "pleasure" and "danger" aspects of women's sexual agency has been influenced by the ground breaking essay of Ellen DuBois and Linda Gordon. See Ellen Carol DuBois and Linda Gordon, "Seeking Ecstasy on the Battlefield: Danger and Pleasure in Nineteenth-Century Feminist Sexual Thought," in Carole S. Vance, ed., *Pleasure and Danger: Exploring Female Sexuality* (Boston: Routledge and Kegan Paul, 1984), pp. 31–49.

2. John D'Emilio and Estelle Freedman, *Intimate Matters: A History of Sexuality in America* (New York: Harper and Row, 1988), p. 262.

3. Karen Anderson, *Wartime Women: Sex Roles, Family Relations, and the Status of Women During World War II* (London: Greenwood Press, 1981), p. 111.

4. For an excellent discussion of this point and the ramifications of the replacement of Victorian sexual ideology with a more liberating sexual ideology in the 1920s and '30s see Christina Simmons, "Modern Sexuality and the Myth of Victorian Repression," in Kathy Peiss, Christina Simmons, with Robert Padgug, eds., *Passion and Power: Sexuality in History* (Philadelphia: Temple University Press, 1989), pp. 169–71.

5. Pseudonymous letter signed "Jack and Bill," to Col. Hobby, concerning Lt. Jones, April 17, 1944, File:Date WAAC Officers, Box 201, Series 55, RG 165, NA.

6. Ibid.

7. Ibid.

8. Barbara Meil Hobson, *Uneasy Virtue: The Politics of Prostitution and the American Reform Tradition* (New York: Basic Books, Inc, 1987), p. 187.

9. R. L. Jenkins, M.D., Michigan Child Guidance Institute, Ann Arbor, "Psychiatry and Morals: A Reexamination of Psychiatry in Its Relation to Mental Hygiene," *Mental Hygiene* 27, no. 2 (April 1943): 177–87. Jenkins identified the moral and scientific approaches as two related methods of controlling human behavior. In particular he argued that psychiatry is and should be influenced by moral issues and judgments. He defined a moral approach for controlling behavior as motivating desirable behavior by disapproval/punishment of bad behavior and rewarding good behavior. In contrast he defined a scientific approach as one which seeks out causes of "that behavior which is considered deviant, undesirable, or bad and trys to remove them" and seeks out causes for behavior "which is considered conforming, desirable, or good and trys to promote them" (p. 182). In Jenkins' description of the "scientific" approach it is clear that cultural norms and standards of morality influence which behaviors scientists will define as "conforming and good" vs. which they will consider "deviant, undesirable, or bad." See also Hobson, pp. 174, 189.

10. Anderson, p. 110.

11. D'Emilio and Freedman, p. 261.

12. Anderson, p. 111.

13. Jenkins, "Psychiatry and Morals," p. 180.

14. Pseudonymous letter signed "Jack and Bill"; cited in note 5.

15. "I Want a Man! I want a Man!" p. 48, File: WAC Songbooks, WAC Files, WAC Museum, Fort McClellan, Anniston, Ala.

16. Margaret D. Craighill, M.D., "Psychiatric Aspects of Women Serving in the Army," *American Journal of Psychiatry* 104 (October 1947): 229.

17. Margaret D. Craighill, M.D., "A Psychological Approach to Social Hygiene for Women," *Journal of Social Hygiene* 32 (April 1946): 200.

18. WAC Social Hygiene Lectures, p. 54, undated, File: Box 145, Series 54, RG 165, NA.

19. Mattie Treadwell, *The United States Army in World War II, Special Studies, the Women's Army Corps* (Washington, D.C.: Office of the Chief of Military History, 1954), p. 585. See also Major Albert Preston, Jr., M.C. "The Mental-Hygiene Unit in a W.A.C. Training Center," *Mental Hygiene* 30, no. 3 (July 1946): 353–80.

20. "The Women," *Newsweek*, May 3, 1943, pp. 27–28; "Wacs in Africa," *Colliers*, October 30, 1943, pp. 16–18; Radio Script, 2d WAC Training Center, "Meet the

WAC," Station WMFJ, Daytona Beach, Fla., November 2, 1943, WAC Files, WAC Museum, Fort McClellan, Ala.

21. Treadwell, p. 373.

22. For example see Treadwell, p. 445.

23. "Cyclone" Forbes Dahlgren, "We Were First: Eglin Field World War II WACs 'We Heard the Guns at Wewak,' " p. 105, from Collection of WAC Memoirs, published and unpublished accounts of women's experiences within the WAC during World War II, WAC Museum, Fort McClellan, Anniston, Ala.

24. "Real Camp Abbott Girl," p. 29, File: WAC Songbooks, WAC Files, WAC Museum, Fort McClellan, Anniston, Ala.

25. Mr. James Fisher to Capt. Westray Boyce, WAAC, July 8, 1943; Mr. James Fisher to Maj. Cora W. Bass, WAC, November 14, 1943. File: 201B, Box 25, Series 54, RG 165, NA.

26. Lt. Colonel James R. Johnson, post inspector general to commanding officer, Fort Benning, re: Report of investigation regarding the conduct of Nancy Blumfield, December 16, 1943, File: 201B, Box 25, Series 54, RG 165, NA.

27. "My First Day at Fort Devens," partially reprinted in *Petticoat Soldiers* 1, no. 2, Fort Devens, WAC Newsletter, June 14, 1943, p. 2, File: Publications Section Report, Box 219, Series 55, RG 165, NA.

28. Pvt. Joan Willis, "Diary of a WAC Private: WAC Walks Guard," *Philadelphia Afro-American*, October 30, 1943, p. 5.

29. Memo from Lt. Colonel Anna W. Wilson, WAC staff director, ETOUSA, to WAC detachment commanders, re: Moral building of WACS in the ETO, June 13, 1944, Letter written by Lt. Elizabeth T. Egan, WAC detachment, Hq Command, ETOUSA. In the memo Lt. Colonel Wilson suggests that WAC detachment commanders use the letter to create suitable narratives of their own to share with women in their command. Appendix 56, pp. 2–4, File: Study of the WAC in the ETO; G-1 Section, #11, V.2 Appendices 1–66 to V.I, Box 502–101–11,-16; 1943–45, Air Force Historical Research Center, Maxwell Air Force Base, Montgomery, Ala.

30. Margaret D. Craighill, "A Psychological Approach to Social Hygiene for Women," p. 200.

31. Memo from Lt. Colonel Anna W. Wilson to WAC detachment commanders, re: Morale building of WACS in the ETO; cited in note 25.

32. For an example, see Col. James R. Johnson, post inspector general to commanding officer, Fort Benning, Ga., re: Report of investigation regarding the conduct of Nancy Blumfeld, cited in note 25.

33. Investigation of Auxiliary Agnes M. Ellard, charge of immoral conduct, July 26, 1943, File: R, Box 29, Series 54, RG 165, NA.

34. Treadwell, pp. 520–22. See also Joanne J. Meyerowitz, *Women Adrift: Independent Wage Earners in Chicago, 1880–1930* (Chicago: University of Chicago Press, 1988), ch. 4, for discussion of similar situations involving organizations like the YWCA, which invoked parental authority, often acting as "surrogate families," in their provisions of services to working class women.

35. Board Proceedings, Auxiliary Agnes R. Skipper, Hq 8th Service Command, Services of Supply, JA Branch to acting chief WAAC Branch, p. 2, July 13, 1943, Box 48, Series 54, RG 165, NA.

36. Meyer WAC Oral History Questionnaires, Edith Wofford, no. 16, Question 28. See also Board Proceedings, Auxiliary Agnes R. Skipper, p. 1; cited in note 35.

37. The most influential work analyzing this phenomenon is Michel Foucault, *The History of Sexuality*, vol. 1: *An Introduction* (New York: Random House, 1980, 1978).

38. Hq. "A" Company Training Battalion, WAAC Branch no. 6, Army Administration School (AAS), Richmond, Ky., To: commanding officer, From: 2d Officer Edith Hines, Subject: Report on Conduct of WAAC Auxiliaries, April 15, 1943, File: 250, Box 48, Series 54, RG 165, NA.

39. Hq. "A" Company Training Battalion, WAAC Branch no. 6, AAS, Richmond, Ky., To: Battalion Hq., From: 3d Officer Mary J. McFall, WAAC, May 17, 1943, re: Conduct on May 15 and 16, 1943, of WAAC Auxiliaries in Lexington, Ky., File: 250, Box 48, Series 54, RG 165, NA.

40. Study of the WAC in the ETO, ch. 3, Association of Officer with Enlisted Personnel, section 1, Background, p. 136, File: Study of the WAC in the ETO, WWII, G-1, #11; V.1, Box 502.101-3–502.101-11, 1943–1945, Air Force Historical Research Center, Maxwell Air Force Base, Montgomery, Ala.

41. For examples of this resentment being expressed and reported by WAC officers, see Memo to Lt. Patricia Lee, editorial officer, WAC Director, from Maj. Helen Woods, WAC staff director, January 8, 1944, File: 095, Box 17, Series 54, RG 165, NA; SWPA 320.2 (4/17/43)E Memo to Maj. General E. S. Hughes, deputy theater commander, NATO from Col. T. B. Catron, military adviser, June 3, 1943, Box 94, Series 54, RG 165, NA. See also Meyer WAC Oral History Questionnaires, Beatrice Brown, no. 6, Question #27.

42. Auxiliary Myrtle Naydeen Grancell, 35th WAAC PHQCO, Fort Custer, Mich., to Rep. Edith Nourse Rogers, March 19, 1943, File: 330, Box 89, Series 54, RG 165, NA.

43. Extract, B-Bat, ETO Stars and Stripes, "Frater-nursie," Appendix 136, May 11, 1945, File: WAC in the ETO; V.III, G-1; #11, Appendices 67–151 to V.I, Box 502.101-11; -16; 1943–45, Air Force Historical Research Center, Maxwell Air Force Base, Montgomery, Ala.

44. Joan Younger, Interview with Oveta Culp Hobby, "Fraternization," *Ladies Home Journal*, February 25, 1952, p. 4, File: *Ladies Home Journal* Article, 1952, Box 9, Hobby Papers, LC. In this interview Hobby explained that from the beginning to the end of the war the WAC went on record as opposing this Army tradition when it came to social engagements between men and women in uniform. See also Treadwell, pp. 511–14.

45. Treadwell, pp. 376, 512–13.

46. Lt. Colonel Mary A. Hallaren, GSC, WAC staff director, ETO, To: Chief of Staff Marshall, September 8, 1945, Subject: Policy governing off-duty associations between commissioned and enlisted personnel, Appendix 148, File: WAC in the ETO; V.III, G-1, #11, Appendices 67–151 to V.I, Box 502.101-11-16. 1943–45, Air Force Historical Research Center, Maxwell Air Force Base, Montgomery, Ala.

47. T. J. Devers, adjutant general, Supreme Headquarters, Allied Expeditionary Force, to General Dwight David Eisenhower, June 7, 1945, Appendix 149, File: WAC in the ETO; V.III, G-1, #11, Appendices 67–151 to V.I, Box 502.101-11-16, 1943–45, Air Force Historical Research Center, Maxwell Air Force Base, Montgomery, Ala.

48. Base Censor Office No. 4, Subject: Summary of Rumors, To: Theater Censor, HQ ETOUSA, August 31, 1943, File: Rumors, Box 192, Series 55; Military Intelligence Division SDBS Military Attaché Report England, Subject: WAC Reaction to British Civilian, From: NYPE Rpt #NYPE 59, August 9, 1944, Box 16, Series 54; All in RG 165, NA.

49. For example, see Basil L. Walters to Hobby, September 17, 1943, File: W Gen Corr, 1943, Box 4, Hobby Papers, LC.

50. For examples of black press articles see: "Say Soldiers in Africa Show Little Interest in Native or White Women," *Philadelphia Afro-American*, January 1, 1944, p. 12; Vincent Tubbs, "Say Australian Girls Just Someone to Talk Home to," *Philadelphia Afro-American*, April 29, 1944, p. 12; Rudolph Dunbar, "American Girls Shunned Foreign Alliances; Wac's Wed Own Boys Overseas," *Philadelphia Afro-American*, April 20, 1946, p. 20.

51. Lucia M. Pitts, *One Negro WAC's Story* (Los Angeles: privately published, 1968), p. 11, File: Minorities—IV-F-22, WAC Museum Historical Files, WAC Museum, Fort McClellan, Anniston, Ala.

52. Ibid.

53. Study of the WAC in the ETO, part 3: Recreation, pp. 114–55; File: WACs in the European Division, ATC, June 1944–August 1945, Box 308.04-1 (January 31, 1945)–308.072 (June 1944–August 1945), Air Force Historical Research Center, Maxwell Air Force Base, Montgomery, Ala.

54. Meyer Oral History Questionnaires, Dorothy Bjornsen, no. 17, Questions 27, 42.

55. For an example, see "The WAC," pp. 246–51, Section 5, Vol. 1, 1942–45, No. V-4, Box 450.01–13, 1941–45, V.2, Air Force Historical Research Center, Maxwell Air Force Base, Montgomery, Ala.

56. Lt. Colonel Mary A. Hallaren, WAC staff director, re: Social associations policy, Appendix 147, p. 6, August 30, 1945, File: WAC in the ETO; V.III, G-1;-11, Appendices 67–151 to V.I, Box 502.101–11;-16, 1943–45, Air Force Historical Research Center, Maxwell Air Force Base, Montgomery, Ala.

57. SPWA 320.2 (4/17/43)E, Col. T. B. Catron, military adviser and executive to Maj. General E. S. Hughes, deputy theater commander, June 3, 1943, NATO (North African Theater of Operations), Box 94 330.31, Series 54; Meeting with Colonels Macy and Catron, Captains Fair, Strayhorn, and Onthank, and Lieutenants Lutze and Bile, Friday, July 1, 1943; Office of the Director, Daily Journal, vol. 1, Box 200, Series 55; all in RG 165, NA.

58. Lt. Colonel Mary A. Hallaren, WAC staff director, re: Social associations policy, cited in note 56.

59. Treadwell, pp. 139–40.

60. Ibid., pp. 453–54.

61. Report of Field Trip to Various WAAC Installations in the 7th and 8th Service Commands in Connection to Changeover to Army Status, 1st Officer Ruth T. Woodworth, Camp Myles Standish, Taunton, Mass., July 10, 1943, File: Unmarked, Box 190, Series 55, RG 165, NA.

62. Meyer WAC Oral History Questionnaires, Edith Wofford, no. 16, Question 27.

63. 3d Officer Westray Battle Boyce, WAAC service command director, To: director, WAAC, Subject: Report of undesirable situation at Wilmington (N.C.) Air Defense

Regional Office involving WAAC AWS 3d Officers, December 5, 1942, File: 322.06 Wilmington Air Defense Office, AWS (12/5/42), Box 88, Series 54, RG 165, NA.

64. Ibid.

65. Ibid.

66. For example, see Board proceedings, Auxiliary Agnes R. Skipper, judge advocates branch, to acting chief, WAAC branch, July 13, 1943, File: 250.1, Box 48, Series 54, RG 165, NA.

67. Treadwell, pp. 446–47. For example of written policies on responsibility for fraternization, see Brig. General R. B. Lovett, Subject: Social associations, June 1945, File: WAC in the ETO; V.III, G-1; no. 11, Appendices 67–151 to V.I, Box 502.101–11;-16. 1943–45; Air Force Historical Research Center, Maxwell Air Force Base, Montgomery, Ala. See also File: WAC Policy File Vol. I, "Off Duty Association Between Commissioned and Enlisted Personnel," Box 197, Series 55, RG 165, NA.

68. For a general discussion of the diverse enforcement of fraternization regulations between men and women, see Treadwell, pp. 401, 447, 512, and File: V.1 January–June 1944; History Army Air Forces Eastern Flying Training Command (EFTC), June–December 1943, chapter 3, "Morale," p. 63, Box 222.01 (January–December 1943)- 222.01 (January–June 1944), Air Force Historical Research Center, Maxwell Air Force Base, Montgomery, Ala.

69. Treadwell, pp. 421–25; "Cyclone Forbes Dahlgren, We Were First: Eglin Field World War II WACs "We Heard the Guns at Wewak," p. 105, WAC Museum, Collection of Memoirs, Fort McClellan, Anniston, Ala.

70. Letter to Rep. Cravens from Lt. Colonel Jessie Rice, executive, WAC, December 22, 1944, File: C 201, Box 25, Series 54, RG 165, NA; WDWAC 314.7, Military Histories, Historical Data and Notes on SWPA WACS, Box 58, Series 54, RG 165, NA; WDWAC 333.2, August 1945, List of complaints on conditions in SWPA and corrective action taken (Summary), File: 333, Box 95, Series 54, RG 165, NA. See also Treadwell, pp. 421–25, 450.

71. Patricia Hill Collins, Black Feminist Thought: Knowledge, Consciousness, and the Politics of Empowerment (London: Unwin Hyman, 1990), p. 177. See also Angela Davis, "Rape, Racism, and the Capitalist Setting," Black Scholar 9, no. 7, pp. 25–28, as cited in Collins.

72. Report on field trip by 1st Officer Treila M. Welch; Discussion of conditions at Grenier Field, Manchester, N.H.; 706th WAAC Post HQ Company, Selfridge Field, Mich., and Camp Gordon, Augusta, Calif.; also Report by 1st Officer Doris E. Epperson on conditions at 410th Post HQ Company, Camp Stoneman, Calif., July 9, 1943; File: Unmarked, Box 190, Series 55, RG 165, NA.

73. Lula Jones Garrett, "Benning WAC's in Varied Jobs; Praised by Colonel and Soldiers," Philadelphia Afro-American, February 12, 1944, pp. 1, 14.

74. Cathy Clark, " 'We Are Pioneers and Models for Our Young,' Clora Bell," Atlanta Daily World, vol. 57, no. 9, October 9, 1984; File: History of WAAC/WAC Black, WAC Museum Historical Files, WAC Museum, Fort McClellan, Anniston, Ala.

75. Report by 1st Officer Treila M. Welch on conditions at Grenier Field, Manchester, N.H., cited in note 72

76. Report by 1st Officer Dorothy Myer, 802d WAAC, Columbus Army Air Base, Columbus, Miss., July 28, 1943, File: Unmarked, Box 190, Series 55, RG 165, NA.

77. Graham Smith, *When Jim Crow Met John Bull: Black American Soldiers in World War II Britain* (New York: St. Martin's Press, 1987), ch. 7.

78. Clare Boothe Luce to Col. Oveta Culp Hobby, May 11, 1945, Concerning a letter from a Wac mailed March 11, 1945, File: 330, Box 89, Series 54, NA.

79. Senator Wayne Morse to the War Department, re: Corporal Vivian K. Roberts, Madigan Hospital, Fort Lewis, Wash., November 13, 1945, File: R, Box 29, Series 54, NA.

80. WAC Director Col. Westray Battle Boyce to Senator Wayne Morse, re: Corp. Vivian K. Roberts, January 8, 1946, File: R, Box 29, Series 54, RG 165, NA.

81. Susan Brownmiller, *Against Our Will: Men, Women, and Rape* (New York: Simon and Schuster, 1975), pp. 76–77. See also Brownmiller's entire ch. 3, pp. 23–118, in which she discusses the relationship between war and rape and the ways in which both "conquerors" (as the Russian and German armies were usually defined) and "liberators" (as British and American forces were defined) were entitled to women's bodies as either "spoils" or "just rewards." The official history of the judge advocate general, ETO, states: "The French people welcomed their liberators, often giving them drink to show their appreciation. . . . The invading soldiers came fully armed. The people were grateful, but they had little or no protection. Many soldiers had the notion that French women generally were both attractive and free with their love. At any rate, whatever the operative factors, the number of violent sex crimes enormously increased with the arrival of our troops in France. . . . Generally speaking, the rape cases of the French Phase fell into one broad pattern characterized by violence, though of different degrees. The use of firearms was common in perpetrating the offense." History Branch, Office of the Judge Advocate General with the United States Forces, European Theater, July 18, 1942–November 1, 1945 at 241 (February 15, 1946) (unpublished manuscript, on file with the Office of the Chief of Military History, Historical Manuscript file, no. 8–3.5 AA v.1); As cited in Madeline Morris, "Rape, War, and the Military," forthcoming *Duke Law Journal* (February 1996), p. 21.

82. Meyer Oral History Interviews, Florence Holmes, no. 2, September 1989. (At WAC Veterans Association Reunion, Fort Des Moines, Iowa.)

83. As feminist theorist Susan Brownmiller has argued, it is probable that the Army tried many rapists on lesser charges, especially since rape was considered a capital crime in the military and convictions could bring a death sentence. Brownmiller, p. 77.

84. Report by 1st Officer Dorothy Myer, cited in note 76.

85. Request from 1st Officer Gretchen Thorp, director, Technical Information Division, via Director's Office, to all WAAC staff directors to report re: Circulating rumors in their area and their source, June 23, 1943; Reply by 1st Officer Katherine R. Goodwin, WAAC staff director, 1st Service Command, Boston; Statement by AFC Martha Chandler, notarized by Maj. William B. Collett, Jr., military intelligence officer, Bangor, Maine, May 29, 1943, File: Rumors Against the WAC, Box 93, Series 54, RG 165, NA.

86. Social Hygiene Lecture to Wacs, cited in note 16.

87. Statement under oath made by Corp. Bernice M. P. Hackett, July 1, 1943; Statement of Auxiliary Sarah K. Huitt, statement of Auxiliary Elizabeth W. Finnell, statement of Auxiliary Claire H. Byrne, statement by Maj. Francis J. McCabe, provost

marshal, Camp Edwards, Mass., July 3, 1943; Lt. Colonel Daniel L. O'Donnell, J.A.G.D. to commanding officer, Camp Edwards, re: Junior Leader Bernice M. P. Hackett, July 9, 1943; Col. Howard S. Patterson, commanding officer, Camp Edwards, to Capt. Josephine T. Dyer, commanding officer, Hq. Company (W), 1114th SCU, Camp Edwards, Mass., July 10, 1943, File: L, Box 28, Series 54, RG 165, NA.

88. Report of investigation regarding alleged criminal assault on member of Women's Auxiliary Army Corps at Keesler Field, Biloxi, Miss., September 25, 1943, To: Commanding general, Army Air Force eastern technical training command, Sedgefield, Greensboro, N.C., From: Lt. Colonel George J. Smith, acting asst. inspector general, p. 4, File: E, Box 26, Series 54, RG 165, NA.

89. Brownmiller, pp. 23–118. One of her main arguments in this chapter is that rape was often used in war as a weapon aimed not only at women but at their husbands, fathers, brothers, etc. (male family and friends). She also contends that during World War II there were numerous examples of women being raped by enemy soldiers in front of their husbands, men insulting and conquering men, using women's bodies as the tool or means of inflicting such humiliation.

90. Report of investigation regarding alleged criminal assault on member of Women's Auxiliary Army Corps, cited in note 88.

91. For one commentary on this military trend, see "Degrees of Rape," *Philadelphia Afro-American*, November 13, 1943, p. 1.

92. For a discussion of differential punishments for white versus black soldiers charged with sex crimes in the ETO during the war, especially in England, see Smith, Introduction and ch. 7.

93. Fort Moultrie, S.C., 1st Lieutenant William Mitchell, post intelligence officer, Subject: Racial Incident, August 25, 1943, File: Rumors, Box 192, Series 55, RG 165, NA.

94. Ibid.

7. The "Lesbian Threat"

1. Donna Penn, "The Meanings of Lesbianism in Post-War America," *Gender & History* 3, no. 2 (Summer 1991): 190–203.

2. Penn, p. 190. For examples of these early works, see Lillian Faderman, *Surpassing the Love of Men: Love Between Women from the Renaissance to the Present* (New York: Morrow, 1981); Blanche Wiesen Cook, "Historical Denial of Lesbianism," *Radical History Review* 20 (1979): 60–65; Blanche Wiesen Cook, "Women Alone Stir My Imagination," *Signs* 4 (1979): 718–739; Adrienne Rich, "Compulsory Heterosexuality and Lesbian Existence," in *Powers of Desire*, ed. A. Snitow et al. (New York: Monthly Review Press, 1983), p. 177–205.

3. For some examples of this literature, see Jeffrey Weeks, "Movements of Affirmation: Sexual Meanings and Homosexual Identities," in Kathy Peiss and Christina Simmons with Robert Padgug, eds., *Passion and Power: Modern Sexuality* (Philadelphia: Temple University Press, 1989): 70–86; Robert Padgug, "Sexual Matters: On Conceptualizing Sexuality in History," in *Passion and Power*, pp. 14–34; Allan Berube, *Coming Out Under Fire: Gay GIs During World War II* (New York: Free Press, 1991). Also Michel Foucault has had perhaps the most influence on the field of

the history of sexuality in general and on gay history in particular. See, for example, Michel Foucault, *The History of Sexuality*, vol. 1: *An Introduction* (New York: Random House, 1980, 1978).

4. The need for "differential" social histories of gay men and lesbians has been noted by several historians of homosexuality. Jeffrey Weeks, for instance, has emphasized the importance of not relying on a single explanation for the development of a "homosexual" identity but rather the need for "differential social histories of male homosexuality and lesbianism." See Jeffrey Weeks, "Movements of Affirmation," p. 81.

5. For examples of works that discuss sodomy laws as the precursor to constructions of homosexuals as a species of people, see Foucault, *The History of Sexuality*; Berube, *Coming Out Under Fire*. For works dealing with the laws against cross-dressing, see " 'She Even Chewed Tobacco': A Pictorial Narrative of Passing Women in America," San Francisco Lesbian and Gay History Project, in Martin B. Duberman, Martha Vicinus, and George Chauncey Jr., eds., *Hidden from History: Reclaiming the Gay amd Lesbian Past* (New York: Penguin Books, 1989), pp. 185–87, 192; Marjorie Garber, *Vested Interests: Cross-Dressing and Cultural Anxiety* (New York: Routledge, 1991).

6. Berube, p. 28.

7. See, for example, " 'She Even Chewed Tobacco,' " pp. 185–87, 192. For a fuller discussion of female cross-dressing historically, see Marjorie Garber, *Vested Interests*. For an analysis of the "performativity" of gender that inheres in cross-dressing and other acts of gender rebellion and disguise, see Judith Butler, *Gender Trouble: Feminism and the Subversion of Identity* (London: Routledge, 1990),

8. John D'Emilio, *Sexual Politics, Sexual Communities: The Making of a Homosexual Minority in the United States, 1940–1970* (Chicago: University of Chicago Press, 1983), pp. 16–17. See also John D'Emilio and Estelle Freedman, *Intimate Matters: A History of Sexuality in America* (New York: Harper and Row, 1988), pp. 193–94.

9. Medical theories that addressed the female sexual invert in the early twentieth century for the most part named gender inversion as a primary characteristic of female homosexuality. Though historian George Chauncey argued in early articles that the issue of sexual object choice came to dominate over gender inversion as a primary criterion for diagnosing a woman as homosexual, it is clear that the mannish woman continued as the popular lesbian archetype for most people. Indeed, Chauncey has indicated in later discussions of this issue that the shift from gender inversion to object choice in the discourse on "female deviance" was always confused and never complete. George Chauncey, "From Sexual Inversion to Homosexuality: The Changing Medical Conceptualization of Female Deviance," in *Passion and Power*, pp. 87–117.

10. Esther Newton, "The Mythic Mannish Lesbian: Radclyffe Hall and the New Woman," in Estelle B. Freedman, Barbara C. Gelpi, Susan L. Johnson, Kathleen M. Weston, eds., *Signs: The Lesbian Issue* (Chicago: University of Chicago Press, 1982, 1983, 1984, 1985): 10. See also Donna Penn, "The Meanings of Lesbianism in Post-War America," for a discussion of this point.

11. Esther Newton, "The Mythic Mannish Lesbian."

12. Elizabeth Kennedy and Madeline Davis, "The Reproduction of Butch-Femme Roles: A Social Constructionist Approach," in *Passion and Power*, pp. 241–58. See also

Elizabeth Kennedy and Madeline Davis, *Boots of Leather, Slippers of Gold: The History of a Lesbian Community* (New York: Routledge, 1993).

13. Leila Rupp, "Imagine My Surprise: Women's Relationships in the 20th Century," in Duberman, Vicinus, and Chauncey, eds., *Hidden from History*, p. 398. Much of the discussion of lesbians generated within the field of women's history has focused on these "romantic friendships" and women's homosocial networks. See Lillian Faderman, *Surpassing the Love of Men*; Cook, "Historical Denial of Lesbianism," Cook, "Women Alone Stir My Imagination," *Signs* 4 (1979): 718–39; Adrienne Rich, "Compulsory Heterosexuality and Lesbian Existence," in *Powers of Desire*, ed. A. Snitow et al. (NY: Monthly Review, 1983):177–205; Carroll Smith-Rosenberg, "The Female World of Love and Ritual," in *Disorderly Conduct: Visions of Gender in Victorian America* (New York: Oxford University Press, 1985).

14. Esther Newton, p. 16.

15. George Chauncey, p. 100.

16. Leila Rupp, p. 407.

17. Maj. Albert Preston, "History of Psychiatry in the Women's Army Corps" (Spring 1946): 4, File: 700, Box 143, Series 54, RG 165, NA.

18. Newton, p. 10; Julie Wheelwright, *Amazons and Military Maids: Women Who Dressed As Men in Pursuit of Life, Liberty, and Happiness* (London: Pandora Press, 1989), pp. 153–54.

19. In 1934 German psychologist Magnus Hirschfeld, president of the World League for Sexual Reform, drew a direct connection between women's desire to enter the military and their potential homosexuality. Hirschfeld believed that female soldiers, because they engaged in the "most extreme" cross-gender behavior, were the most confused sexually. Wheelwright, p. 153.

20. Letter to commanding general, Fourth Air Force, to commanding general, Western Flying Training Command, re: Results of January 1944 Gallup Poll, pp. 249–50, February 8, 1944, section 5, 4th Air Force Historical Study, no. V-4, Box 450. 01–13, 1941–45, vol. 1, Air Force Historical Research Center, Maxwell Air Force Base, Montgomery, Ala. See also Maxson F. Judell to Col. Hobby , re: Uniforms, April 24, 1944, and James E. Dunlap to Col. Hobby, re: Uniforms, February 21, 1944, Box 21, Series 54. Memo for the Record, From: Maj. H. M. Boutell, GSC chairman, Subject: Plans and policy committee meeting, November 8, 1948; Item 3: "Discussion: Uniform consideration," October 27, 1948, File: WAC Committee Chairman's Book, Box 222, Series 55; all in RG 165, NA. "Reform for a Uniform," *Colliers*, June 3, 1944, p. 82. Mattie Treadwell, *The U.S. Army in World War II, Special Studies, the Women's Army Corps* (Washington, D.C.: Office of the Chief of Military History, 1954), pp. 158–66.

21. Treadwell, 156–58, 160—61.

22. Milton Caniff, "Know Which Arm You're In," from "Male Call," 1944, in Peter Poplaski, ed., *Male Call Rejects Featuring Miss Lace* (Princeton, Wisc.: Kitchen Sink Press, 1987). While Coniff was best known for his syndicated civilian comic strip "Terry and the Pirates," his military comic strip, "Male Call," was distributed by the Camp Newspaper Service and appeared in over 3,000 military newspapers in the United States and overseas. I am indebted to Allan Berube for bringing this material to my attention.

23. Historian, WAC section, Hq., Fourth Air Force, January 1, 1944–September 30, 1945, p. 46, Historical Section Files, pp. 249–50, section 5, 4th Air Force Historical Study, no. V-4, Box 450.01–13, 1941–45, vol. 1; Field uniform, Part 2: "Plans and Policies," ch. 2, p. 73, "Supply," File: Study of the WAC in the ETO, V.I, Box 502.101-3–11 (1943–45) ETO, Air Force Historical Research Center, Maxwell Air Force Base, Montgomery, Ala.

24. Berube, *Coming Out Under Fire*, pp. 59–61. Correspondence: May 19–October 15, 1943, Elizabeth Arden Corp. on WAAC hairstyles, File: 062.001, 1942–43, Box 9, Series 54, RG 165, NA.

25. Field Uniform, Part 2: "Plans and Policies," cited in note 23. See also chapter 4 of this book in which I give the example of the male commander in the ETO who refused to assign a shipment of female mechanics to the appropriate duties because did not want them to wear trousers.

26. Miss Louisa Givogre, Los Angeles, to the adjutant general, re: WAAC Uniforms, March 11, 1942, Box 19, Series 54, RG 165, NA.

27. Historical Record of WAC Detachment, Hq., USASOS, June 1945, Historical Record C-2417, D-1, AFWESPAC, Box 7, RG 319, NA.

28. Treadwell, p. 38. Although historian Lillian Faderman has argued that pants and the public acceptance of women wearing them became a symbol of a lesbian style in the 1940s, wearing slacks in the WAC was always contested. Lillian Faderman, *Odd Girls and Twilight Lovers: A History of Lesbian Life in Twentieth-Century America* (New York: Columbia University Press, 1991), p. 126.

29. Capt. Ethel F. Hoffman, Hq. USAFISPA to Lt. Colonel Jessie Pearl Rice, deputy director, WAC, Washington, D.C., May 28, 1944, File: 314.81, Box 57, Series 54, RG 165, NA.

30. Army policies addressing male homosexuals and WAC procedures for dealing with lesbianism differed during World War II. Historian Allan Berube has meticulously documented the influence of modern psychiatry on the development of the Army's antihomosexual apparatus. The most significant change in Army policies toward male homosexuality was a movement away from long-standing regulations criminalizing sodomy, and thus punishing identifiable homosexual acts, toward policies that defined the homosexual soldier as mentally ill and therefore in need of psychiatric treatment and rehabilitation, not imprisonment. Berube contends that this change allowed the military to cast a substantially wider net in screening for homosexuals and thus affected a much larger number of gay men than had the original sodomy restrictions. Berube, pp. 8–33. It should also be noted that Berube makes clear in his study that this change was not smooth nor complete during the war and that some gay men continued to be imprisoned under the older sodomy regulations.

31. Maj. Albert Preston, *History of Psychiatry in the Women's Army Corps* (Spring 1946): 8–10. File: 700, Box 143, Series 54, RG 165, NA.

32. "WAAC News," *WAAC Newsletter* 1, no. 33 (June 5–12, 1943): 3, Fort Des Moines, Iowa, Box 212, Series 55, RG 165 NA.

33. Memo for the adjutant general, Appointment and Induction Branch, Attn.: Recruiting and Induction Section, Col. Sailor, Subject, WAAC recruiting, From: Lt. Colonel G. T. Gifford, director, Personnel, WAAC, November 19, 1942, File: Enrollment of Auxiliaries with Physical Defects or of Doubtful Reputation, Box 111,

Series 54, RG 165, NA. I am indebted to Allan Berube for bringing this document to my attention.

34. Tab A, Memo to the adjutant general, Appointment and Induction Branch, Attn.: Col. Sumner, From: 3d Officer Virginia Beeler Bock, executive officer, Personnel Division, WAAC, For the Director, December 5, 1942; Lt. General Somervell, adjutant general to commanding general, All Service Commands, Subject: Enrollment of WAAC Auxiliaries with Doubtful Moral Standards, December 15, 1942, File: cited in note 33.

See also Report from Col. J. A. Hoag, commandant, Fort Des Moines, Iowa, First WAAC Training Center, To: director, WAAC, Subject: Summary of pending disciplinary cases, December 15, 1942, File: 250.1, Box 48, Series 54, RG 165, NA.

35. Berube, p. 30.

36. "Life in the WAAC," File: 062.001, 1942–43, Box 9, Series 54, RG 165, NA. That some women's desire to join the women's corps in order to "be with other girls" was an indication of possible lesbianism was also addressed by an Air Force personnel officer after the war. In his report on the future utilization of the WAC in the Air Force he argued that "group living" was a problem for most "normal, healthy women" who joined the armed services. He went on to note that though there were many women who "enjoyed" such situations, "they are not the type of women we are looking for or desire in our establishment." Maj. John L. Harris, "The Utilization of the WAC Within the Regular Air Force" (1948), Air University Air Command and Staff School thesis, Air University Library, Maxwell Air Force Base, Montgomery, Ala.

37. Maj. Albert Preston Jr., History of Psychiatry in the Woman's Army Corps, pp. 9–10, See also Treadwell, pp. 602–6.

38. TB MED 100, War Dept. Technical Bulletin, 1944, "WAC Recruiting Station Neuropsychiatric Examination," File: 320.2, Box 64, Series 54, RG 165, NA. See also Berube, Coming Out Under Fire, p. 32.

39. Lecture Series on Sex Hygiene for Officers and Officer Candidates, WAAC. See in particular "Sexual Relationships," and "Homosexuality," pp. 45–55, Box 145, Series 54, RG 165, NA.

40. War Dept. Pamphlet 35-1, p. 25, Box 145, Series 54, RG 165, NA.

41. See Berube's discussion of this point though he does not address class as an issue in defining which same-sex relationships were perceived as "queer" and which were seen as acceptable. Berube, pp. 44–45.

42. War Dept. Pamphlet 35-1, p. 26, cited in note 40; Lecture Series on Sex Hygiene, pp. 53–55, cited in note 39. It should be noted that this type of same-sex relationship, involving hero-worship, is addressed by historian Leila Rupp in her discussion of the various forms taken by middle- and upper-class, white women's relationships. Rupp, p. 398. These techniques for handling "lesbian" relationships, especially the suggestions for redirecting or channeling women's energies into so-called moral behaviors, are reminiscent of the methods, described by historian Martha Vicinus, that were used within English girls' schools to "regulate and control" female romantic friendships in the late nineteenth and early twentieth centuries. See Martha Vicinus, "Distance and Desire: English Boarding School Friendships, 1870–1920," in Duberman, Vicinus, and Chauncey, eds., Hidden from History, pp. 212–29.

43. War Dept. Pamphlet 35-1, p. 26, cited in note 40; Lecture Series on Sex Hygiene, "Homosexuality," pp. 53–55, cited in note 39.

44. Berube, pp. 59–61. See also War Dept. Pamphlet 35-1, p. 26, cited in note 39.

45. War Dept. Pamphlet 35-1, p. 26, cited in note 39; Lecture Series on Sex Hygiene, "Homosexuality," pp. 53–55, cited in note 39.

46. War Dept. Pamphlet 35-1, p. 27.

47. Margaret D. Craighill, "Psychiatric Aspects of Women Serving in the Army," *American Journal of Psychiatry* 104 (October 1947): 228.

48. Lt. Martha B. Hayes, Case #5; WDWAC 201, 11th IND, War Department Office of Director, WAC to Commanding General, Army Service Forces, Attention: Director of Military Personnel, May 8, 1944, File: Data WAAC Officers, Box 201, Series 55, RG 165, NA.

49. Report of Proceedings of a Board of Officers in the Case of Technician 4th Grade Julie L. Farrell, WAAC, WAAC Branch no. 6, AAS, July 22, 1943, Richmond, Ky., File: P, Box 29, Series 54, RG 165, NA.

50. Letter from Pvt. Ruth Ricci to friend in United States (intercepted by post censor), October 1, 1944; Letter to Hobby from Lt. Colonel Elizabeth Strayhorn, re: Pvt. Ricci's accusations of widespread homosexuality, October 12, 1944; Report of conditions for Wacs in New Guinea, October 28, 1944, File: 330, Box 89, Series 54, RG 165, NA.

51. Berube, p. 193.

52. Memo to Lt. Colonel Brown from Maj. General Frink, re: List of recommendations made by Brown for SWPA, October 23, 1944; Memo to Col. Coursey from Lt. Colonel Brown, November 24, 1944, File: 330, Box 89, Series 54, Rg 165, NA.

53. D'Emilio and Freedman, *Intimate Matters*, pp. 260, 288–89. See also John Costello, *Love, Sex, and War: Changing Values, 1939–45* (London: Williams Collins, 1985); Berube, p. 6; and Elaine Tyler May, *Homeward Bound: American Families in the Cold War* (New York: Basic Books, 1988), p. 69.

54. Berube, *Coming Out Under Fire*, p. 22; Faderman, *Odd Girls and Twilight Lovers*, p. 125.

55. Meyer Oral History Questionnaires, nos. 4 and 11, Martha Ward and Anne Brown, respectively, Question 29.

56. Faderman, p. 125.

57. Ibid., no, 18 Bessie Weaver, Question 29.

58. Ibid., nos. 12, 18, and 7, Florence Fox, Bessie Weaver, Anne Clark, respectively, Question 29.

59. Ibid., nos. 8 and 19, Catharine Thompson and Bee Charles, respectivelly, Question 29.

60. Jane G. Williams, Bloomington, Ind., to Col. Hobby, re: Fort Custer, Mich., and the 4621 Service Unit, November 15, 1943; 1st Lieut. Mary L. Hart, Investigation of complaint and response to Col. Hobby, December 27, 1943, Box 91, Series 54, RG 165, NA.

61. Letter to Col. Hobby from Capt. Smith's mother, March 20, 1944; Transcription of phone conversations between Col. Hobby and Col. Morrisette, judge advocate general's office, concerning this situation, March 28 and 31, 1944; WDGAP 201—"Report on Relief of WAC Officer from Active Duty," October 17, 1944, File: Data, WAAC Officers, Box 201, Series 55, RG 165, NA.

62. Ibid.

63. Pat Bond, "Tapioca Tapestry," in Marcy Adelman, ed., *Long Time Passing: Lives of Older Lesbians* (Boston: Alyson, 1986), p. 165.

64. Report of Proceedings of a Board of Officers in the Case of Tech. 4th Grade Julie Farrell, WAAC, pp. 18–19, 22–25, cited in note 48.

65. Berube, p. 104. Here Berube discusses the "rule of thumb" developed by most gay men and lesbians to protect their existence in the military. This rule included talking to no one explicitly about their homosexuality.

66. Report from Lt. Colonel Birge Holt and Capt. Ruby Herman, Inspector General's Office, to acting inspector general, Subject: Investigation of conditions in the 3d WAC Training Center, Fort Oglethorpe, Ga., July 29, 1944, File: 333.9, 3d WAC Training Center, RG 159, NA. Hereafter the report will be referred to as Report, Fort Oglethorpe. I am indebted to Allan Berube for bringing this report to my attention and for furnishing me with a copy of the document.

67. Berube, p.43.

68. Report of Proceedings of a Board of Officers in the Case of Tech. 4th Grade Julie Farrell, WAAC, pp. 75–76, cited in note 49.

69. Report, Fort Oglethorpe, pp. 29–30, cited in note 66.

70. Berube, p.102.

71. Bond, p.166, in Adelman, ed., *Long Time Passing*.

72. Berube, *Coming Out Under Fire*, p. 113. See also Freedman and D'Emilio, pp. 288–9. See also my discussion of such vice laws during the war in chapter 5. For a wonderful discussion of gay and lesbian nightlife in urban communities during the war, see Berube, pp. 98–127.

73. Bond, pp. 169–70, in Adelman, ed., *Long Time Passing*.

74. Allan Berube argues that popular beliefs that portrayed all homosexuals as "perverts" who "could not be loved and were not worth loving . . . robbed many gay men and women of the self-esteem and mutual respect upon which they could build long-term relationships" (p. 118).

75. "Johnnie Phelps," in Mary A. Humphrey, ed., *My Country, My Right to Serve: Experiences of Gay Men and Women in the Military, World War II to the Present* (New York: Harper Collins, 1988), p. 39.

76. For a terrific discussion of this point, see Berube, pp. 34–67. He argues that gay GIs developed their own methods of self-expression within military frameworks, practices that the military adapted itself to during the war because of the manpower shortage. For example, gay men's participation in gay drag and military sanctioned "camp" shows and butch lesbians' visibility in the few traditionally masculine jobs, like the motor corps, available to Army women during the war.

77. "Johnnie Phelps," in Humphrey, ed., p. 38.

78. Nellie Gruber, Oral History Interview no. 3, September 1989. Interviewed at WAC Veteran's Association Reunion, Fort Des Moines, Iowa.

79. Report of Proceedings of a Board of Officers in the Case of Tech. 4th Grade Julie Farrell, WAAC, pp. 7–9, cited in note 49.

80. See Berube, p. 40, for his discussion of a similar point.

81. Letter from former 1st Sgts. Joan G. Pound and Norma L. Chambers, to Congressman John M. Coffee, December 7, 1943; Honorable John M. Coffee to Col. Oveta Culp Hobby, director, Women's Army Corps, December 19, 1943; File: 330.14, Box 91, Series 54, RG 165, NA.

82. Ibid.

83. Ibid. See also Memo, Lt. Col. R. Hippelheuser, assistant adjutant general, to 1st Lieutenant Gloria Joyce Gomila, WAC, Subject: Result of investigation conducted at 2d WAC Training Center, Daytona Beach, Fla.; Report, Lt. Colonel, assistant adjutant general to commanding general, Army Service Forces, Attn.: Director Women's Army Corps, March 6, 1944, File: 330.14, Box 91, Series 54, RG 165, NA.

84. Letter from ex-Wac Frankie Casey to Col. Oveta Culp Hobby, WAC director, April 30, 1945, File: C, Box 26, Series 54, RG 165, NA.

85. Ibid. See also Hon. John Coffee to Col. Hobby, cited in note 81.

86. For an extensive discussion of the development of "undesirable" discharge policies by the military during World War II, see Berube, pp. 139, 141, 149–76.

87. Frankie Casey to Col. Oveta Culp Hobby, cited in note 84.

88. Charity Adams Earley, *One Woman's Army: A Black Officer Remembers the WAC* (College Station: Texas A & M University Press, 1989), pp. 180–81.

89. Letter from Farrell to "Little George," identified as Lt. Pines, in July 22, 1943, Report of Proceedings of a Board of Officers in the Case of Tech. 4th Grade Julie Farrell, cited in note 49.

90. Ibid., pp.68–70.

91. Report, Fort Oglethorpe, Letter from Mrs. Adams to commanding general, judge advocate, War Dept., May 12, 1944; Report from Lt. Col. Birge Holt and Capt. Ruby Herman, Subject: Investigation of conditions in the 3d WAC Training Center, Fort Oglethorpe, Ga., cited in note 66.

92. Report, Fort Oglethorpe, pp. 9, 20.

93. Ibid., pp. 9–10, 24.

94. Ibid., pp. 16–18, 20.

95. For a more extensive discussion of military interrogation tactics and their impact on gay men and lesbians during World War II, see Berube, pp. 203–10.

96. Tab A and B, Invesstigation at Fort Oglethorpe, Ga., File: Data WAAC Officers, Box 201, Series 55, RG 165, NA.

97. Report, Fort Oglethorpe, p. 24; see also Berube, pp. 205–9.

98. Report, Fort Oglethorpe, pp. 3, 14.

99. Ibid., p. 14. In an interesting sidenote ex-Wac Pat Bond has discussed making this connection in a humorous fashion in the comedy shows she performed for lesbian audiences in later years. In one skit Bond explained to a young woman what she needed to do to be a "real" lesbian. "Bunny, if we're going to be real dykes, you gotta make love to 'em with your mouth," Bond, p. 170.

100. Tab A and B, Investigation at Fort Oglethorpe, Ga., August 26, 1944, cited in note 96.

101. Report, Fort Oglethorpe, pp. 27–28; cited in note 66.

102. Ibid., pp. 30–31.

103. For example, see Memo for the commanding general, Army Air Forces, Attn.: Air WAC officer, from Col. Oveta Culp Hobby, director, WAC, Subject: Homosexual practices, August 26, 1944, Box 201, Series 55, RG 165, NA. For the testimony concerning these women, see Report, Fort Oglethorpe, Appendix, pp. 1–8.

104. Bond, "Tapioca Tapestsry." For a discussion of the impact of these purges particularly for gay men and the "legacy" of the war for gays and lesbians, see Berube, *Coming Out Under Fire*, pp. 203, 262–63 and ch. 10. These purges of lesbians similar

to those of gay men were primarily motivated by the demobilization of the armed forces and the need to cut personnel. This pattern is no different today than it was fifty years ago, as homosexuality might be tolerated when the military needs personnel and then gays and lesbians are purged when the need is gone. The extent of these postwar purges has been the subject of debate by scholars. What the evidence does demonstrate for the Women's Army Corps is that the highest numbers of honorable discharges for "inaptitude or unsuitability" and "other than honorable discharges" (the categories under which many lesbians were discharged) occurred in 1945, with the majority taking place after June 1945. In other words, after V-E day. Treadwell, *The U.S. Army in World War II*, table 12, Enlisted Personnel Separated from the Women's Army Corps: August 1942–December 1946, p. 778.

105. Maj. Helen H. Hart, WAC supervisor, 6th Army Hq., Presidio, San Francisco, to Maj. Helen E. Hanson, Office of the Director of WAC, June 24, 1946, File: H, Box 27, Series 54, RG 165, NA.

106. Pat Bond, pp. 166–67.

107. Ibid., p. 166.

108. Capt. Robert C. Longan Jr., Medical Corps, Neuropsychiatry Consultants Division, to Col. Emmett R. Litteral, Letterman General Hospital, San Francisco, Subject: Psychiatric screening of WAC personnel, September 16, 1946; Maj. Helen Hart, WAC staff director, Hq., 6th Army, Presidio, San Francisco, to Maj. Helen Hanson or Selma Herberts, WAC Director's Office, Subject: Psychiatric screening for Wacs, August 20, 1946, File: H, Box 21, Series 54, RG 165, NA.

Epilogue

1. Meyer Oral History Questionnaires, Martha Ward, no. 4, Question 48.

2. "The Woman Veteran," August 31, 1946, Reprints from Research Studies, MPR-2, Research Service Office of Coordination and Planning, Veterans Administration, Washington, D.C. "Readjustment Experiences and Problems Met Three to Four Months After Separation," based on a survey of enlisted women discharged from the Army and Navy in February 1946, Box 51, Series 54, RG 165, NA. See also Dovey Johnson, "Former Negro Servicewomen FACE FORWARD" (1945), in Dovey Johnson Roundtree Papers, Bethune Museum and Archives, Washington, D.C.

3. Meyer Oral History Questionnaires, Loretta Howard, no. 20, Question 48.

4. Meyer Oral History Questionnaires, Juanita Waters, no. 5, Question 50.

5. Meyer Oral History Questionnaires, Laura Frank, no. 21, Questions 48–50.

6. Doris E. Samford, *Ruffles and Drums* (Boulder, Colo.: Pruett Press, 1966), p. 164.

7. Cynthia Enloe, *Does Khaki Become You? The Militarization of Women's Lives* (London: Unwin Hyman, 1988), p. 212.

8. Barbara Kantrowitz, "The Right to Fight," *Newsweek*, August 5, 1991), p. 23.

9. As quoted in Barbara Kantrowitz, "The Right to Fight," p. 23.

10. "Military Witchhunt Victims Charge Sexual Harassment, *National NOW Times* (April 1989): 5.

Index